PILGRIMAGE AND TOURISM TO HOLY CITIES
Ideological and Management Perspectives

CABI RELIGIOUS TOURISM AND PILGRIMAGE SERIES

General Editors:
Dr Razaq Raj, Leeds Business School, Leeds Beckett University, UK.
Dr Kevin Griffin, School of Hospitality Management and Tourism, Dublin Institute of Technology, Ireland

This series examines the practical applications, models and illustrations of religious tourism and pilgrimage management from a variety of international perspectives. Pilgrimage is not only a widespread and important practice in Islam, Judaism and Christianity, but also in other major religious traditions such as Buddhism, Hinduism and Sikhism.

The series explores the emergence and trajectories of religious tourism and pilgrimage. Inclusive of all denominations, religions, faiths and spiritual practices, it covers evaluations of religious tourism and pilgrimage, management guides, economic reports and sets of represented actions and behaviours within various cultural, management and marketing contexts. A key strength of the series is the presentation of current and diverse empirical research insights on aspects of religious tourism and pilgrimage, juxtaposing this with state-of-the-art reflections on the emerging theoretical foundations of the subject matter.

The series illustrates the principles related to religion, pilgrimage and the management of tourist sites. It aims to provide a useful resource for researchers and students of the subject, and increase understanding of this vital aspect of tourism studies.

PILGRIMAGE AND TOURISM TO HOLY CITIES

Ideological and Management Perspectives

Edited by

Maria Leppäkari

Swedish Theological Institute in Jerusalem and Åbo Akademi University, Finland

and

Kevin Griffin

Dublin Institute of Technology, Ireland

CABI is a trading name of CAB International

CABI	CABI
Nosworthy Way	745 Atlantic Avenue
Wallingford	8th Floor
Oxfordshire OX10 8DE	Boston, MA 02111
UK	USA
Tel: +44 (0)1491 832111	Tel: +1 (617)682-9015
Fax: +44 (0)1491 833508	E-mail: cabi-nao@cabi.org
E-mail: info@cabi.org	
Website: www.cabi.org	

A catalogue record for this book is available from the British Library, London, UK.

Library of Congress Cataloging-in-Publication Data

Names: Leppäkari, Maria, editor. | Griffin, Kevin A., editor.
Title: Pilgrimage and tourism to holy cities : ideological and management
  perspectives / edited by Maria Leppäkari, Swedish Theological Institute
  in Jerusalem & Åbo Akademi University, Finland, and Kevin Griffin, Dublin
  Institute of Technology, Ireland.
Description: Boston, MA : CAB International, 2016. | Series: CABI religious
  tourism and pilgrimage series | Includes bibliographical referenc4650es
  and index.
Identifiers: LCCN 2016029185 | ISBN 9781780647388 (alk. paper)
Subjects: LCSH: Pilgrims and pilgrimages. | Pilgrims and pilgrimages--Social
  aspects. | Tourism--Religious aspects. | Tourism--Management.
Classification: LCC BL619.P5 P5197 2016 | DDC 203/.51--dc23
LC record available at https://lccn.loc.gov/2016029185

ISBN-13: 978 1 78064 738 8

Commissioning editor: Claire Parfitt
Editorial assistant: Emma McCann and Alexandra Lainsbury
Production editor: Lauren Povey

Typeset by SPi, Pondicherry, India.
Printed and bound in the UK by CPI Group (UK) Ltd, Croydon, CR0 4YY.

Contents

PART II. MANAGING PILGRIMAGE SITES IN HOLY CITIES

Contributors

Ibrahim Al-Marashi is associate professor of Middle East history at California State University San Marcos. He received his MA in Arab studies from Georgetown University in 1997 and his PhD from the Department of Modern History, St Antony's College, University of Oxford in 2004 for his thesis 'The nineteenth province: the invasion of Kuwait and the 1991 Gulf War from the perspective of the Iraqi state'. He has published and presented a broad range of papers focusing on the Middle East, the following being a sample of his more recent outputs: 'Sadrabilia: the visual narrative of Muqtada Al-Sadr's Islamist politics and insurgency in Iraq' (2013); 'The 2003 Iraq War did not take place: a first person perspective on government intelligence and Iraq's WMD program' (2014); and 'Reconceptualizing sectarianism in the Middle East and Asia' (2014). Mailing address: Department of History, California State University San Marcos, San Marcos, California, 92096, USA. E-mail: ialmarashi@csusm.edu

Yaakov Ariel is a graduate of the Hebrew University and the University of Chicago. Ariel is a professor of religious studies at the University of North Carolina at Chapel Hill. His research focuses on Christian–Jewish relations in the modern era, on Christian attitudes towards the Holy Land and Israel and on Jewish and Christian New Religious Movements and the effect of the counterculture on Jewish and Christian groups. His book *Evangelizing the Chosen People* won the Outler Prize of the American Society of Church History. His latest book, *An Unusual Relationship: Evangelical Christians and Jews*, was published by New York University Press in 2013. Mailing address: University of North Carolina at Chapel Hill, Department of Religious Studies, CB# 3225,125 Saunders Hall, UNC-Chapel Hill, Chapel Hill, NC 27599-3225, USA. E-mail: yariel@email.unc.edu

Simon Coleman is Chancellor Jackman Professor at the Department for the Study of Religion, University of Toronto. Previously, he was Chair of the Department of Anthropology, University of Sussex. He has been editor of the *Journal of the Royal Anthropological Institute*, and is co-editor of *Religion in Society*, as well as co-editor of the book series *Routledge Studies in Pilgrimage, Religious Travel and Tourism*. He has carried out fieldwork in Sweden, the UK and Nigeria, and is currently part of a team working on pilgrimage to English cathedrals. Books include *Reframing Pilgrimage: Cultures in Motion*, edited with John Eade (2004, published by Routledge). Mailing address: Department for the Study of Religion, Jackman Humanities Building, Rm.333, 170 St George Street, University of Toronto, Ontario, M5R 2M8, Canada. E-mail: simon.coleman@utoronto.ca

Tariq Elhadary is the Acting Head of Admission and University Preparation at United Arab Emirates (UAE) Ministry of Presidential Affairs, Scholarships Office. He is a former lecturer of English language and translation at Ajman University for Science and Technology. He received his MPhil in English studies and educational methods from the University of Glasgow in 1998, and his PhD in applied linguistics and Qur'anic studies from the University of Leeds in 2008. His current research activities are in the fields of religious studies, religious tourism and academic advising. Mailing address: Ministry of Presidential Affairs, Scholarships Office, 73505 Al Najda St., Abu Dhabi, UAE. E-mail: tariqelhadary@yahoo.com

Aron Engberg is a PhD candidate in religious studies at Lund University. His PhD is based on fieldwork among international evangelical volunteer workers in Jerusalem and he analyses the relationship between individual life stories and religio-political narratives in order to explore the symbolic role of Israel in evangelical identity formation. Mailing address: Centre for Theology and Religious Studies, Lund University, CTR, LUX, Box 192, 221 00 Lund, Sweden. E-mail: aron.engberg@ctr.lu.se

Vreny Enongene is currently a PhD candidate at the Dublin Institute of Technology. She has a background in tourism marketing and management, and is currently undertaking a PhD in religious tourism. She also has interest in the broad area of cultural heritage tourism management, as well as in the emerging trends and issues in tourism in the emerging tourism destinations of the Global South. Mailing address: School of Hospitality Management and Tourism, Dublin Institute of Technology, Cathal Brugha Street, Dublin 1, Ireland. E-mail: vreny.enongene1@mydit.ie

Kevin Griffin is a lecturer in tourism at the Dublin Institute of Technology, where he teaches students from undergraduate to PhD level. His research interests are broad, but primarily encompass a range of tourism themes such as heritage, culture, social tourism, the pedagogy of fieldwork and in particular religious tourism and pilgrimage. He is co-founder of the *International Journal of Religious Tourism and Pilgrimage*, and has published widely. His main recent publications include: *Cultural Tourism*, (2013, edited with Raj and Morpeth); *Religious Tourism and Pilgrimage Management: An International Perspective*, 2nd edn (2015, edited with Raj); *Conflicts, Challenges, Religion and Culture* (2017, edited with Raj). Mailing address: School of Hospitality Management and Tourism, Dublin Institute of Technology, Cathal Brugha Street, Dublin 1, Ireland. E-mail: kevin.griffin@dit.ie

Göran Gunner is Associate Professor in Mission Studies, Uppsala University, and Researcher at the Church of Sweden Research Unit, Uppsala. Dr Gunner is also Senior Lecturer at Stockholm School of Theology, Stockholm, Sweden. His research areas include religious minority situations in the Middle East and issues related to human rights. He is also the editor of the Church of Sweden Research Series. Among his publications are *An Unlikely Dilemma: Constructing a Partnership between Human Rights and Peace-Building* (co-authored with Kjell-Åke Nordquist, 2011) and *Genocide of Armenians: Through Swedish Eyes* (2013). He is also co-editor of *Lutheran Identity and Political Theology* (2014), *Justification in a Post-Christian Society* (2014) and *Comprehending Christian Zionism: Perspectives in Comparison* (2014). Mailing address: Church of Sweden Research Unit, Svenska kyrkan, SE-751 70 Uppsala, Sweden. E-mail: goran.gunner@svenskakyrkan.se

Motti Inbari is an associate professor of religion at the University of North Carolina at Pembroke. Dr Inbari focuses his research on Jewish fundamentalism mostly in Israel, but also in the USA and Europe. He is the author of: *Jewish Fundamentalism and the Temple Mount* (2009, State University of New York (SUNY) University Press); *Messianic Religious Zionism Confronts Israeli Territorial Compromises* (2012, Cambridge University Press); and *Jewish Radical Ultra-Orthodoxy Confronts Modernity, Zionism and Women's Equality* (2016, Cambridge University Press). Mailing address: Religion and Philosophy, The University of North Carolina at Pembroke, One University Drive, PO Box 1510, Pembroke, NC 28372-1510, USA. E-mail: mordechai.inbari@uncp.edu

Moshe Kalian is now retired. In the last 10 years of his civil service he held the position of the District Psychiatrist of Jerusalem in the Israeli Ministry of Health. During his long professional career he was the head of a psychiatric ward in Kfar Shaul hospital in Jerusalem and then the District Psychiatrist of the Central Region of Israel. He was also twice the chairman of the Jerusalem branch of the Israeli Psychiatric Association and the chairman of the Israel Society for Forensic Psychiatry. He wrote several dozen scientific publications in issues of forensic psychiatry and 'Jerusalem syndrome'. He is the co-author of the book *Jerusalem of Holiness and Madness*, published in Hebrew in 2013. Mailing address: Ben-Gurion University, Mental Health Center, Ben-Gurion University of the Negev, Beer-Sheva 84170, Israel. E-mail: kalian@netvision.net.il

Maria Leppäkari is Director of the Swedish Theological Institute in Jerusalem, a research and study institute run by the Church of Sweden since 1951 in Israel. Her work in Jerusalem is characterized by interreligious dialogue, sustainable development and religious-political perspectives. Dr Leppäkari is Associate Professor in Comparative Religion at Åbo Akademi University (Finland). Her academic work has focused on Jerusalem as a meaning-creating symbol; the study of religion and violence in apocalyptic settings; and pilgrimage and health promotion. See: *Apocalypti Representations of Jerusalem* (2006) and *Hungry for Heaven: The Dynamics of Apocalyptic Violence* (2008). Dr Leppäkari was Visiting Researcher at Hebrew University 1998–1999, Visiting Scholar at the Swedish Theological Institute in Jerusalem 1998 and Visiting Research Fellow at the University of California Riverside 2007. Mailing address: Swedish Theological Institute in Jerusalem, PO Box 37, IL-910001 Jerusalem, Israel. E-mail: maria.leppakari@abo.fi

Razaq Raj is an internationally renowned academic with over 15 years higher education experience of teaching and research in the UK, Malta, Portugal, Spain, Italy, Germany, China and South Korea. He is Principal Lecturer and is a visiting professor at the Kedge Business School, France and University of Vitez, Bosnia. He has published work on strategic management, economic and financial impacts, cultural festivals, sustainable tourism and religious tourism. He has both organized international conferences and delivered keynote speeches. He has published in a number of peer-reviewed journals and conference proceedings. He has substantial experience of developing international partnerships in Germany and the Middle East and also sits on voluntary sector management boards. He is often sought out by news media for his views on international terrorism and has been a guest on BBC and Sky News. Mailing address: Leeds Business School, Leeds Beckett University, 520 The Rose Bowl, Portland Gate, Leeds, LS1 3HB, UK. E-mail: r.raj@leedsmet.ac.uk

Irfan Raja is a researcher in the School of Music, Humanities and Media at the University of Huddersfield, with expertise in areas such as human resources, communications and media. His publications and conference papers include: book chapter – 'Emerging power of new media and post-election violence in Iran' (2013); conference paper – 'Framing Pakistan, Islam and the War on Terror' (2013); conference paper – 'Old conflict, new perspective: social media and news from Gaza' (2011); and conference paper – 'The mosque as a religious place and institution for Muslims and the myth of British media' (2011). Mailing address: School of Music, Humanities and Media, University of Huddersfield, Huddersfield, HD1 3DH, UK. E-mail: irfan.journalist@gmail.com

Anna Trono who has been awarded the national scientific qualification of full professor in Geography, is now Associate Professor of Political and Economic Geography at the Department of Cultural Heritage, University of the Salento, where she teaches PhD, Masters and Bachelor Degree courses. Her special research interests are regional and urban policies, cultural and environmental heritage and sustainable tourism. She has published numerous essays and books on these themes. As chief scientist or other component of work groups, she is actively involved in the preparation and management of numerous national and international research projects and conferences on religious tourism and cultural itineraries. Mailing address: Political Economic Geography, Department of Cultural Heritage, University of Salento, Via Dalmazio Birago 64, 73100, Lecce, Italy. E-mail: anna.trono@unisalento.it

Eliezer Witztum is a full professor in the Division of Psychiatry, Faculty of Health Sciences, Ben-Gurion University of the Negev and Director of the School for Psychotherapy, Mental Health Center, Beer Sheva. He specializes in cultural psychiatry, trauma and bereavement, strategic and short-time dynamic psychotherapy treatment of paedophiles and history of psychiatry. He has written more than 200 scientific publications. His recent books include *Sanity and Sanctity* (2001) and *King Herod: A Persecuted Persecutor: A Case Study in Psychohistory and Psychobiography* (2007). Together with Professor Lerner he wrote *Genius and Madness* (Hebrew) (2009) and *Working With the Bereaved: Multiple Lenses on Loss and Mourning* (2012) and together with Professor Rubin, Dr Malkinson and Dr Moshe Kalian *Jerusalem of Holiness and Madness* (Hebrew) (2013). Recently he wrote *Social, Cultural and Clinical Aspects of Ethiopian Immigrants in Israel* (2014) with Dr Nimrod Grisaru. Mailing address: Mental Health Center, Ben-Gurion University of the Negev, Beer-Sheva 84170, Israel. E-mail: elyiit@actcom.co.il

Introduction

1 Western Holy Cities and Places – An Introduction

Maria Leppäkari[1]* and Kevin Griffin[2]

[1]Swedish Theological Institute in Jerusalem and Åbo Akademi University, Finland; [2]Dublin Institute of Technology, Dublin, Ireland

This book is about a Western conception of pilgrimage as it is understood and referred to from three specific perspectives, that of Judaism, Christianity and Islam. The original idea of the book was to serve as an aid to site managers, students of religion and tourism, as well as others seeking to understand the complex world of religiously motivated travel. Being the first volume in the CABI *Religious Tourism and Pilgrimage Series*, it provides new perspectives on old, familiar and well-documented themes with a fresh approach in relation to perspectives on ideological motives, history, management, mental health and religious perceptions. The volume collects for the first time between the covers of a book and presents in an interdisciplinary perspective, the thoughts of authors from various academic fields. This heterogeneity allows a broad span of expertise, information and knowledge that previously can be found only through a thorough search of books and journals. Here practical applications, models and illustrations of religious tourism and pilgrimage management are being studied from a variety of international perspectives. The chapter authors explore the emergence and trajectories of religious tourism and pilgrimage while including a variety of denominations, religions, faiths and spiritual practices. Each author demonstrates in his or her own fashion how intrinsic details play a crucial role within the various pilgrimage management processes.

As presented in the book, multidisciplinary approaches are paramount for generating holistic perspectives when exploring and understanding complex management concepts in relation to pilgrimage phenomena in what is here referred to as 'holy cities' (i.e. places or specific spots in Western cities prescribed with the noun 'sacred' and thus constituting pilgrimage sites). Many times, these sites are referred to as 'holy cities' in Judaism, Christianity and Islam. In a blended manner, the chapters account for current and diverse empirical research insights

*maria.leppakari@abo.fi

which highlight aspects of religious tourism and pilgrimage by juxtaposing state of the art reflections on emerging theoretical foundations of the subject matter. Our wish is that the reader will find this a fresh approach when working through the various aspects that are accounted for here: ideological motives, history, safety management, mental health, technology and sustainable development in combination with an understanding of different religious perceptions.

Words such as 'religion', 'pilgrimage' and 'meaning-creating processes' are addressed and problematized in the chapters, and a concluding remark on the use of the words is presented in the book's final chapter in order to tie together the different chapters and perspectives which span over time, space and place. The final chapter also attempts to finally discuss the role of 'religion' in terms of these concepts. Essentially, this book is about understanding the impact and identifying the trajectories of religiously motivated travel, how religiously conceptualized places are imbued with special meaning; special meaning which creates qualities and promotes the importance of reflection in relation to general assumptions about such concepts.

The existential dimension of the 'holy place' and 'holy city' is defined as a place that is evocative of affective inner structures and this is often considered to be an underlying constituent of human patterns of action, thinking and relating, and therefore is of tremendous importance for understanding both religiosity and worldview. A 'place' or 'city' is not only considered as physical. Humans as moral subjects inhabit places, which are constituent of symbolical sets and references. As a comprehensive model, such existential dimensions of a 'place' bring together the varying foci of different theoretical perspectives on a more general level.

Here 'place' or 'city' is defined as a *centre of meaning shaped by memories, expectations, stories of real and imagined events and visceral feelings*. As a symbol, *a place* sensitizes us and blurs the boundary between the world and ourselves. Through the senses a place is also evocative of an existential dimension. An existential place, *the city* acknowledges emotional, interpretative and phenomenological dimensions. Sites that are prescribed with sanctity in Judaism, Christianity and Islam have deep roots in contributing to societal development and reshaping global scenery.

It is evident that multidisciplinary approaches are paramount when generating an holistic perspective, when exploring and understanding management concepts. We hope that the reader will appreciate the holistic perspectives presented in the following chapters and through them develop a broader understanding of cultural sustainability, which here is particularly promoted through the combination of cases representing three monotheistic faith-traditions. A religious tourism industry has grown considerably in recent decades based on the 'holy cities' of Judaism, Christianity and Islam, which have, through history, drawn pilgrims and religious tourists, adventurers, authors and entrepreneurs. This growth is demonstrated, not only in economic terms in the number of visitors, but also in the number of tourism and cultural management courses integrated and established at universities. It is also apparent by the number of cultural, entertainment and business-related facilities operating in the industry. Such a growth of interest simultaneously calls for ethical reflection and reminds us that there is a multitude of factors which every traveller has to consider regarding the implications of his/her visit to 'holy places'; all visitors leave a mark, and we must ensure that through years of interaction between site and visitor that we protect against physical, societal, ethical and identity erosion.

The aim of this book is to provide an eclectic collection of contemporary perspectives on central Western sites prescribed with sanctity. The book provides perspectives on old, familiar and well-documented themes with a fresh and unique approach in relation to ideological motives, history, safety management, mental health and religious perceptions. Thus, bringing together experts, information and knowledge that previously could only be found through extensive research in disparate disciplines/publications. The basic idea here is to demonstrate to the reader that certain intrinsic details play a crucial role within the pilgrimage management process. Here, multidisciplinary approaches are paramount for generating an understanding of holistic perspectives when exploring and comprehending management concepts.

Most books that deal with monotheistic faith-traditions are oriented towards a more-or-less classic understanding (i.e. historical perspectives, history of religions, political perspectives on cultural conflicts and so forth) of the pilgrimage phenomenon in relation to holy cities, therefore this volume is innovative in its approach. As we see it, this book contrasts with what is available at present in the market. Our multi-faith approach to sacred spaces, with emphasis on a practical application of religious tourism and pilgrimage management, will hopefully be a valuable reference for academics, students and practitioners as it is a timely text on the future of faith-based tourism and pilgrimage. In the end, if we want to understand 'the big picture' we need to explore different aspects of different faiths, different forms of different activities to help us to contextualize what we are dealing with, and further develop our global understanding of this activity which we call pilgrimage.

Structure of the Book

Part I of the book, 'Western Pilgrimage to Holy Cities in Judaism, Christianity and Islam', provides us with perspectives on both past and present, time and space. In **Chapter 2, (*Judaism – Jewish and Israeli Pilgrimage Experience: Constructing National Identity*)** Motti Inbari provides contemporary and historical perspectives on Jewish pilgrimage. The chapter focuses on the Jewish custom of visiting tombs as an act of pilgrimage. The author argues that the modern Jewish experience continues an ancient custom (in the State of Israel and by diaspora), and it now exhibits both spiritual and national dimensions. Ancient Judaism demanded pilgrimage three times a year to the Temple in Jerusalem, as a religious duty which was constituted in the Bible. These pilgrimages continued until the destruction of the Second Temple in 70 CE; however, after this destruction, the religious authorities issued a ban over Jewish visits to the Temple Mount. Another ban on mass immigration to the Land of Israel was also imposed, out of fear of an eruption of messianic fervour. From medieval times, the focus of Jewish pilgrimage turned to visiting tombs of biblical figures and holy men. In modern times, the Jewish people have gone through strong trends of secularization. Therefore, some of the pilgrimage activities exhibit both secular and national dimensions. This chapter describes two aspects of pilgrimages in modern Judaism – spiritual and national. Examples of spiritual pilgrimage include visits to the graves of holy men such as Rabbi Menachem Mendel Schneeorson's Lubavitcher Rebbe burial site in Brooklyn New York or the grave of Rabbi Israel Abuhatzeira (the Baba Sali) in Netivot, Israel. The chapter then describes two Zionist national pilgrimage sites – the death camps in Auschwitz Poland and Masada archaeological site in Israel.

Chapter 3 by Vreny Enongene and Kevin Griffin (***Christianity – Contemporary Christian Pilgrimage and Traditional Management Practices at Sacred Sites***) explores contemporary Christian pilgrimage experiences, with emphasis on where pilgrimage fits in the life of a contemporary believer. In so doing, it addresses the changing demands of contemporary pilgrims, as well as the factors that are shaping current pilgrimage patterns. The chapter explores how the changing needs and expectations of contemporary pilgrims are altering traditional management practices at sacred sites, and provides examples of innovative management approaches adopted in catering to these needs. It further analyses the implications of such pressures on management at sacred sites and the future of contemporary pilgrimage experiences, and questions where pilgrimage fits in the life of a contemporary Christian, and whether or not traditional pilgrimage practice has really undergone a fundamental change in recent times.

Christianity – Christian Pilgrimage to Sacred Sites in the Holy Land: a Swedish Perspective is the title of Göran Gunner's chapter (**Chapter 4**) which takes a past and present perspective on Swedish Christian pilgrimage; examining how the Reformation in Sweden put a ban on pilgrimage and travels to Jerusalem and Rome as well as stopping domestic pilgrim routes. Swedes travelling to Jerusalem took the shape of explorers, some of them fairly successful. A more popular alternative emerged whereby travellers sought to see as much as possible of the land, people and sites. Many had the ambition to write a travel story to spread awareness at home. The pattern of their activity is clear – there was no tradition of honouring the traditional holy sites but instead the authors described them in rather negative terms. The authors instead developed new scenarios, attracting Swedes to the garden of Gordon's Golgotha or the Sea of Galilee. At the same time, the Holy Land was placed centrally in churches and chapels in Sweden through maps, pictures and hymns, and the 19th-century revival movement transferred biblical sites to their own premises named as Bethlehem, Zion, Tabor and so forth. Modern pilgrims follow the same pattern with an intention to see as much as possible, briefly visiting holy places during a tour while admiring – when they come in contact with them – 'original places' in nature. During the last 20 years, pilgrimage has received a boost in Sweden.

Providing an Islamic perspective, **Chapter 5** by Razaq Raj and Irfan Raja (***Islam – Contemporary Perspectives***) contextualizes Islam within contemporary societal development in Europe, wherein Western societies have begun to view Islam as incompatible with, and a security threat to, their secular and liberal way of life. In the chapter it is discussed that this is mainly because most often sections of the media, polity and conservative writers present a distasteful view of Islam, featuring it as a source of social ills and all sorts of troubles in the world. Several notable studies are offered to provide convincing analysis that the media has an important role in building misperceptions and misunderstandings of Islam. Accordingly, the authors note that such narratives of Islam present a view which suggests that Islam is an old-fashioned, authoritarian, outdated religion. Focusing on the motivation for Muslims to attend mosques on a daily basis, the chapter attempts to highlight the loving nature of the Islamic faith.

Chapter 6 by Tariq Elhadary (***Islam – Spiritual Journey in Islam: The Qur'anic Cognitive Model***) has two objectives. First, to acquaint the reader with certain Islamic matters which they should grasp before embarking on an Islamic-related religious journey, or more specifically visiting Muslim religious historical places, if they wish to reach a more than superficial understanding of the Qur'an. Second, the chapter illuminates the major tenets of faith referred to in the Qur'an. Thus, the chapter attempts to clarify the concept of pilgrimage in Islam and to address questions about Islam that commonly arise in the mind of the non-Muslim tourist (and/or pilgrim). These notions are drawn out and explored by utilizing the Qur'anic Cognitive Model (or QCM) and thus, present the basic claims of the Qur'an and thereby minimize the degree of deviation from mainstream Islam. The chapter focuses on Islamic monotheism, on the essential comprehensive characteristics of Islamic doctrine and its primary bases. It also illustrates the relationship between God's omnipotence and monotheism. The theme of prophethood and the message of the Qur'an are discussed in some detail and linked to an investigation of the human mission on earth – particularly exploring the search to achieve and maintain balance.

Part II of the book, 'Managing Pilgrimage Sites in Holy Cities', addresses a range of management issues in relation to holy spaces and contested places, and continues the breadth of perspectives presented in the introductory chapters.

Simon Coleman's chapter (**Chapter 7**) entitled ***Pilgrimage Policy Management: Between Shrine Strategy and Ritual Improvisation*** challenges conventional models of managing pilgrimage sites in the West, which often see administrators and managers as needing to 'protect' the sacred from tourists who lack the knowledge to engage in appropriate ways with the shrine and its environs. In addition, it is often assumed – at least by many scholars of religion – that the area of primary interest and focus in a shrine is at its religious and liturgical centre, where the core of believers/pilgrims tend to be concentrated and also to act in relatively more predictable ways. Drawing on his own work on pilgrimage shrines and cathedrals in England, as well as on wider literature on pilgrimage sites around Europe, the author questions both of these assumptions. The author carefully considers the implications which his arguments have for the management of shrines – what if we seek to relocate or at least to recognize key points of engagement by pilgrims and tourists away from apparent liturgical and aesthetic 'centres', and thus widen our perspective to examine the wider locales around shrines as places of complex, often unpredictable, but certainly not trivial engagement? One implication of such an approach is to blur the boundaries between sacred and secular, but also between shrine and wider environment.

Chapter 8 by Moshe Kalian and Eliezer Witztum (***The Management of Pilgrims with Malevolent Behaviour in a Holy Space: a Study of Jerusalem Syndrome***) presents a fascinating discussion on the health implications of travel in general, and more specifically about pilgrimage and mental health. The authors are professors in psychiatry and have a wealth of both clinical-practice-based and theoretical perspectives in addressing challenges and opportunities when it comes to both pilgrims and religious tourists. Though their explicit area of expertise in health studies is the popularly known 'Jerusalem Syndrome', their chapter discusses general Western perspectives on mental health, meaning-creating processes and personal crises when travelling. The authors address the relevance of religious traditions (Judaism, Christianity and Islam) in mental health work among pilgrims and religious travellers.

Chapter 9 by Anna Trono explores some of the key *Logistics at Holy Sites* and discusses how management is a complicated task because planners and managers have to cater for the needs of various market segments and remember that the spiritual experience is paramount – these are not primarily tourism sites. Focusing on pilgrimage as an opportunity for local development, the chapter considers the holy site as an economic and cultural asset and analyses how small and big organizations of pilgrimage and local/regional authorities manage tourist flows at their sites, ensuring availability of infrastructure, transport, communication, facilities and private businesses, including tour operators and hotel providers. The author also discusses positive factors, limitations, threats and opportunities for an optimal management of sacred sites looking at a range of studies in Western countries.

In **Chapter 10** (*Protestants and Pilgrimages: the Protestant Infrastructure in Jerusalem*), Yaakov Ariel discusses the historical development of Protestant pilgrimage infrastructure in Jerusalem, as a substantial element of Western pilgrimage organization. In theory, Protestants have not recognized the concept of holy sites and pilgrimages, but since the 19th century 'the Holy Land', and especially Jerusalem, has been treated pretty much as a land embodied with special meaning. The chapter studies the formation of Protestant pilgrimage infrastructure from its early beginnings in the 1820s until 1948. It also explores the theological views that motivated or enhanced such projects. It points to the long-term impact of the agencies and the efforts of Protestants when undertaking this work. The chapter highlights the roots of pilgrimage infrastructure development and its consequences for modern-day religious tourism.

In his chapter (**Chapter 11 – *The Impact of the Islamic State of Iraq and Syria's Campaign on Yezidi Religious Structures and Pilgrimage Practices***) Ibrahim Al-Marashi discusses how the Islamic State of Iraq and Syria (ISIS), through the expulsion of Iraqi Christian Chaldean and 'heterodox' Yezidi and Sabean communities, and the destruction of their religious churches, temples and practices, seeks to create a homogenous neo-Salafi space by 'religious cleansing' of persons and physical structures. The chapter considers the ramifications of such a campaign and how it stretches beyond the local. Eliminating these religious sites severs the opportunity for religious pilgrimage for these minority diaspora and destroys the only spiritual link these exile and refuge communities possess to their ancestral lands. The destruction of sites of non-Muslim sacred architecture is embedded in a process of deporting Iraq's minorities, and crushing any religious focal point that could unite their diasporas to the area controlled by Islamic State through the act of pilgrimage, resembling the destruction of the Temple by the Roman Empire.

In **Chapter 12**, Aron Engberg presents the position of *Evangelical Volunteers in Israel as Long-term Pilgrims: Ambassadors for the Kingdom*. This chapter explores the boundaries between tourism, volunteer work and pilgrimage. What is the role of religious discourse in the production of sites and practices as sacred? The author explores these questions in relation to contemporary evangelical Christian volunteer work in Israel as an example of 'long-term pilgrimage'. In discourses on the volunteer, seemingly secular and political sites and practices are placed within eschatological narratives and infused with other-worldly meaning. The author argues that what makes it reasonable to conceptualize these trips as 'pilgrimage' is not found in their engagement with traditional sacred spaces but rather in the seemingly secular ones. Such observations are important for understanding the role of ideological narratives in the production of religious sites and practices.

Providing a conclusion to the book, in **Chapter 13**, Maria Leppäkari's discussion on *Redeeming Western Holy Places and Contested Holy Cities* addresses 'holy places' in relation to 'holy cities' and challenges pilgrimage and tourism research when addressing religious concepts. 'Holy cities' are cities like any others, yet they are not. Cities described as holy are more complex in character than 'ordinary' urban settlements. Within the sphere of religion certain geographical sites are of intrinsic importance, as sacred places, and attract people in a very special way. Such sites have come to signify something 'holy'. A 'city' is not only to be considered as physical, it also comprises space occupied by humans as moral subjects, inhabiting symbolic sets and references to specific places. In this chapter, the author's reflections on the impact of this collection of chapters, provides new perspectives on old, familiar and well-documented themes and brings forth a fresh approach in relation to ideological motives, ethics and justice, history, management, mental health and religious perceptions.

In conclusion, sustainable development in dialogue and conflict settings is addressed as part of a delicate societal development. Here, identity-making abilities and living symbolisms are identified, highlighted and further described in order to expand the reader's perspectives. This final discussion takes management beyond traditional perspectives and in the end, the author argues that pilgrims and religious tourists might think they are redeeming a city (as discussed widely in tourism literature), but it is actually the opposite, in the three monotheistic religions which have been explored in this volume, there are clear signals that place is an important element in redeeming the pilgrim.

Part I Western Pilgrimage to Holy Cities in Judaism, Christianity and Islam

2   Judaism – Jewish and Israeli Pilgrimage Experience: Constructing National Identity

MOTTI INBARI*

The University of North Carolina at Pembroke, Pembroke, USA

Introduction

Pilgrimage to the holy city of Jerusalem was a major ancient Jewish ritual. This chapter will discuss how this ancient tradition was transformed in the modern, secular, Israeli–Jewish experience. To this end, three different contemporary pilgrimage locations are presented, along with an explanation of how these new shrines are used for the creation of a national myth. New pilgrimage sites have helped develop Israeli identity, and even secular locations were sanctified. This process was promoted by the State of Israel, thus turning them into political pilgrimages. A different type of pilgrimage was also created from grass roots, by popular participation in newly dedicated shrines of North African Jewish saints. Thus, the renewed Jewish national home on the biblical borders of the Land of Israel also renewed ancient rituals of Jewish life, but in different locations and with different meanings.

According to sociologist Victor Turner, a pilgrimage is a sacred journey of spiritual ascension to a spiritual centre, a mythical land of pristine existence. Later on, pilgrimage became a form of non-instrumental travelling in traditional and particularly peasant societies (Turner and Turner, 1978). A pilgrimage has two elements: (i) the external journey to the sacred site; and (ii) the internal journey as a transformative spiritual experience. In addition, pilgrimage can also be used in secular contexts – for example, pilgrimages to war graves, celebrities' homes and football stadia (Blackwell, 2014).

Eric Cohen in his seminal piece on pilgrimage argues that a pilgrimage is a journey to one's centre which is beyond the boundaries of the immediate life space. Modern tourism, Cohen claims, involves gradual abandonment of the traditional,

*mordechai.inbari@uncp.edu

© CAB International 2017. *Pilgrimage and Tourism to Holy Cities:*
Ideological and Management Perspectives (eds M. Leppäkari and K. Griffin)

sacred image of the cosmos, and the awakening of interest in culture, social life and the natural environment of others. He argues that pilgrimages and modern tourism are thus predicated on different social conceptions of space and contrary views concerning the kind of destination worth visiting. As a result, they involve opposite directions: in pilgrimage the destination is from the periphery towards the cultural centre, but in modern tourism, it is away from the cultural centre into the periphery (Cohen, 1979).

This chapter will review the tradition of Jewish pilgrimage to the ancient Temple, explain its purpose and meaning, and discuss the reasons for its termination. Modern pilgrimages to state-sponsored locations in Masada and to death camps in Poland such as Auschwitz-Birkenau, Majdenek and Treblinka will then be presented. The third type that will be reviewed is a grass-roots pilgrimage to a venerated saint's shrine which lies in Israel's periphery.

Historical Perspectives

Jerusalem holds a unique place in Jewish imagination, and its pre-eminence in the heart of the Jewish people cannot be overestimated. In Jewish legends, the Temple Mount in Jerusalem holds the foundation stone of the world (Babylonian Talmud, Yoma 54a); The Bible mentions Mt Moriah as Issac's binding place (Genesis 22).

In the Bible it is written that upon the cessation of a plague, King David purchased the Temple Mount in Jerusalem in order to erect an altar. David wanted to construct a permanent temple there, but as his hands were desecrated by blood he was forbidden to do so himself, so the task was left to his son, Solomon, who completed it (2 Samuel 24: 18–25).

The Bible lays out the divine authorization for pilgrimage to Jerusalem's First Temple: 'Three times in a year you shall hold a festival for me' (Exodus 23: 14). The three times are specified in Deuteronomy 16: 16 as the Jewish festivals of *Passover*, *Shavu'ot* and *Sukkot*. These pilgrimages were mandatory in historical times, but applied only for men. They required a personal appearance in Jerusalem and were linked directly to key moments in the agricultural cycle and required pilgrims to bring a portion of their harvest with them as a gift for the Temple. The ancient spring festival of Passover, with its offering of young lambs and sheaves of first-cut barley, became the occasion for the recounting of the events of the exodus from Egypt. Shavu'ot, the festival of the wheat harvest 7 weeks after Passover, commemorated God giving the Laws to Moses on Mount Sinai. And Sukkot, in early autumn when the first fruits and grapes were gathered, came to recall the 40-year period of wandering in the desert (Gitlitz and Davidson, 2006, p. 25).

The Second Temple (built to replace the destroyed First Temple) was built after Cyrus' declaration that can be found in the Book of Ezra (1: 1–6). This structure was also central for the life of the Jewish nation. During the festival of *Aliya laregel* (literally meaning ascension or pilgrimage in Hebrew) there was a commandment to bring sacrifice and to bow down in front of the Temple's gates. Many visitors used to watch the priests conducting their work and it was known that the study of the Torah was taking place in the Temple yard. In order to maintain the Temple, the administration collected special taxes. The Sanhedrin sat at the Temple's gates and served as a judicial authority as well as a religious one. Therefore, pilgrimages to the site were important tools for communication and exchange of information between the small minority of Jews living in the Land of Israel and the majority that were living in exile.

Although the official commandment of pilgrimage in Judaism requires travelling three times a year, it is possible that not every Jew went on them all, but probably sacrifice was sent with the envoys. Entering Jerusalem required special purifications, and ritual baths were built at the Temple gates. During pilgrimage, the city was packed with visitors, which scholar Shmuel Safrai estimated to be several tens of thousands. During the time of the pilgrimage, it was believed that the sacredness of the Temple was expanding towards the whole city so that sacrifice offered inside the city, but not in the Temple which was overcrowded, was regarded as sufficient fulfilment of the commandment (Safrai, 1965).

During pilgrimages, Jewish pride grew and inflamed several revolts against Rome that took place on these occasions (Hengel, 1989). In the year 70 CE, the Great Revolt against Rome failed and the Temple was burned to the ground. Since then, Judaism, as a religion, functions without an operating Temple, and synagogues replaced the Temple as the place of worship. With the destruction of the Temple, pilgrimages to the holy city were terminated. In fact, through the generations, rabbis actually banned Jews from visiting the Temple site. According to Halacha (Jewish religious law), all Jews are considered to be impure due to contact with the dead, since they have come into contact with deceased persons or with others who have at some point been in such contact. During the Second Temple period (536 BCE – 70 CE) Jews were cleansed from the impurity of the dead by virtue of the 'sin water' – the ashes of the red heifer mixed in water. Since the destruction of the Second Temple, red heifers have not been available. Moreover, the precise dimensions of the Temple have been lost, including the location of the *Kodesh Kodashim* – the most sacred site – identified as the dwelling place of the *Shechina*, the Divine Presence. Entry into this section of the Temple was absolutely prohibited, with the exception of the High Priest (who was cleansed with the 'sin water' before performing his sacred duties) on the Day of Atonement. Since the location of the Temple was no longer known, and since red heifers were unavailable, it was ruled that Jews were prohibited from entering the entire Temple Mount area, even though this area is known to be bigger than that of the Temple itself. Accordingly, a person who enters the Temple Mount area incurs the (theoretical) penalty of *Karet* (the Divinely-imposed death penalty). This position that prohibits Jews from entering the Temple Mount has been supported in numerous Halachic rulings (Sheffer, 1968).

Jewish existence is encapsulated in two dichotomous rabbinical perceptions – exile and redemption. Since the destruction of the Second Temple, the Jewish people have been in exile. Rabbinical exegesis views this exile as spiritual as well as physical. The End of Exile can come only through prophetic leadership and miracles leading to ultimate and complete redemption. Thus, the rabbis demanded messianic passivity. The miraculous approach, based mainly on the rulings of Rashi (1040–1105), a famous medieval French rabbi, argues that the Temple will descend ready-made from the skies. Therefore, human action is not required in order to reconstruct it (Inbari, 2009).

In 691 CE the Dome of Rock mosque was completed on the Temple Mount in Jerusalem, by the order of Abd Al-Malik, the Muslim ruler of Damascus, for Jerusalem is considered the third holiest site to Islam, after Mecca and Medina in the Arab Peninsula. In the 1967 war, the State of Israel occupied the Temple Mount. Since that war, Israeli governments have sought to mitigate the tension raised by this action, and have allowed two major mosques to be located on the mount, and have thus allowed the Muslim Waqf to maintain its control of the Temple Mount. This status quo arrangement was introduced by Moshe Dayan, Israeli Minister of Defence, following the occupation of the holy sites, and stated that the Temple Mount would continue to serve as a Muslim place of prayer, while the Western Wall would be a Jewish place of prayer. Due to Jewish religious restrictions on entering the most sacred areas of the Temple Mount, the Western Wall has become, for practical purposes, the holiest generally accessible site for Jews to pray at (Inbari, 2009).

From a historical and theological level, the Land of Israel, and particularly Jerusalem, holds significance in Jewish memory. Zionism, the modern Jewish national movement, was intended to secularize the Jewish people, and to separate political action from religious philosophies. Zionism opposed Jewish passivity when it came to the question of immigration to the Land of Israel. Thus, early Zionist immigrants were secular in most cases; however, their act of immigration was couched in religious language. Immigration was called *Aliya*, which means accent, and it is the same term that was used for Jewish pilgrimage to the Holy Temple (*Aliya laregel*) during ancient times. The blurring of the lines between religious and secular was made on purpose, and a link between national traditions and religious rituals was created. With that, the State of Israel also sanctified national shrines, some which previously had meanings, but also it was bound to change them according to newly created national needs (Gitlitz and Davidson, 2006, pp. 189–192).

Pilgrimage to Masada

One of the new national pilgrimage sites was Masada, an ancient fortress on a high plateau overlooking the Dead Sea and the Judean desert. King Herod the Great (73–4 BCE) chose to build on this site a palace and a place of refuge. However, this place was used as the last stronghold of the Jewish revolt against Rome. The story of the fall of Masada was recorded by Flavius Josephus, the Jewish historian who was a contemporary to the events he recorded. Josephus reported that the Romans besieged Masada and prepared a massive break into the walls of the fortress. Once the leader of the Jewish rebels, Elazar ben Yair, realized there was no other way of escaping, he decided to commit an act of communal suicide, martyrdom, so that he and his supporters would not fall as slaves to the Romans. The next day, when the Romans entered the fortress, they found 960 dead bodies. The story of Masada recorded by Josephus was never popular among Jews, and the story wasn't documented in any other Jewish source of antiquity, like the Talmud (Brighton, 2009).

The new secular interest in ancient Hebraic past prepared the ground for Masada's odyssey from the periphery of historical chronicles to the centre of modern Jewish historical consciousness. The Zionist interest in the ancient national past encouraged a fascination with the Judean war of liberation. When the Hebrew translation of Josephus's *Wars of the Jews* was published in Palestine in 1923, the pioneers hailed it as a major text of historical and national significance (Ben Yehuda, 1995). In 1927, the publication of a poem entitled 'Masada' by Yitzhak Lamdan provided an important stimulus to the reintroduction of Masada into the newly created *Yeshuv* (Jewish settlement) collective memory. As a result, the site turned into a pilgrimage location.

Reaching remote Masada was a complex and rather risky undertaking during the pre-state period. Field trips often lasted a week or longer under difficult conditions. According to Yael Zrubavel, the site's appeal contributed to the development of special rituals that underscore the growing importance of Masada as a national myth (Zrubavel, 1995, p. 64).

Youth trips to Masada took place during the 1910s to 1940s. This turned into a popular tradition, although it resulted in some accidents along the way. The trips emphasized Jewish heroism and the love of freedom. The high degree of physical fitness and strong willpower contributed to a growing fascination with the site.

During the 1950s, an archaeological interest in the ruins had arisen. The first systematic survey of the site was conducted in 1955–1956 by archaeologists from the Hebrew University of Jerusalem. In the 1960s another archaeological expedition was conducted on the site, headed by Professor Yigal Yadin, which received much publicity and government support, and transformed Masada from a neglected cliff in the Judean desert into a major tourist attraction in Israel. As the result of enormous publicity, Masada's history became better known to Israelis and non-Israelis (Zrubavel, 1995, p. 68).

The rituals around Masada developed in various stages. During the first stage, the ritual focused on the long and perilous trip to Masada in its surroundings. When these trips became more common, youth groups began to elaborate their rituals on the top of Masada, and the stay on the site became more significant. Travelling to the site enhanced patriotic education, as the direct encounter of the student with the site left a strong impression on them. Zrubavel argues that field trips were considered a sacred activity through which Hebrew youth could reclaim their roots in the land (Zrubavel, 1995, pp. 120–121). The route served as a symbolic re-enactment of the Jewish struggle for survival. From the 1940s, ceremonies on the mount started to develop. Sections from Josephus's text dramatically quoting Elazar ben Yair's speech about the desire to die free rather than to be enslaved by the Romans was particularly forceful, and so was Lamdan's poem 'Masada'. In addition, youth groups often prepared fire inscriptions stating: 'Never Again Shall Masada Fall'. The dramatic impact was sure to leave a lasting impression on the participating youth (Zrubavel, 1995, p. 128).

From the 1960s the state took control of the site and developed it as an important archaeological centre. The resultant construction of new roads and hotels, and the declaration of the site as a national park, opened a new era of development. A cable car was built to allow travellers a safe and quick entrance, and tickets were sold at the gate. Nowadays, the archaeological ruins are the core attraction for visitors, while the trip itself has lost its significance. Masada had turned into a major tourist attraction, second only to the Western Wall (Zrubavel, 1995, pp. 133–137). The discovery of the ancient synagogue on site gave the place a spiritual dimension, and since 1967 schools developed a new tradition of Bar Mitzvah ceremonies at the discovered synagogue. Thus, the new tradition imbues another rite of passage ceremony on the mount.

Zrubavel argues that Masada, as a sacred shrine, has given rise to various interpretations, each of which promotes a different memory and different ritual tradition. Masada is thus a site of secular folk pilgrimage that serves as a bridge between the ancient past and the present and suppresses the memory of exile. At the same time, it is an official sacred site for national ceremonies. Yet, it is also a religious site that offers a continuity of religious tradition from antiquity to the present. Finally, it is a touristic site that marks all these definitions of sanctity for a wide range of visitors, Israelis, Jewish and non-Jewish (Zrubavel, 1995, p. 137). In 2010, Masada attracted more than 700,000 visitors, and it was named the most visited touristic site in Israel, according to a news report (News1, 2011). Additionally, Masada is second only to the Western Wall in terms of preferred Bar and Bat Mitzvah locations in Israel (Masada, 2015).

Pilgrimage to Auschwitz-Birkenau, Majdenek and Treblinka

Other new important Israeli shrines have been dedicated, interestingly, overseas in Poland at the ghettos, concentration camps and death camps. In Israel, the Shoah (Holocaust), the murder of 6 million Jews by Nazis and their helpers, has left an indelible mark on the national psyche. Scholar Jackie Feldman argues that from the 1990s, both curricula and ceremonies have increasingly been focused around youth voyages to Poland, which have become the most intensive encounter of Israeli youth with the Shoah. Tens of thousands of Israeli teenagers travel to Poland each year for state-sponsored trips that Feldman identifies as secular pilgrimages, which focus on transmitting the students' experience as lessons learned from the past in order to understand the present as Jews and Israelis. Feldman argues that these youth trips can best be understood as ritual re-enactments of survival. The voyage is a civil religious pilgrimage, which transforms students into victims, victorious survivors, and finally *olim* (immigrants) to the land of Israel (Feldman, 2008).

In order for the students to become participants rather than spectators, they must come to feel coexistence with the events themselves. The voyage facilitates the students to leave their taken-for-granted life centre, travel to the death world, and when they come back home, they should be emotionally different from when they left. The inner rhythm of the itinerary requires some balance. The trip takes about a week in which the most intense element is a heavy Holocaust day, with visits to sites such as death camps like Auschwitz-Birkenau, Majdenek or Treblinka. This is followed by a lighter day, with visits to sites of the Jewish past, Polish tourist sites or free time. The trip begins and ends at the transition site of the Warsaw Ghetto Monument. At each site, the visitors perform fairly standard liturgical and ritual activities, often in a fixed order. As in other pilgrimages, the markers in the landscape are narrated through sacred texts. The rituals assist in transforming the participants from victims to survivors and later into brave soldiers. The rituals allow the students to transit from exile to redemption, from passivism to activism, from holocaust to Israel.

According to Feldman (2008), the voyage to Poland is not a study trip. It is a rite of transformation, designed to transmit understanding through identification of embodiment and experience. At a pivotal stage in their development, shortly before joining the army (in Israel there is a draft duty of 3 years for men and 2 years for women at the age of 18), the teenagers participate in this intensive week-long pilgrimage that preforms the history of the Jewish people and the paradigm of Jewish destruction and redemption. The students 'witness' the destruction of the Jews in exile. But there, they 'survive' to return to witness their triumphant ascent to Israel. The heroism of the Warsaw Ghetto warriors helps the students to identify with life and with the role of Israel as the protector of Jews.

The death camps voyages take the participants into absolute evil, which is not a place of worship or the centre of the universe (Turner and Turner, 1978). The students enter the demonic death world only to conquer it through the symbols of the state. In doing so, Feldman argues, the student can overcome Auschwitz with great difficulties and costs. In embodying Israel at the death camps, re-enacting a drama of suffering, death and rebirth, Auschwitz becomes the birthplace of the State. The students' increased awareness of existential danger and sense of overcoming that danger through the presence of the State, for example by holding Israeli flags while visiting the camps, generates a real commitment to national and cultural values (Feldman, 2008, pp. 255–258).

Folk Pilgrimage to Saints' Tombs

The modern Israeli pilgrimages to Masada and Poland are examples of political pilgrimages that serve to build collective memory and national identity. However, the modern Israeli experience has developed additional types of sacred voyages: grass-roots phenomena that can be explained as serving a similar purpose. While the state-sponsored rituals are secular in nature, although containing religious and ritualistic symbolism, the following case is religious, and from the outside might be viewed as having nothing to do with the State.

During the 1950s and 1960s, the State of Israel observed waves of Jewish immigration from North Africa, mostly from Morocco. The immigrants were transferred into newly created 'development towns' on Israel's periphery, with inadequate sources of job opportunities and low-quality educational institutions. These towns were mostly populated with homogeneous groups of new immigrants, and throughout the years they have turned into slums (Picard, 2013).

Jews and Muslims in North Africa shared many cultural beliefs and customs, despite their religious differences. The folk veneration of saints was an important component in the lives of Moroccan Jews. This is also the hallmark of Maghreb Islam. Jewish saints have usually been described as charismatic rabbis who combined sublime qualities, exemplary living and proficiency in esoteric lore. This combination granted them special spiritual powers. The tombs of such saints were the loci of pilgrimage, and the geographical distribution of these sites reflects the traditional distribution of Jewish communities in Morocco. Most of the saints' graves were manifestly of local nature. The central event for the saint's cult was a pilgrimage to their tomb on the anniversary of their death, and a festival held on that occasion. The anniversary of the saint's death was considered an especially good time for believers to prostrate themselves on their grave, because it is believed that on this day their presence at the site is felt with great force, and the saint is amenable to fulfil their requests. During the first half of the 20th century, the festival of some of these saints turned into a huge celebration that drew thousands of believers from various regions of Morocco. These visits were based on the belief that the saint could offer succour for a wide range of problems. Those in need beseeched the saint and vowed to bring a thanksgiving feast to their tomb if they interceded in their favour. Such saints were a constant presence in their believers' lives. They dreamed about them and called their name in dire straits (Bilu, 2010, pp. 17–28).

As mentioned, Jewish Moroccan immigration to Israel is not regarded as a success story. The Moroccans vented their feelings of discrimination, frustration and anger produced by the problems of absorption, into social protest, riots and eventually into political engagement that shifted Israeli politics from the 1970s. During the initial years after the establishment of the State of Israel, immigrants felt heavy pressure to shed what was perceived by the country's elite as primitive and irrational traditions, as part of forming a modern Israeli identity. In this climate, the veneration of saints was viewed as a particularly vulnerable custom, given the fact that migration to Israel left the saints' graves far off and inaccessible. Separation from the saints was even harder in times of hardship and misery that the immigrants had to go through.

From the 1970s, the saints' cult began to flourish again in Israel. During that time, Moroccan Jews started shaping Israel's political arena, first by voting en masse for the Likud party and bringing it into power in the 1977 elections, and later some shifted their political alliance with the rise of Shas, as an Orthodox *Mizrahi* (oriental) party. The sense of ethnic pride that embodied their politics also stood behind the rise of the saints' cult in Israel. The colourful nature of the *hillula*, a celebration to commemorate the saint's departing day which combines fervour and spirituality alongside earthly pleasures like eating and drinking, made them attractive to a wide variety of the population. Young people who have grown distant from religion find the *hillula* to be a convenient way to spend time outdoors and meet members of the opposite sex. For women, the *hillula* is an opportunity to break free from household burdens and express devotion to the saint without constraints, as equals among equals. Finally, the mass gathering is a fine opportunity to get together with family and friends. According to Yoram Bilu, the cult of saints grew within a crisis-ridden matrix as a system of cultural significance which is manifestly of a popular religious character, adopted largely by traditional Mizrahi Jews (especially those from North Africa) in particular, as a way of coping with personal and collective problems of life in Israel (Bilu, 2010, pp. 40–41).

Bilu identifies several 'paths' along which Moroccan Jews have expressed their veneration for saints. The first path includes the adoption of well-known local holy graves, whose status is based on long traditions of pilgrimages. This refers to graves of charismatic figures from the Bible and Talmud, Middle Ages' mystics or Hasidic rabbis of recent centuries. Such places include the tomb of Rabbi Shimon Bar Yochai on the slopes of Mt Meron, the tomb of Rabbi Meir Ba'al Ha-Nes near the hot springs of Tibberias, and the cave of Elijah the Prophet on the outskirts of Haifa. The *hillula* of Rabbi Shimon and Rabbi Meir are the most important pilgrimages among the venerable saints' cult in Israel. The *hillula* of Rabbi Shimon has been celebrated since the Middle Ages, and it is a colourful festival that attracts hundreds of thousands of visitors each year.

The second group of sites which Moroccan Jews are adopting are the graves of holy individuals who were discovered in the vicinity of their homes in the development of towns and farming villages. These communities celebrate *hillulot* (plural of *hillula*) at these sites in their familiar Moroccan style. Bilu mentions the establishment of the *hillula* of Honi Ha-Me'agel (Honi the Circle Maker), a legendary miracle-worker from the second Temple period, in Hatzor Haglilit in the upper Jordan Valley. The festival for this individual is celebrated each year on Israel's Independence Day.

A third path is the creation of new, modern saints. The most impressive process of sanctification of this sort is the rise of Rabbi Yisrael Abu-Hatsera, popularly known as Baba Sali, to the rank of an Israeli national saint in the 1980s and early 1990s. Baba Sali died in 1984 at the age of 94, and he was recognized as a saint during his lifetime. An ascetic who dedicated his life to kabalistic study, prayer and healing, he was perceived as a worthy scion of his family, headed by his grandfather Rabbi Yaakov Abu-Hatsera (1807–1880). After his death, Baba Sali's tomb in Netivot, a development town in the Negev, quickly became the most popular *hillula* in Israel, after those of Rabbi Shimon Bar Yochai and Rabbi Meir Ba'al Ha-Nes. His grandson, Baruch Abu-Hatsera, has turned his grandfather's tomb into a complex that includes a dome in traditional Maghrebi style, an adjoining synagogue, yeshiva and preschool. The complex is built at the outskirts of the cemetery and it is intended to host big crowds. The site was turned into an official Israeli holy site in 1996.

A different path is involving the transfer of North African saints to Israel via dreams. This is a spontaneous initiative of ordinary men and women, to whom a revered saint from the Maghreb appears in a dream and tells them he has decided to be settled in the Holy Land, close to his former believers. In all of these cases, the saint orders the dreamer to set aside a place in their home, to announce his arrival to the Moroccan community, and to invite them to celebrate his *hillula* in his new abode. For example, a number of sites devoted to Rabbi David u-Moshe were dedicated in Israel, with the most notable being in a housing project in Safed.

The final path is transporting the remains of Jewish saints from North Africa for reburial in Israel. This type is rare since Moroccan authorities have usually objected to transferring the bones of the dead to Israel. The most famous case under this category is that of Rabbi Chaim Pinto, buried in Ashdod, whose bones were smuggled from Morocco to Israel. The Pinto dynasty was considered esteemed in Morocco, and nowadays they compete with the Abu-Hatsera dynasty for prestige and influence (Bilu, 2010, pp. 41–51).

This tradition of saints' veneration can be observed as cultural resistance to Israel's secular hegemony. It might be viewed as a retreat into a tradition that characterized Jewish life in the Maghreb, a rejection of the new Israeli identity and a refusal to accept its authority. Yoram Bilu argues for the contrary, that reviving the cult of saints is a dynamic process that reflects the sense of home felt by ethnic North African immigrants in Israel, but at the same time rejects the old model of being Israeli and contributes to its destruction. The cult of saints is participating in reshaping Israeli identity in directions that take it far from the Zionist ethos of Israel's early years and brings it closer to a more pluralistic social reality. This process has taken place in Israel's periphery – the development town highly populated by Moroccan Jews. The inhabitants of these towns with bad reputations were searching for an ideological justification for their existence and to consolidate local identity. They thus constructed a local myth by creating or annexing holy sites. Therefore, the rise of these holy sites with their new rituals may be viewed as a consolidation and developing a sense of identity and attachment to Israel's topography.

Conclusion

This chapter offers a wide scoping view of the role which Jewish pilgrimage has played in the story of Israel, ancient and contemporary. Pilgrimage is a sacred duty in Jewish ritual that survived destruction and immigration. The Temple in Jerusalem was the centre of ancient rituals, but its destruction in 70 CE transformed Judaism in many ways. With the absence of the Temple, and the many ritualistic and political complications that are associated with the Temple's site, Jews preferred to identify different locations for pilgrimage. The rise of the State of Israel in 1948 has pushed for recognition of new locations in the Holy Land. The goal of the State was to build its own national symbols and pride. Thus, new sites were sanctified in order to tell the Zionist story. These places symbolized death and survival, destruction and heroism, according to the new Zionist ethos. Also in the periphery, a way was found to harness old cultural traditions in order to develop a sense of pride in the new locale, and Moroccan Jews used the veneration of saints to combine their cultural traditions with Zionism. Thus, the re-emergence of pilgrimage sites in the new land is a remarkable story of how ancient traditions have been able to reshape and take new meanings in the modern secular State of Israel.

References

Ben Yehuda, N. (1995) *The Masada Myth: Collective Memory and Mythmaking in Israel*. University of Wisconsin Press, Madison, Wisconsin.

Bilu, Y. (2010) *The Saints' Impresarios: Dreamers, Healers, and Holy Men in Israel's Urban Periphery*. Academic Studies Press, Brighton, Massachusetts.

Blackwell, R. (2014) Motivation for pilgrimage: using theory to explore motivations. In: Tore Ahlbäck (ed.) *Pilgrimages Today*. Scripta Instituti Donneriani, Åbo, Finland, pp. 24–37.

Brighton, M.A. (2009) *The Sicarii in Josephus's Judean War: Rhetorical Analysis and Historical Observations*. Society of Biblical Literature, Atlanta, Georgia.

Cohen, E. (1979) A phenomenology of tourist experience. *Sociology* 13, 179–201.

Feldman, J. (2008) *Above the Death Pits, Beneath the Flag: Youth Voyages to Poland and the Performance of Israeli National Identity*. Berghahn, New York.

Gitlitz, D. and Davidson, L. (2006) *Pilgrimage and the Jews*. Praeger Publishers, Westport, Connecticut.

Hengel, M. (1989) *The Zealots: Investigations into the Jewish Freedom Movement in the Period from Herod I until 70*. T. & T. Clark, Edinburgh, UK.

Inbari, M. (2009) *Jewish Fundamentalism and the Temple Mount: Who will Build the Third Temple?* SUNY Press, Albany, New York.

Masada (2015) Available at: http://www.masada.org.il (accessed 29 April 2016).

News1 (2011) Available at: http://www.news1.co.il/Archive/001-D-266419-00.html (accessed 29 April 2016).

Picard, A. (2013) *'Olim bi-meśurah: mediniyut Yiśra'el kelape 'aliyatam shel Yehude Tsefon Afriḳah, 1951–1956 [Cut to Measure: Israel's Policies Regarding the Aliyah of North African Jews, 1951–1956]*. Ben Gurion Institute for the Study of Zionism and the State of Israel, Sede Boker, Israel. (in Hebrew)

Safrai, S. (1965) *Ha-'Aliyah le-regel bi-yeme ha-Bayit ha-sheni [Jewish Pilgrimage During Second Temple Period]*. Am ha-sefer, Tel Aviv, Israel. (in Hebrew)

Sheffer, S. (1968) *Har habayit – keter tifartenu [The Temple Mount – Crown of Our Glory]*. Yefe Nof Publishers, Jerusalem. (in Hebrew)

Turner, V. and Turner, E. (1978) *Image and Pilgrimage in Christian Culture: Anthropological Perspectives*. Columbia University Press, New York.

Zrubavel, Y. (1995) *Recovered Roots: Collective Memory and the Making of Israeli National Tradition*. University of Chicago Press, Chicago, Illinois.

3 Christianity – Contemporary Christian Pilgrimage and Traditional Management Practices at Sacred Sites

Vreny Enongene* and Kevin Griffin

Dublin Institute of Technology, Dublin, Ireland

Introduction

This chapter seeks to explore contemporary pilgrimage experiences, with emphasis on where pilgrimage fits in the life of a contemporary Christian. In so doing, it addresses the changing demands of contemporary pilgrims, as well as the factors that are shaping current pilgrimage patterns. The chapter further discusses how the changing needs and expectations of contemporary pilgrims are altering traditional management practices at sacred sites, and provides examples of innovative management approaches adopted in catering to these needs. It further analyses the implications of such pressures on management at sacred sites and the future of contemporary pilgrimage experiences, and questions where pilgrimage fits in the life of a contemporary Christian, and whether or not traditional pilgrimage practice has really undergone a fundamental change in recent times.

Christian Pilgrimage: A Brief History

Pilgrimages have been performed from time immemorial. The first record of general pilgrimage in the Bible dates as far back as the 4th century before the birth of Christ, when aristocrats and other religious persons, more precisely Jewish males, travelled to the Holy Land of Jerusalem on pilgrimage three times a year, to celebrate Passover and the feasts of Shavu'ot and Sukkot (widely known as pilgrimage festivals – see Deuteronomy 16: 6), as prescribed by their God.

Among the early biblical individuals who left their homes for religious reasons (often called pilgrimages) were Abel, Enoch, Noah, Abraham and Sarah, his wife, Isaac and Jacob. These characters acknowledged themselves as pilgrims

*vreny.enongene1@mydit.ie

on earth as illustrated in the book of Genesis (23: 4) when Abraham recounts 'I am a stranger and sojourner with you' identifying himself as a traveller on pilgrimage. Jacob, speaking to the Pharaoh in Genesis (47: 9), states:

> The days of the years of my pilgrimage are a hundred and thirty years: few and evil have the days of the years of my life been, and have not attained unto the days of the years of the life of my fathers in the days of their pilgrimage.

Further reference to pilgrimage occurs in the Book of Psalms (39: 12):

> Hear my prayer and my request, Lord Jehovah, and give heed to my tears and do not be silent, because I am an inhabitant with you and a Pilgrim, like all my fathers.

For Christians, perhaps the clearest demonstrations of pilgrimage are evident in the life of Jesus, as He followed his parents on pilgrimage to Jerusalem:

> Every year his parents went to Jerusalem for the Feast of Passover. When he was twelve years old, they went up for the feast, according to the custom of the feast. When they had fulfilled the days [of the feast], his parents started home, unaware that the boy Jesus had stayed behind in Jerusalem.
>
> (Luke 2: 41–43)

Perhaps pilgrimage is evident when Jesus spent 40 days fasting in the desert: 'Jesus, full of the Holy Spirit, left the Jordan and was led by the Spirit into the wilderness.' However, some theologians argue that Christian pilgrimage really commenced after the death of Jesus, with the first of such journeys undertaken by an Ethiopian eunuch to Jerusalem where he went to worship, and was confronted by Philip, baptised and conferred with the gift of evangelism (Acts 8: 26–40).

It is in line with the above that we see the foundations of pilgrimage for contemporary Christians. Christian beliefs are deeply embedded in the supernatural, and in keeping with the faith of the believers' predecessors. One such element of belief is the value of embarking on these journeys called pilgrimages where the traveller seeks meaning and a quest for answers to certain concerns, as well as developing their self-identity.

Some scholars are of the opinion that the authentication of Christian sites that marked the life, death and resurrection of Jesus Christ by Queen (Saint) Helena (mother of Saint Constantine), laid the foundation for the journeys of future Christians. Large numbers of Christians believed in her investigations and visited the churches, which she had built across the landscape (Belhassen *et al.*, 2008, p. 675), treating them as places where Christ had revealed himself in a special way.

In recent times, the number of Christian pilgrimages to the Holy Land and its sacred sites (to include Bethlehem and Nazareth) have seen a remarkable rise, with approximately 700,000 pilgrims making these trips on an annual basis (Collins-Kreiner and Kliot, 2000); and all this, despite our increasingly secularized society. As Jansen puts it:

> In present-day Europe pilgrimage is flourishing, despite trends in secularization and a notable decline in church attendance … journeys to sacred places for religious

and other purposes have a long, if sometimes marginalised, history, but now such journeys are taking centre stage, attracting new groups and new meanings.

(Jansen, 2015, p. 1)

However, some changes in the traditional practice of pilgrimage are visible among modern pilgrims.

The Changing Nature of Contemporary Christian Pilgrims

Kartal *et al.* (2015) note that a typical faith-based tourist is no longer who they used to be, in terms of their needs, expectations and purchasing behaviour. They have become sophisticated and so are their demands. Among these changing demands is the growing need for entertaining experiences and satisfaction from the spiritual renewal services (Ambrose and Ovesenik, 2011). This is in stark contrast to traditional pilgrimage, which involved leaving behind the pleasures of the earthly world, and instead desiring the supernatural/heaven more than the comforts and enjoyments of this life. None the less, while there is sufficient evidence that pleasure formed an element of early pilgrimage (see commentary on the 15th century Canterbury pilgrimage in Griffin and Raj, 2015), the need for entertainment is identified as taking centre stage during modern pilgrimage journeys. The major shift from traditional forms of pilgrimage ritual to a more sophisticated ritualistic approach, questions the role which pilgrimage plays in the life of contemporary Christians. Concurrently, some scholars claim that in the face of scientific rationality, religion's influence on all aspects of life from personal habits to social institutions is in dramatic decline (Pavicic *et al.*, 2007). Inherent in this overall discussion is the assumption that people have become, or will become 'less religious'.

It is therefore no surprise that Swatos and Christiano (1999) observed people today being in admiration of human achievements, not divine forces, and as such, societies of the future will be constructed around these, not antiquity's notion of the 'sacred'. Such observations reinforce Schnell's argument that a large number of pilgrims are either not explicitly religious at all or only moderately religious. So, why then do they submit to these ancient Christian rituals and what are the longitudinal psychological consequences (Schnell and Pali, 2013, p. 888)? This brings us to the question: what role does pilgrimage play in the life of contemporary Christians, who may be either explicitly religious, or only moderately religious? More importantly, this raises the question as to where pilgrimage fits in the life of contemporary Christians.

It is against this background that current research stresses the importance of what the pilgrims themselves say about their pilgrimage experiences, given that they are the main 'element' in the process (Collins-Kreiner and Kliot, 2000, p. 55). This is important, since recent literature on pilgrimage emphasizes the lack of understanding regarding what these pilgrims are saying about their experiences. The above arguments and observations are testament to the changing nature of the contemporary pilgrim and their pilgrimage experiences, as well as the role pilgrimage plays in the life of the contemporary Christian pilgrim and results in operational challenges for sacred site managers.

Managing the Pilgrim's Experiences at Sacred Sites (From Tradition to Modernity)

The changing nature of the contemporary pilgrim, as well as emerging challenges in the management of contemporary pilgrims' experience, have been highlighted by Collins-Kreiner and Kliot, in their 2000 paper 'Pilgrimage tourism in the Holy Land: the behavioural characteristics of Christian pilgrims', where emphasis was placed on the importance of management awareness for the needs of modern-day pilgrims to Israel. These changing needs and expectations of contemporary Christian pilgrims have significant implications in the management of sacred sites. This is particularly the case when such demands include the need for entertaining experiences, which are often in contrast (and sometimes conflict) with the traditional norms and practices of these sacred places (Shackley, 2001). The original purpose and mission of many such sites was to provide an environment and space conducive to worship, prayer and other forms of activity that provided pilgrims and other religious cohorts with a feeling of closeness to their creator.

Such pressures for 'entertainment', in turn pose operational challenges for sacred site managers, particularly where there is a need to adapt traditional management practices in ways that meet the needs and expectations of these ever-changing Christian pilgrims. A shift is expected from tradition to modernity. There is growing evidence of a need for a shift to a more modernized approach in management at sacred sites that effectively caters to the needs of contemporary pilgrims. This is seen in recent calls for innovative management approaches at sacred sites, exemplified in the promotion of competitive innovative products and services by religious and pilgrimage tourism scholars as espoused at the Bethlehem Declaration on religious tourism that took place on the 15–16 June 2015. Kartal *et al.* (2015) suggest that religion has become a product, witnessing increased competition not just from religions, but from secular leisure activities. Thus, effectively catering for these needs necessitates the introduction of innovative product and service development strategies aimed at fulfilling the contemporary pilgrim's growing desire for entertaining experiences.

Innovative Approaches to the Management of Contemporary Pilgrim Needs and Expectations at Sacred Sites

Innovation has emerged as a recurring theme for the sustainability and competitiveness of the tourism and hospitality industry. For faith-based tourism, the many and ongoing changes within the demographics and purchasing behaviour of the market segment in the past 10–20 years (Wright, 2013), calls for innovative approaches in catering to the changing needs and expectations. Simultaneously, there are demands to maintain the sacred and emotive qualities, and attractiveness of these places. As a result, quite recently, religious and pilgrimage scholars have begun to advocate a shift from traditional to a more modern approach in managing visitor's experiences at holy places (Bethlehem Declaration, 2015; Wiltshier, 2015). This necessitates that management at sacred sites adapt traditional practices to suit the needs of modern Christian pilgrims, while protecting their core values – and this constitutes one of the most pressing missionary challenges in contemporary holy sites.

Pilgrim trails and routes

In line with recent emphasis on the need to provide sacred site visitors (including modern-day pilgrims) with meaningful and satisfying experiences, administrators are expected to shift from traditional management to a more modern approach. This must consider innovative management strategies and the development of competitive products and services aimed at satisfying the changing demands of the contemporary pilgrim market segment. One innovative approach involves the development of trails (i.e. themed trails in honour of saints, or routes to important/ancient holy sites) which is emerging as a global practice. Some trails (see Table 3.1) are based on well-established ancient pilgrimage routes; however,

Table 3.1. Examples of historical pilgrimage trails (based on ancient routes).

Country	Trail	Description
Ireland	Croagh Patrick Trail	A 61 km trail culminating in the ascent of Croagh Patrick (764 m) which was a pre-Christian site
USA	Mormon Pioneer National Historic Trail	A 2092 km route which members of The Church of Jesus Christ of Latter-day Saints travelled in the 19th century – now part of the United States National Trails System
Tibet	Mount Kailash	A 52 km trail circumnavigating this mountain which is an important pilgrimage for followers of Hinduism, Buddhism, Jainism and Bon
India	Char Dahm Pilgrimage Route	Links pilgrims to India's four sacred sites of Badrinath, Rameswaram, Dwarka and Puri – a pilgrimage trail popular with Hindus
Norway	St Olav's Way	A 1000-year-old, 643 km trail from Oslo to Trondheim
Spain	Camino de Santiago (St James's trail)	This is recognised as a European Cultural Route. This famous Christian pilgrimage trail comprises a range of routes converging on Santiago from multiple starting points in Spain, France, Portugal, Switzerland, Italy and even the UK and Ireland
Italy	Via Francigena	A medieval trail originating in Canterbury, England, and ending in Rome. In recent years, as the 'route' has developed there are linkages to Germany, The Netherlands, Spain and even Jerusalem
International	The Confraternity of Pilgrims to Jerusalem	This is an organisation that encourages and assists individuals who seek to walk or cycle from Canterbury to Jerusalem (and even on to Mecca)

others, while linked to historically important individuals or events, may not have previously existed as identifiable trails, and are developed to serve the modern pilgrim/tourist.

In addition to the international plethora of historic pilgrimage trails (as illustrated briefly in Table 3.1), many of which have been lately revitalized, there is a recent growth of new pilgrimage 'trails' and 'routes' (see an eclectic range of new and old routes recognized by the Council of Europe at www.culture-routes. net). Without entering into a discussion on whether these are being developed as tourism attractions, or as genuine pilgrimage experiences (a debate for another paper), these 'products' seem to be serving a growing public interest in following walking, or driving, trails for pilgrimage or religious tourism motives. Many pilgrimage routes are organized to the highest international standard, with the provision of traditional tourism management tools such as interpretation materials, signage, literature and ancillary facilities including accommodation (see Fig. 3.1).

Fig. 3.1. Selection of 'traditional' pilgrimage trail management tools. (a) Interpretation (Mormon Trail); (b) signage (Via Francigena); (c) brochure (St Olav's Way); (d) accommodation (Camino de Santiago). (From (a) Light, C., 2007; (b) Tørrissen, B.C., 2012; (c) Netpublicator, no date; (d) Bitesizedtravel, 2015.)

In addition to these traditional tools, a range of new technological, digital interpretation and guidance supports are now being utilized to assist in the management and development of holy places.

Technology in the Contemporary Pilgrimage Experience

The use of technological tools in mediating the pilgrim's experience is quickly gaining prominence. Confirmation of this is evident in a burgeoning scholarly investigation into the use of technology in enhancing both the on-site and the off-site experiences of faith-based tourists. Some recent examples include: (i) Marine-Roig (2015) who has evaluated visitors to la Sagrada Famíla using over 1000 online reviews; (ii) Cantoni *et al.* (2012) who have examined the use of online communications during Catholic World Youth Day; and (iii) Prats *et al.* (2015) who have explored the use of social media by religious sites.

Audio guides

A common tool, which has roots in 'pre-digital' technology, is the humble audio guide. Developed to facilitate self-guided visits to important museums, galleries and religious sites, these range from simple audio-only recordings with a linear narrative (Fig. 3.2a), to devices where the visitor can self-select their route by listening to particular tracks (Fig. 3.2b). Many recordings in religious sites include musical content with a variety of professionally written and presented narratives, to establish a more peaceful ambience, and thus assist in the creation of a spiritual environment for reflection and prayer. More recent innovations include the integration of visual technology (Fig. 3.2c), whereby additional archival material, close-ups of particular elements and a variety of viewer-led content is provided. One of the greatest benefits of this technology is the possibility to present information in aural and visual form in a wide variety of languages. This basic form of audio content can also be integrated into modes of transport – the usual example being a city bus tour, but equally these technologies can be bundled with novel approaches such as the Segway tour illustrated in Fig. 3.2d.

Static digital displays

An industry 'standard' in catering for the modern 'pilgrim' is the introduction of static digital interpretation tools at major cathedrals around the world. The growing use of such methods in contemporary pilgrimage experiences is exemplified in an Irish example, whereby €250,000 has recently been invested in technology at Dublin's St Patrick's Cathedral (D'Arcy, 2015). This investment includes the introduction of touch screens and audio-visuals, in addition to a newly developed app that provides a detailed story of the cathedral. This technology has been introduced to bring St Patrick's Cathedral to life, providing interactive insight into 800 years of history and architecture. As evidenced in Fig. 3.3,

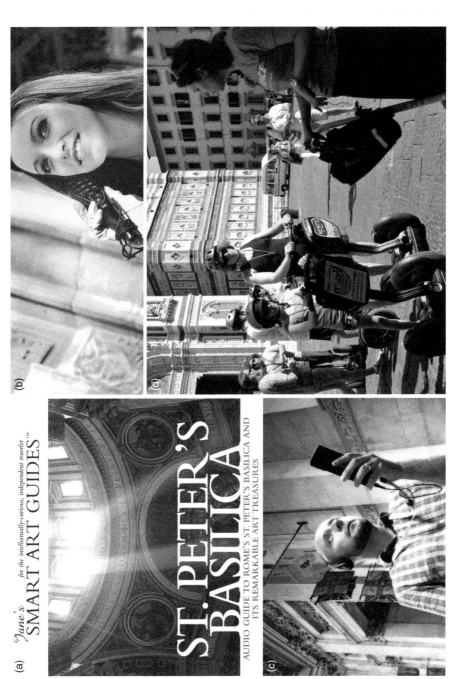

Fig. 3.2. Evolution of audio guides. (a) Double CD of St Peter's Basilica; (b) audio 'wand'; (c) multimedia audio guide, St Paul's London; (d) Segway tour of Florence with audio guide. (From (a) Janessmartart, no date; (b) Rouen Tourisme, no date; (c) TessDrive, no date; (d) St Paul's, no date.)

a similar programme of technological innovation has recently been undertaken in Great St Mary's Church in Cambridge, UK.

Fig. 3.3. Technology appealing to all generations at Great St Mary's Church in Cambridge. (From GSM Heritage, no date.)

Apps and location-based technology

Keeping up to date with modern technology is now becoming quite a challenge for managers of religious sites: what digital platform to use, what hardware is required on-site, or does one rely on visitors having downloaded material in advance of visiting (see Fig. 3.4a), or being 'live' online as they walk around a site (see Fig. 3.4b and c)? One of the biggest challenges is receiving objective information, which interrogates the flood of promotional material provided by technological companies. The next wave of such development would appear to be focusing on augmented/virtual reality.

Some sites are now developing data-provision points based on Bluetooth beacons (small, relatively cheap broadcasting units which provide location-specific data to a smartphone via low-energy Bluetooth communication channels); others are providing information via off-line, global positioning system (GPS)-activated software, which has been downloaded before the visitor leaves home; others are providing information via live downloads from open-access wifi networks. The examples, demonstrated in Fig. 3.4, are based on pre-trip downloads, but this technology is set to develop exponentially with more competitive roaming charges for mobile data, in tandem with a booming 'wearable devices' industry. While far from universal, some municipalities, such as Tel

Fig. 3.4. Location-based tools. Downloadable augmented reality guides for
(a) Berlin, (b) Milan and (c) London. (From (a) http://media.148apps.com/screenshots/
1015419514/us-iphone-2-berlin-travel-guide-and-offline-city-map-beetletrip-augmented-
reality-germany-bahn-metro-train-and-walks.jpeg; (b) Screen capture from https://
www.youtube.com/watch?v=kd8ZFStGO48; (c) http://www.createtomorrow.co.uk/en/
article/augmented-reality.)

Aviv, Israel (60 'hot spots' introduced in October 2013), have followed the
likes of Milwaukee, USA (wifi spots introduced in 2003) in introducing free
wifi in public spaces. Many individual sites, hotels, restaurants, etc. provide
free, unlimited wifi to all guests. Thus, religious sites, in order to prepare for
the pilgrim-visitor of the 21st century, must seriously consider exploring this
market. The technological possibilities for visitors entering a site of worship,
with suitable digital devices, engaging in tailor-made, visual and aural 'experience' are fascinating. It is posited here that flexibility in terms of content
and delivery could mean that linguistically, culturally and religiously heterogeneous groups, following multiple faith paths, could engage in deeply spiritual, individually tailored activities, at the one time, in a suitably managed site.
The implications of this for contested sites, which must be managed with the
utmost care, is exciting.

Connecting remotely

In addition to on-site facilities, modern technological developments provide a range of engagement opportunities pre- and post-visit. Indeed, the 'pilgrim' may never move beyond their virtual experience. The first manifestation of this is for the 'pilgrim' to look up information on a range of websites, or for a more intimate experience, to watch the chosen site of their faith via webcam. Table 3.2 illustrates just three of the many such sites that exist in the holy cities for the three faiths under consideration in this book.

Table 3.2. Holy city webcams.

Holy city	URL for webcam
Western Wall	http://english.thekotel.org/cameras.asp
Mecca	http://live.gph.gov.sa/
Vatican	http://www.vaticanstate.va/content/vaticanstate/en/monumenti/webcam.html

Virtual pilgrims

A related theme, which illustrates the power of the web in the context of faith practices, is the opportunities which exist online for religious and spiritual engagement. In addition to the multitude of informative and instructional online videos on YouTube and other media-sharing platforms, multi-denominational sites such as www.beliefnet.com/ and www.postaprayer.org/ provide a broad range of religious opportunities for reflection and prayer (see Fig. 3.5a as an example). Islamic-specific websites range from those which provide tuition in the tenets of the faith (www.meaningfulprayer.com/) to apps (such as www.muslimpro.com/) which assist in providing accurate prayer times and a Qibla Locator, to indicate the direction to Mecca for prayer. Jewish Internet users can have an actual bespoke prayer note placed in the Western Wall by logging in to www.aish.com/w/note/ and sending their intentions remotely, or can find their daily prayers online at www.onlinesiddur.com/. At www.sacredspace.ie/ (see Fig. 3.5b), which was founded in 1999, and attracts over 5 million visits on an annual basis, Christians can find prayers and reflections in 23 different languages, which they can follow privately. Alternatively, they can join a global online prayer group such as http://www.prayerchainonline. net. This use of online technologies extends to an astonishing range of religion-delimited activity such as Catholic sites for lighting a candle (www.catholic.org/prayers/candle/), Jewish sites for finding a partner (http://www.jewishsoulsearch.com/) or Islamic sites for entertaining children (www.islamicplayground.com/).

Virtual retail

A further aspect of modernization and 'virtuality' are the attempts made by religious sites to raise much-needed funds via online shops. While many churches,

Fig. 3.5. Virtual pilgrimage. (a) Gratefulness.org – light a candle page; (b) Sacred Space, prayer site; (c) Vatican Facebook page; (d) the Pope's Twitter account. (From (a) Gratefulness.org, no date; (b) Sacred Space, no date; (c) Facebook, no date; (d) Twitter, no date.)

cathedrals, monasteries and religious sites have traditionally depended on income from 'entry fees', donations and retail to maintain their properties, many are now moving 'online' with their retail offering (for an interesting paper on the production and resultant online sale of produce by monasteries and convents in Hungary, read Clarke and Raffay, 2015). The symbolic meaning of gifting and receiving these commercial objects, which are imbued with divine presence, is reasonably well understood, but purchasing traditional items virtually, without visiting the site is little understood (see Doney, 2013 for a discussion which deals with this). However, it is suggested here that this remote purchasing is in fact a modern means of engaging in an important pilgrimage practice.

WEB 2.0-sharing

The diverse technological applications outlined above (and many other media platforms beyond the scope of this chapter) are based primarily on one-way data provision, by the holy site itself, or by commercial providers. However, a further fascinating category of user-generated interpretation, evaluation and critique is available via so-called Web 2.0 systems. Online platforms not only provide for the reporting of first-person narratives, they also create an avenue for sharing, responding and reacting to other people's pilgrimage and religious experiences. Many commercial companies are using blog software to engage with their 'customers' before, during and after their pilgrimage (one randomly chosen site – holyland2016.weebly.com/ – provides a range of practical information for clients who will be travelling on pilgrimage in the near future, ranging from the price of postage stamps from Israel to the USA to weather predictions).

True, Web 2.0 systems, however, facilitate the creation of content by the general user, in an organic, and sometimes even anarchic manner – depending on the perspective. Many travellers choose to post their thoughts and opinions online – in fact at the time of writing this chapter, 6468 individuals have posted comments on the TripAdvisor page for the Old City of Jerusalem. While many observations for the likes of Jerusalem and other holy cities focus on the practicalities of travel (accommodation, food and entertainment), there are many submissions containing reflections and thoughts on pilgrimage, faith, prayer and spirituality. Finally, in this regard it is worth noting the use of social media platforms such as Facebook and Twitter, which abound with user-generated content on all aspects of life, with religious travel and pilgrimage to holy places being well represented (see Fig. 3.5c and 3.5d to see the Vatican Facebook page and the Pope's Twitter account, respectively).

The modern church visitor

The use of these many technologically mediated approaches to enhancing the visitor experience at holy places is indicative of a very significant shift in the delivery of pilgrimage experiences away from religious adherence following a strict pattern to what has been pejoratively described as 'a la carte' Christianity. However, reflecting on the word of God as represented in the Bible ('I was a stranger, and you welcomed me', Matthew 25: 35b), all visitors to Christian holy places should be welcomed without judgement. In fact, 'welcome' and 'invitation' are core gospel values: God welcomes the outsider (1 Corinthians 1: 26–31), seeks the lost (Luke 15), and invites all into the community of the kingdom (1 Timothy 2: 4). Christian theology stresses the depth and breadth of God's welcome, teaching that no one is beyond the reach of God's love (Methodist.org, 2015). Therefore, critically judging these new means of encouraging visitors to engage with 'church' is in fact contrary to the entire Christian message.

Reflection

This leads one to question whether the experience and benefit accrued from undertaking these spiritual journeys in an enhanced manner mediated by technology, or even doing so digitally or virtually, in the comfort of your own home is the same as performing them in a traditional manner. After all, according to Father Svetozar Kraljevic in Medjugorje, pilgrimage is based on introspective prayer, focused on the self. He notes further that another word for pilgrimage is prayer, which can be considered as a cultural way of living, a whole mentality and a whole way of life. Of course, he has set up a website (www.mir.ie/fr-svet.html) to discuss and illustrate his thoughts in this regard.

We are further told by Father Svetozar that 'in pilgrimage we are being thrown into a mill and crushed, our old ways are crushed so that we can receive new ways' (Kraljevic, 2009). How does this fit in the life of contemporary Christians who wish to cling to old habits while at the same time desire increased leisure and entertainment opportunities? Are modern Christians abandoning their traditional faith as they search for meaning via new methods of interpretation? Perhaps, faith is evolving to allow such a technologically mediated experience. And thus, in the context of this chapter, perhaps it is the traditional pilgrimage practices (not the spiritual significance of the holy place) which are being 'crushed' and reshaped, rather than the 'pilgrim'.

The aim of this chapter is to examine the ways in which pilgrimage fits in the life of contemporary Christians. We are especially interested in the changing needs and expectations of these modern pilgrims, with particular focus on how changing demands are altering traditional management practices at sacred sites. It is important to reflect on the long-standing rituals of pilgrimage and the many recently revived and modified ritualistic practices, in order to determine the effect which change has on the management of these sacred resources – especially in view of society's changing perceptions/expectations regarding individual faith.

A form of faith travel, which deserves mention here, is the emerging practice of 'extreme pilgrimage', a title used for and by the contemporary Anglican pilgrim-Vicar Peter Owen-Jones, whose multiple 'celebrity' pilgrimages have drawn attention from around the globe. Described online as 'Spiritual leader, TV presenter, explorer and author', Owen-Jones visits famous places of pilgrimage in an attempt to practice a range of world methods of spirituality and enlightenment.

This 'maverick 21st century priest' has undertaken a global trek to visit a multitude of pilgrimage sites including: (i) the Shaolin Monastery of Henan Province in central China; (ii) the Kumbh Mela festival in India; and (iii) the Egyptian caves of St Anthony in the desert, where he mimicked the desert fathers and spent 21 days in prayerful solitude, all the time being recorded for a very well-received television programme.

What does this say about contemporary Christian pilgrims who now wish to undertake journeys that do not conform to their inherited faith? Essential for a Christian, 'a pilgrimage is the celebration of [their] own faith – a manifestation of a cult which needs to be lived faithful to tradition – with intense religious sentiments and a realization of ... paschal existence' (Papal document *Pellegrinaggio*, No. 32, cited in Kraljevic, 1999). What benefits are there if a pilgrimage fits comfortably into the life of the contemporary Christian, without challenging them in any way? This discussion does not suggest that pilgrimage must be as intense as that undertaken by the Confraternity of Pilgrims to Jerusalem, an eclectic group of 'extreme pilgrims' who travel a combination of ancient and contemporary pilgrimage routes from Canterbury Cathedral to Temple Mount in Jerusalem.

Roth and Steven's view presented in 1985 suggests that:

> Pilgrimages are walking Zen; step by step the practitioner makes his or her way through blue sky temples and white cloud monasteries. Conducted in the traditional manner – on foot, in old-fashioned garb, carrying no money, accepting whatever comes – Pilgrimages are among the most demanding, and therefore most rewarding of all religious disciplines.
>
> (Roth and Steven, 1985, p. 108)

Is it possible for our digitally connected contemporary pilgrim, who is said to be increasingly demanding entertaining experiences, to fit into the traditional pilgrimage practice? Can the armchair pilgrim, in their 'virtual' experience, compete or compare with the biblically prescribed pilgrims who were ordered to 'Take nothing for the journey, neither staves nor scrip, neither bread neither money; neither have two coats apiece' (Luke 9:8) as they search for meaning, peace and love?

The Future of Pilgrimage

Regardless of the diverse claims and perspectives in relation to traditional and contemporary pilgrimage practices, Swatos and Christiano (1999) observed that people today are in admiration of human achievements, not divine forces, and as such, societies of the future will be constructed around these, not antiquity's notion of the 'sacred'. In part, this explains the changing nature and demand for faith-based travel, of which modern-day Christian pilgrims are a subset. Indeed, some of the Christians on the Camino to Compostela in Spain are 'pilgrims' who are not even moderately religious. So where then does pilgrimage fit in the life of contemporary Christians? Why, despite protesting and refuting their engagement with religion, do they submit to these ancient Christian rituals, and what are the longitudinal psychological consequences of such events on them (Schnell and Pali, 2013, p. 2)? More importantly, what is the future of pilgrimage for the contemporary Christian? According to Barbarić (1999) in his thoughts on pilgrimage:

> Although the basis and primary motive of every pilgrimage is the longing for God, leaving behind everyday life and opening oneself to God, there certainly are secondary reasons for modern pilgrimage – getting to know the world, people and their customs, however, if these secondary motives become the most important, then we are dealing with tourism.
>
> (Barbarić, 1999, p. 1)

Therefore, can the modern Christian activity, which we have discussed at length, be considered as pilgrimage, or is it in fact tourism? Or is it gradually becoming tourism? Will it become tourism? Furthermore, are the traditional ritualistic practices of pilgrimage going to be a 'thing of the past', only to be undertaken by the 'extreme pilgrims'? Considering the factors that are shaping and altering traditional pilgrimage practices as well as the management practices at sacred sites, what are the inherent challenges to ensure that visitors with varying motives are provided with the help they need to have a truly spiritual and rewarding experience of 'pilgrimage'?

Conclusion

An examination of contemporary pilgrimage experiences and their impact on management practices at sacred sites raises concern as to the role pilgrimage plays in the life of contemporary Christians. The observations and discussions presented in this chapter have shed light on the complex nature of present-day pilgrims and their requirements. The chapter also opens a new area of scholarly discourse on the future of pilgrimage, given the identified shift from traditional Christian pilgrimage practice/ritual to a modern approach exemplified in the demand for entertaining experiences at holy sites. The challenge lies in satisfying the needs of these contemporary pilgrims, while maintaining the numinous quality of the holy site. As demonstrated in the discussions throughout this chapter, it is evident that changing pilgrimage patterns, in addition to the needs and expectations of the modern-day pilgrim, will have significant operational implications for management at sacred sites the world over, as well as for future pilgrimage experiences.

Throughout the chapter, significant changes in religious adherence have been highlighted, which in part can be explained by an ever-increasing materialistic and secularized society. The chapter also presents a range of innovative approaches adopted by management at sacred sites to meet the ever-changing needs of contemporary pilgrims. Current trends include the development of walking trails linking prominent pilgrimage destinations, and now technology is transforming the pilgrimage experience, acting as the most valuable tool in bringing these pilgrimage resources to life. To a certain extent, site managers are utilizing such approaches as an attempt to meet the desire for entertaining experiences by modern-day pilgrims and religious tourists. To this end, changes in traditional management and operational approaches show that site mangers are not static entities, but instead are flexible by responding to the changing nature of the visitor experience being sought.

These contemporary pilgrim demands and the ways in which they are altering traditional management practices emphasize the need for in-depth analysis on the actual role which pilgrimage experience plays in the life of contemporary Christians. The literature reveals a new approach to contemporary Christian pilgrimage (extreme pilgrimage experiences) that is not always in conformity with participants' beliefs and faith. This may be indicative of a shift in traditional Christian pilgrimage practices and values. A substantial literature suggests that society is in constant search for increased gratification in terms of material possessions. However, there is also a clear trend in recent years (perhaps in response to increasing materialism) indicating a search for self-actualization and fulfilment and a desire to belong to a particular social stratum/class. This is a further influence, globally, on the changing nature of Christian pilgrimage.

Globally, there is a growing interest in Christian pilgrimages as well as curiosity regarding the factors that are driving their growth and evolution. The question is: what role is pilgrimage playing in the life of a contemporary Christian, and how are the changing nature and demands of faith-based/contemporary pilgrimage impacting on the traditional management practices at holy sites? We can clearly see that management at sacred sites are adapting their traditional approaches to suit the needs of these modern pilgrims. Through the development of innovative products and services, while not losing sight of the underlying spiritual, historical and ritualistic experiences, site managers are sensitively responding to the changing demands of society. Contemporary pilgrims' needs and expectations are changing when they visit historical holy sites. There is evidence of visitors drifting away from traditional religious practices and rituals. However, being mindful of tradition and heritage, while being open to new methods, tools and practices, Christian holy sites can stand up to scrutiny and be confident for the future, in a world where they are witnessing increased competition not only from religions, but from secular leisure activities (Kartal *et al.*, 2015).

References

Ambrose, M. and Ovesenik, R. (2011) Tourist origin and spiritual motives. *Management* 16(2), 71–86.

Barbarić, Fr S. (1999) Anthropological–Biblical and Religious–Spiritual dimensions of a Pilgrimage, as they apply specifically to Medjugorje. Available at: http://www.mir.ie/files/Anthropological_xm366uv5.pdf (accessed 19 November 2015).

Belhassen, Y., Caton, K. and Stewart, W.P. (2008) The search for authenticity in the pilgrim experience. *Annals of Tourism Research* 35(3), 668–689.

Bethlehem Declaration (2015) *Bethlehem Declaration on Religious Tourism as a Means of Fostering Socio-Economic Development of Host Communities*. Religious Tourism Declaration from World Tourism Organization (UNWTO)-sponsored conference 16 June 2015. Available at: http://www.bethlehem.edu/document.doc?id=3240 (accessed 21 November 2015).

Bitesizedtravel (2015) Available at: https://bitesizedtravel.ca/2015/01/08/accommodations-sleeping-camino-de-santiago/#jp-carousel-8551 (accessed 28 October 2016).

Cantoni, L., Stefania, M. and De Ascaniis, S. (2012) Online communications of the Catholic World Youth Day. In: Griffin, K. and Raj, R. (eds) *Reflecting on Religious Tourism and Pilgrimage*. ATLAS, Arnhem, The Netherlands.

Clarke, A. and Raffay, Á. (2015) Religion, local produce and sustainability at religious sites in Hungary. *International Journal of Religious Tourism and Pilgrimage* 3(2), 33–47. Available at: http://arrow.dit.ie/ijrtp/vol3/iss2/3 (accessed 21 November 2015).

Collins-Kreiner, N. and Kliot, N. (2000) Pilgrimage tourism in the Holy Land: the behavioural characteristics of Christian pilgrims. *Geo-Journal* 50(1), 55–67.

D'Arcy, C. (2015) Technology helps bring St Patrick's Cathedral to life. *Irish Times*, 5 August 2015. Available at: http://www.irishtimes.com/culture/heritage/technology-helps-bring-st-patrick-s-cathedral-to-life-1.2307666 (accessed 21 November 2015).

Doney, S. (2013) The sacred economy: devotional objects as sacred presence for German Catholics in Aachen and Trier, 1832–1937. *International Journal of Religious Tourism and Pilgrimage* 1(1), 62–71. Available at: http://arrow.dit.ie/ijrtp/vol1/iss1/6 (accessed 21 November 2015).

Facebook (no date) Vatican Facebook page. Available at: https://www.facebook.com/Vaticancom (accessed 19 November 2015).

Gratefulness.org (no date) Available at: http://www.gratefulness.org/light-a-candle/ (accessed 19 November 2015).

Griffin, K. and Raj, R. (2015) The globalization of pilgrimage tourism? Some thoughts from Ireland. In: Raj, R. and Griffin, K. (eds) *Religious Tourism and Pilgrimage Management – an International Perspective*, 2nd edn. CAB International, Wallingford, UK, pp. 57–78.

GSM Heritage (no date) Available at: https://gsmheritage.files.wordpress.com/2015/11/dsc_1240.jpg (accessed 19 November 2015).

Janessmartart (no date) Available at: http://www.janessmartart.com/assets/stpetersbooklet.pdf (accessed 19 November 2015).

Jansen, W. (2015) Old routes, new journeys: reshaping gender, nation and religion in European pilgrimages. In: Jansen, W. and Notermans, C. (eds) *Gender Nation and Religion in European Pilgrimage*. Ashgate, Abingdon, UK.

Kartal, B., Tepeci, M. and Atli, H. (2015) Examining the religious tourism potential of Manisa, Turkey with a marketing perspective. *Tourism Review* 70(3), 314–231.

Kraljevic, Fr S. (1999) Thoughts for Pilgrims. Available at: http://www.mir.ie/fr-slavkos--thoughts-for-pilgrims.html (accessed 19 November 2015).

Kraljevic, Fr S. (2009) Set out on a spiritual visitation .... Pilgrimage is prayer. Available at: http://www.mir.ie/files/fr-svet.html (accessed 19 November 2015).

Light, C. (2007) Available at: https://commons.wikimedia.org/wiki/File:Wayside_on_Mormon_Trail_Nebraska.JPG (accessed 19 November 2015).

Marine-Roig, E. (2015) Religious tourism versus secular pilgrimage: the Basilica of La Sagrada Família. *International Journal of Religious Tourism and Pilgrimage* 3(1), 25–37. Available at: http://arrow.dit.ie/ijrtp/vol3/iss1/5 (accessed 19 November 2015).

Methodist.org (2015) Welcome and Invitation. Available at: http://www.methodist.org.uk/mission/welcome-and-invitation (accessed 19 November 2015).

Netpublicator (no date) Available at: http://np.netpublicator.com/netpublication/n21771829 (accessed 19 November 2015).

Pavicic, J., Alfirevic, N. and Batarelo, V.J. (2007) The management and marketing of religious sites, pilgrimages and religious events: challenges for Roman Catholic pilgrimages in Croatia. In: Raj, R. and Morpeth, N.D. (eds) *Religious Tourism and Pilgrimage Festival management*. CAB International, Wallingford, UK, pp. 48–63.

Prats, L., Aulet, S. and Vidal, D. (2015) Social network tools as guides to religious sites. In: Raj, R. and Griffin, K. (eds) *Religious Tourism and Pilgrimage Management: an International Perspective*. CAB International, Wallingford, UK, pp. 146–159.

Roth, M. and Steven, J. (1985) *Zen Guide: Where to Meditate in Japan*. Weatherhill, New York.

Rouen Tourisme (no date) Available at: http://www.rouentourisme.com/audio-guides/ (accessed 19 November 2015).

Sacred Space (no date) Available at: http://www.sacredspace.ie/ (accessed 19 November 2015).

Schnell, T. and Pali, S. (2013) Pilgrimage today: the meaning-making potential of ritual. *Journal of Mental Health, Religion & Culture* 16(9), 887–902.

Shackley, M. (2001) *Managing Sacred Sites, Service Provision and Visitor Experience*. Continuum, London.

St Paul's (no date) Available at: https://www.stpauls.co.uk/SM4/Mutable/Uploads/imported_media/Multimedia_guides.jpg (accessed 19 November 2015).

Swatos, W.H. and Christiano K.J. (1999) Secularisation theory: the course of a concept. *Sociology of Religion* 3, 209–228.

TessDrive (no date) Available at: http://www.tessdrive.com/2015/07/west-east-its-segway-all-way (accessed 19 November 2015).

Tørrissen, B.C. (2012) Available at: https://commons.wikimedia.org/wiki/File%3AVia-Francigena-Signposts-In-Italy-2012.jpg (accessed 19 November 2015).

Twitter (no date) The Pope's Twitter account. Available at: https://twitter.com/Pontifex?ref_src=twsrc%5Egoogle%7Ctwcamp%5Eserp%7Ctwgr%5Eauthor (accessed 19 November 2015).

Wiltshier, P. (2015) Derby Cathedral as a beacon: the role of the Church of England in tourism management. *International Journal of Religious Tourism and Pilgrimage* 3(2), 65–76. Available at: http://arrow.dit.ie/ijrtp/vol3/iss2/7 (accessed 19 November 2015).

Wright, K. (2013) How to innovate in faith-based tourism. *Leisure Group Travel Magazine*, October. Premier Travel Media, Willbrook, Illinois.

4 Christianity – Christian Pilgrimage to Sacred Sites in the Holy Land: A Swedish Perspective

GÖRAN GUNNER*

Church of Sweden Research Unit, Uppsala, Sweden

Introduction

Through centuries, Jerusalem and the Holy Land has been a goal for pilgrims, researchers, travellers, and more recently for tourists. Whatever the purpose of the tour has been, a visit to the sacred places has been part of the journey. This chapter will use Swedish travellers – predominantly Protestant Christians – to Jerusalem and the Holy Land, (to Palestine and Israel) to explore the idea of Western pilgrimage to sacred sites, and uses historical as well as present day examples in order to discuss what a pilgrim may face and react to when visiting a sacred place like Jerusalem.

An inquisitive traveller in the Holy Land was and is usually dependent on a tour leader or a tour guide showing attractions and places of interest. Possibly, the traveller can make the trip with the help of a guidebook. Whether the trip is made with a guide or more independently, preparations have to be done at home, in advance, reading guidebooks and previous travel books. Once the traveller reaches the destination, experiences at sites and encounters with people blend with what was written in the travel books. The nature of the landscape, the villages and towns offer not only a journey in what is seen, but also an experience which is mediated by what is contained in the guide or guidebook's narratives. Through these interpretations, a place, a building or an outdoor experience often becomes a journey through time. As often as possible, the guides (written and oral) link a site to the events that occurred at the site throughout time, and in particular connections to scripture are emphasized.

This exploration is based on the interpretation of travel accounts through the years. While these fascinating sources offer many opportunities for exploring the overall theme, the following headings have been chosen for the focus of the chapter:

*goran.gunner@svenskakyrkan.se

- Jerusalem as the sacred place between heaven and earth;
- driven by adventure and curiosity;
- you will find what suits your purpose;
- fact is fact but another place may be better;
- witness to radical change in society; and
- sacred places as political watersheds.

Jerusalem as the Sacred Place Between Heaven and Earth

On the wall of a cabin in Småland, southern Sweden, hung a glazed poster from the late 1800s. The image is a ship named *Gospel* sailing across the sea of time. Every detail is a symbol hinting at a Christian life in the light of a Pietistic tradition and evokes a common desire for Jerusalem – the heavenly city. The background is a rather poor countryside where people aim for a better future. Whoever embarked on the ship left the city blight and thereby the billiard room, the pub and the dancing hall of these heathen countries. By doing so, they became totally subordinate to the captain Jesus. On the grand staircase to the golden tabernacle stand angels singing. The sea of time has passed in an instant and eternity becomes an anticipated and awaited reality. The pilgrim saw the goal of this imagery, and a language rich in images bridged the gap between a life in misery and streets of gold in the heavenly city Jerusalem (see Fig. 4.1).

Fig. 4.1. Poster of the ship named *Gospel* sailing across the sea of time to the heavenly city of Jerusalem.

Eternity could not really be imagined or described since the goal was so totally different from human conditions and so elusive to describe with human words. Still, eternity was accessible through the mythical language in which divine events still were clothed in human words, with a focus on Jerusalem. All the hymns and songs gave a language for the desire: hymns about moving towards eternity, to the sky, to the golden city, the other side, the heavenly Jerusalem. Even the names of the hymn books from the 1800s reminded the user of being a pilgrim in this world on the way to something else: *Pilgrims' Harp, Pilgrim's Songs on the Way to Heaven, Songs of Zion*. Thus, for the pious person, Jerusalem became the heavenly city of Jerusalem.

Christians, who lived their entire life in Sweden, had the feeling that Jerusalem was always present in one or another way. The pictures shown in Sunday school (which I still have) showed biblical stories and Jerusalem as the city of Jesus. In sermons, Jerusalem turned out to be a historical city – the city of the Bible. Every Sunday followers walked on these streets together with Jesus, the disciples, and a bunch of people and animals. This was also a city on the map of the Holy Land – a city to remember and honour as the city of the life of Jesus, his burial and resurrection.

Beginning in the 1890s something happened among small groups of Swedish Pietistic people. They became influenced by new thoughts coming from America. Jerusalem was no longer the city connected to the life of Jesus and the city of resurrection. It was transformed into the axis of world history with a focus on the future – the Second Coming of Christ as well as an upcoming battle of Armageddon. For some it became a new theological focus. While daily life continued in the village as before, for a few it became a dramatic change. My father was born in a village close to Nås in Dalarna and he sometimes talked about the farmers who had left everything to go to Jerusalem and settle in the American Colony. They were convinced that they were going to meet with Christ in the very near future. Jerusalem was no longer a dream but became a solid reality, where people tried to survive in a new environment while Jesus still did not appear.

The idea of farmers travelling to Jerusalem from a small village in a remote area of Sweden may seem peculiar, but these people were only part of a bigger pattern. The population of Sweden was facing severe problems with starvation and an overpopulated countryside and hundreds of thousands went to the (other) Promised Land – America. At the same time, for the small group going to Jerusalem it became a well-documented adventure and resulted in travel stories and a huge amount of very important contemporary photos of Jerusalem.

Individuals, who could afford it and got the opportunity, travelled to what were considered faraway places to see something new and experience other countries. In many cases, they felt a duty to tell about their experiences, which they did through lectures, articles in newspapers or through writing a book. The priest and orientalist Jacob Berggren explains this in his book from 1826:

> After longer and comprehensive trips in the Eastern countries, happily returning to the Fatherland, I feel a duty, to hereby provide the general public a short story about what I have, during my wanderings, had the opportunity to see and experience of the world and of human beings.
>
> (Berggren, 1826)[1]

In the last 50 years, it has become realistic for the common man and woman in Sweden to travel to Palestine/Israel. Before, the economic realities were a hindrance resulting in only a moderate flow of travellers. The European states began in the 1930s to establish a network of air routes making it possible to fly to the Holy Land. Previous travellers were dependent on a long voyage before they reached the port city of Jaffa on the way to Jerusalem. When the Crown Prince Couple, Princess Ingrid and Prince Bertil travelled to the Near and Middle East in 1932–1933 it was still by boat with their homecoming 4 months later (Lagerberg, 1935, p. 9). For other Swedish travellers and especially in recent times it is significantly shorter trips of 1–2 weeks. Some authors wrote against the background of having lived in the Holy Land for a long time, but surprisingly many published their books after a single short trip to the area.

So, when talking about Jerusalem (and the Holy Land) authors are writing about a city existing in reality and at the same time a symbolic expression of faith and hope for Christian religious manifestations in relation to history, the present time and the future. For the pilgrim or traveller, therefore, it seems possible to view Jerusalem as:

- the heavenly city;
- the city of Jesus and the biblical story;
- the place of the Second Coming of Jesus; and
- a goal/destination to visit for some days or weeks.

Driven by Adventure and Curiosity

In this part of the chapter, I will give a few examples, from history, of reasons for travelling to the sacred sites by pious people, researchers or adventurers. It is known from written sources that a small number of Nordic pilgrims in the 1000s and the 1100s travelled to major places of pilgrimage such as Jerusalem, Rome and Santiago de Compostela. As an example, on rune stones it is possible to read the likes of: 'Estrid let raise these stones after Östen, her husband, went to Jerusalem and died away in Greece.' The trip, maybe with the aim to die in Jerusalem, is considered to have taken place about 1030–1040 (Edberg, 2006, p. 343).

We know that the Nordic Vikings travelled all the way to Constantinople and to Jerusalem, by them named *Jorsala*. The 10th century Muslim writer Ahmad Ibn Faḍlān describes the Vikings he met when travelling far north as having the most perfect bodies, tall as palm trees, with blonde hair and ruddy skin. They were tattooed 'from the tip of their toes to their neck' with 'dark-green lines' and other pictures. Ibn Faḍlān recorded a rather long story about those foreigners always being armed with an axe, a sword and a long dagger as well as being the 'filthiest of all Allāh's creatures', drinking beer day and night and appearing like 'asses that roam' (Montgomery, 2000, pp. 5–8).

At this point, I need to mention a very well-known pilgrim – Saint Bridget (in Swedish *Heliga Birgitta*) – who converted to Catholicism and spent her days in Rome. She also made a pilgrimage to Jerusalem in 1373 where she had visions at the Holy sites (see for example: Searby and Morris, 2008; St Bridget of Sweden, 2015).

The Reformation in the Nordic folk churches stressed the word of God and put aside ceremonies involving icons, pilgrimage and incense; while these were not forbidden from the beginning they needed a correct interpretation. As an example it was better to hand over candles to poor people than burning them in front of pictures of saints. The Reformation can be looked upon as a gradual process and in the Parliament of 1544, prohibitions were registered against pilgrimage, holy water, salt, wax, incense and monstrance. The purpose of church buildings was to meet and listen to the Word of God and not for any 'strange' worship of God (Andrén 1999, pp. 63, 111).

How then to perceive the Swedish travellers to Jerusalem and the Holy Land after the Reformation? In 1733, Carl Fredrik von Höpken and Eduard Carlsson were sent to Jerusalem by the Swedish Board of Commerce to investigate trade in the Levant. They entered into Jerusalem through the Damascus gate and commented that the gate was only allowed for Christian Europeans. They needed a permit from the pasha as well as paying a tribute before entering. They remarked that he did not mind at all getting the money. They were taken care of at St Saviour's Monastery. The monks first washed their feet and then asked if they were coming out of curiosity or for devotion (von Höpken and Carlsson, 1789). Von Höpken and Carlsson were Christians but the answer to the question was: curiosity. That is the crucial question for some of the Swedish travellers through the years as many travelled out of curiosity, as researchers.

Some of the most interesting Swedish encounters are from the 18th century, beginning in the time of king Charles the XIIth, who is known as one of the Swedish warrior kings. After a battle, in Poltava in present-day eastern Ukraine, the king settled for 6 years together with his 2000 soldiers in Bender in the Ottoman Empire. From here he sent explorers throughout the East and not least to the Holy Land. They were described as three young, beautiful gentlemen, with experience in fortification and the art of drawing. They returned 1 year and 3 months later with a large number of drawings of landscapes, cities and ruins. Unfortunately most were destroyed by fire during a skirmish in Bender when the King was forced to go back to Sweden. The most important remaining item from this episode is a very detailed map of the Ottoman Empire. Other researchers followed. Among the most important are the disciples of Carl Linnaeus (Carl von Linné). His system for naming, ranking and classifying organisms is still in wide use today and he enlisted the help of his students. Linnaeus sent his people to different parts of the Middle East. One example is Fredrik Hasselquist who systematically collected information about 601 plants and animals in the Holy Land. While he died in Smyrna in 1752, the results of his work were published in a book in 1757: *Iter Palaestinum eller Resa til Heliga Landet* (Hasselquist, 1969 [1757]).

In more recent centuries, people from the Nordic countries travelled out of curiosity and for adventure more than as ordinary pilgrims. It may be a backpacker, a Lutheran vicar, a Free church-leader or the Crown Prince of Sweden – afterwards, they have all done the same – they tell a story. Usually the stories are accompanied by detailed descriptions of history, archaeology, geography, culture, religion and in some cases references to the Bible. All travellers want to visit as many places as possible and usually they stay a short time in each location.

You Will Find What Suits Your Purpose

Before the modern way of travelling appeared, the Pietistic tradition had its own way to deal with this. Simply, the Holy Land was embodied at home. When prayer houses, chapels and churches were built in Nordic villages and towns they were in many cases named after places such as Bethany, Bethel, Bethesda, Bethlehem, Elim, Emmaus, Salem, Tabor and Zion. All these names were seen on the biblical maps and were, thus, more than abstract names for a building or congregation. Every Sunday school had a map of the Holy Land on the wall, in order to illustrate the biblical history. Contemporary visual aids were widely in use, one such item was a flannel board – a thin blanket stretched over a stand. On this foundation were added figures, and a biblical landscape could emerge with palm trees, buildings with their flat roofs, animals and people in their robes. All of these fabric elements could be moved as a story progressed. This created in the children an image of how Palestine looked.

At the same time a minor flow of Christian leaders and travellers started to tour the Holy Land and to visit Jerusalem. As with earlier generations, one common way to communicate their experiences was through publishing a book with their travel story. Sometimes the travellers used a camera or a sketch pad. When doing so they needed to choose their images carefully due to the increased printing costs. Interestingly, they seem to have looked for visuals which were familiar to their pre-understanding (i.e. what they expected according to their own ecclesial environments). When Paul Waldenström included a picture of the Palestinian farmer travelling with his wife, of course it reminded the reader of many presentations of Mary and Joseph on their way to Bethlehem (Waldenström, 1896). In the same way, illustrated Bibles for children also have pictures of the Holy Family on their way to Bethlehem to be taxed or fleeing to Egypt from Herod. It is easy to overlook that in Waldenström's image, the man is sitting on the donkey while the woman is walking and in the pious pictures it was Mary who sat on the donkey. In the image shown in Fig. 4.2,

Fig. 4.2. Images of Mary and Joseph travelling in Bethlehem. Paul Waldenström's picture of the Palestinian farmer travelling with his wife (from Waldenström, 1896, p. 384).

Mary is seen wearing a long headscarf and Joseph an ankle-length robe with a Palestinian shawl on his head.

It is easy to identify motives for travellers' photographs among the posters used in Sunday school. This is especially true for agricultural imagery. For example, the Sunday school poster of 'sowing and reaping' compares well with the photo of farmers threshing wheat (see Fig. 4.3) and it is important for travellers to represent Palestinian farmers still performing sowing and reaping according to the biblical method, wearing the same clothes and using the same agricultural tools. The images are not about Palestinian farming but about replicating biblical images in the present.

Fig. 4.3. Replicating biblical images in the present. (a) Sunday school poster of 'sowing and reaping'; (b) traveller's photograph of farmers threshing wheat (from Launis, 1950, p. 99).

Many Sunday schools handed out memory cards, often in connection with birthdays. In the example shown in Fig. 4.4, a memory card with the Good Shepherd is shown. This is a popular recurring motif for photographers. The halo motif can even be discerned on the Palestinian shepherd.

A similar image of the rural idyll can be seen represented in the Sunday school image and the traveller photograph shown in Fig. 4.5. In this case, the Sunday school poster shows the disciples on the way to Emmaus under the heading 'Jesus in conversation with his disciples' with the city in the background. The poster and the traveller's photo are strikingly similar. It is possible to conclude that the reader of the book, in the first instance, is expected to think of the time of Jesus, rather than pious men in present-day Jerusalem.

Fig. 4.4. Replicating biblical images in the present. (a) Image on a Sunday school memory card depicting the Good Shepherd; (b) traveller's photograph of a shepherd with his sheep (from Lüpsen 1958, p. 54).

Fig. 4.5. Replicating biblical images in the present. (a) Sunday school poster showing the disciples on the way to Emmaus under the heading 'Jesus in conversation with his disciples'; (b) traveller's photograph taken in Jerusalem in the 1950s (from Lüpsen, 1958, p. 35).

Sometimes, it is obvious that the images are arranged to match the photographer's expectations as illustrated in Fig. 4.6. This arrangement of Palestinian shepherds and their sheep cannot be misunderstood by the reader. The addition of artificial lighting for the photograph causes some of the shepherds to place their hands as a protection for the light – which clearly suggests that they are looking at something special. For the photographer, the contemporary shepherds are completely uninteresting but he has managed to produce an image of the shepherds at the birth of Jesus. Thus, this is a photographic representation of the shepherds seeing and hearing the heavenly choir praising God (Luke 2: 13–14).

Fig. 4.6. Traveller's photograph of contemporary Palestinian shepherds arranged in such a way as to produce an image of the shepherds at the birth of Jesus (from Launis, 1950, p. 21).

It was this type of image that the traveller wanted to see – images somehow alluding to biblical times. Photos and pictures of contemporary Eastern life, such as clothing, agriculture, handicrafts, depictions of women at the well and fishermen on the lake all helped readers to see the life of Jesus. Everything was pre-prepared through Sunday school and sermons at home, and through these images gave the trip to the Holy Land a sense of recognition and one that became a positive experience. Maybe this was what the traveller (and reader of the book) expected and wanted to see as a step in demonstrating and strengthening their own faith. The pre-understanding of what it looked like in Jerusalem and Palestine in the time of Jesus had been confirmed.

During the 1800s and early 1900s, the images are of the Palestinian population in the villages. This did not change when the Jews began to settle more frequently in kibbutzim and towns because they were mainly dressed in Western-style clothes – so the travellers did not photograph them when they wanted biblical 'images'. Right up to the present day, motifs with Palestinians are used. A Scandinavian traveller with a religious heritage can hardly pass a sheep or a flock of goats or Bedouin tents without bringing biblical times to mind. Today's Palestinians become visual aids in order to illustrate the time of the Patriarchs or the New Testament.

Fact is Fact but Another Place May be Better

Some travel stories create suspicion in relation to traditional holy sites. Which biblical locations are correct and how to interpret them? A Scandinavian visitor should not really trust the information they get, even if it is correct, it is just about ceremonies or business and not about faith. One example is when Waldenström, on horseback, made the journey from Kana in Galilee to the village el-Mesched where, according to tradition, the prophet Jonah was buried. In order to be allowed to visit the tomb the travellers were asked to pay 5 francs and Waldenström tells that the guardian on the spot was very firm. When they prepared to leave the place and began to leave on their horses, the guard ran after them and offered to show the tomb for 3 francs. Now the travellers were firm:

> Now, it was our turn ... and we let him know that he could go his way. We did not want to disturb the Prophet in his sleep. Thus, from us he had nothing to expect. By the way, the tomb of Jonah is even to be seen in other places, namely at Hebron, and in the vicinity of Sidon. Those who do not get the opportunity to see it in one place get to do it in any of the other two! Long live competition!
>
> (Waldenström, 1896, p. 338)

All travellers agreed on the fact that the Holy Sepulchre was the correct site of the crucifixion and burial as well as the resurrection of Jesus. But obviously, the site as such and what they experienced and saw did not correspond to the anticipations they had of the place. A contributing factor was probably that the tour guides fuelled their discomfort through stories about monks who were fighting for space among church altars and chapels. Added to this was the guides' unfamiliarity with northern European pious traditions which contrast strongly with Eastern Christianity which is punctuated with processions, incense, vestments, etc. Some visitors became fascinated and curious while the majority appear to have become confused.

Efraim Briem, Professor in theological prenotions and theological encyclopaedia, described in detail the tomb of Christ and Golgotha and then remarked:

> Of course, everyone who visits the Holy Sepulchre must be seized by doubt, whether one is faced with authentic monuments. Christ's tomb was blasted into a cliff, but there is no cut, only a recess on a smooth surface. And Calvary reminds least of all of a hill and is, moreover, only a few dozen meters away from the tomb.
>
> (Briem, 1938, p. 44)

Birger Pernow was a priest who became director of the Swedish Israel Mission. In his travel guide to the biblical lands he writes several pages describing the interior of the Holy Sepulchre, following closely the words of Briem. But he adds:

> Even a Protestant visitor can hardly fail to sense any holy awe of this place, even though it is difficult to find the right devotions and worship within these walls because of the crowd – especially during Easter, which is very noisy with large throngs and troublesome murmur – 'Lamp-exhibition' and haggling with sacred memories that take place here.
>
> (Pernow, 1958, p. 73)

In order for the visit to be successful, the traveller is expected to search for devotion and worship. So, you undertake various actions, even if you know for sure you are heading to the wrong historic place. Pilgrims go to the Garden Tomb which suits the images they have carried from home. They gather in groups in the Garden reading the Gospel, singing well-known songs from home and celebrate communion – all in their own language. Pernow explains that the Garden Tomb: 'gives a clear idea of how Calvary looked like when Christ's cross was erected there and ... [invites] ... Protestant pilgrims who cannot find the desired calm places of worship in the Holy Sepulchre' (Pernow, 1958, p. 74).

Pastor Nils Tägt states that a visit to this garden for present-day pilgrimage is among the richest experiences in Jerusalem:

> Outside roars the city life. Inside the herb garden you will experience a paradisiacal beauty, serenity and tranquillity. That's the way you want to imagine the place where Jesus got his final resting place. Here you experience, that you have entered a stillness, dwelling in the midst of a noisy city, you have arrived into an oasis, where you are surrounded by beauty and serenity, which also creates a sense of calm in a rushed contemporary human being's inner world.
>
> (Tägt, 1979, p. 92)

For Scandinavian pilgrims the garden, birds' song and the tomb in the rock creates an atmosphere for prayer and holiness. This is the spot for declaring 'He is risen, He is not here'. That is the moment the travellers talk about with tears in their eyes. Thus, historicity does not matter.

When the travellers' expectations are not met the assessment of what they are experiencing is tough. This applies particularly to sacred places where churches have been built, such as the Church of the Nativity in Bethlehem and the Holy Sepulchre in Jerusalem. Here you will be given an illustrative example of something that occurs in virtually every travel story. When Lewi Pethrus arrived in Bethlehem, he had probably hoped to recognize sites, using the Bible as his guide. He is not at all interested in describing the sights in the Church of Nativity or any other churches or chapels. For him the sites being built up had no importance at all. He wanted to see something else:

> How much more wonderful would it not have been to come to Bethlehem and see the Birth Cave as it was ... But so little discernment have great churchmen and generation after generation of religious leaders. When you are in this cave and look around there, you prefer to close your eyes and exclude all marble and all the lamps and candles, all the saints and wax dolls and imagine the cave as it once was: rough and untrimmed, filled – not by the Catholic priest's incense – but with true Palestinian

stable odour. When you in your imagination have swept out all the religious lumber which in this way has vandalized the room and robbed it of its holy simplicity, you experience something of the big event, which took place on the first Christmas night.
(Pethrus, 1922, pp. 62–63)

The journey is not just about travel and experience to see historical holy sites, it is also about travelling in a way that reinforces and strengthens personal tradition.

Sometimes it is with mixed feelings that the travellers observed the devotion of local Christians. It was not the tradition of the traveller but still they were attracted by the devotion. Charlotta Heijkenskiöld travelled to Jerusalem in 1834 and died the same year on her trip in Syria. When standing in the Holy Sepulchre at the place of the crucifixion she expressed her feelings in a rather common Swedish Pietistic way:

The same sense of sanctity and piety I experienced at the Lord's table, captured me, and the power of the blood of Jesus spoke unconditionally, that what is stated in the revealed Word and the Holy Scripture is truthfully true.
(Murray, 1973, p. 13)

Waldenström expresses this well when standing at the Stone of Anointing, watching all the people kneeling: '[I went] forward and kneeled in order to pray at the same place. It really attracted me'. Days later when standing at Calvary he saw pilgrims kneeling down praying, and he writes: 'But isn't it just Catholics who do so? you ask. Yes, in general. But this evening one could see two Swedish Lutherans crawling in there on their knees. And no one but God and they knew their names' (Waldenström, 1896, p. 501).

So Jerusalem and the holy sites are also places where travellers have changed their minds, disrupted their own traditions and experienced something new.

Witness to Radical Change in Society

Also in times of great change, pilgrims and tourists have been present. A crucial moment is of course what happened in the years around 1948. The war, the flourishing State of Israel, the catastrophe for the Palestinian population, the immigration of Jews and the Palestinians becoming refugees all activated travellers. Besides describing their traditional visits to holy sites they try to comprehend what is going on.

Of course, it is possible to consider travel and guidebooks as an expression of not only what the author formulates but also their interpretation of what prevailed at the time of their trip, and it is important to note that the narrator takes precedence in the interpretation. The listener is for good or for bad at the mercy of the informant and the interpretation offered. The problem is that the narrator's words are often equated with truth. By adding together such stories from different times it is possible to see how a place or phenomenon evolves and changes. Then the stories, taken together, can indicate a journey such as the move from an agrarian to a modern society, or illustrate that the manner of worship, for example in the Holy Sepulchre, has not changed over time. A journey through time with the help of travel books could possibly also give some idea of what changes have occurred in the interpretations. Here, an example is taken of authors describing what has taken place in the Jezreel Valley. A lot of visits include this valley in the trip since the holy site of Mount Tabor is located here.

From horseback, travellers up to the end of the 1800s saw a completely or partly cultivated plain that was denoted as the most fertile plain of Galilee. 'I was surprised to see these rolling cornfields as far as the eye could reach, which reminded of American plains' (Franson, 1889, p. 52). Surprise is expressed over the 'extent and fertility of this land' (Stave, 1893, p. 369). Nordlander describes these as 'Palestine's biggest and richest fields and we now had ample opportunity to study farming' (Nordlander, 1899, p. 180). A few years later the plain is characterized as an 'extraordinarily fruitful land to a large extent' and those who cultivate the land are Arabs who live on the mountain slopes (Aurelius, 1913, p. 76).

The first Jewish colony on the plain was established in 1911 and this was followed over the next decade by a further ten or so colonies. During the 1920s: 'the harvest of the colony is good, but presents nothing particularly remarkable, when compared with the Arabs' (Saxon, 1921, p. 315) and it is also noted that the plain is being used as pasture for the Bedouin animals (Pethrus, 1922, p. 295). The Arabs harvested in the traditional way (Rangman, 1923, pp. 157–160) while after visiting a Jewish colony the conclusion is 'they are usually poor farmers' (Walder, 1925, p. 291).

Change follows, and creates an impact in the 1930s. The Jews are described by 'their enthusiasm to rebuild their old country' (Wærn-Bugge, 1931, p. 109). A pamphlet published by Keren Hayesod is quoted and the conclusion is that the plain during the last year's rebirth of the country has become a breadbasket and the country's pride constituted by grain fields, gardens and cultivated land (De Heer, 1931, p. 43). The previously barren marshland and malaria source of infection had turned into a fertile agricultural plain (Pernow, 1936, p. 96). This fact is retold by various authors: 'The Jews have transformed the valley, once the sump region and malaria area, to the fertile land' (Andrén, 1949, p. 12) and 'Jezreel plain ... was then a swampy and plagued area, but now a thriving cultural district with the most fertile soil in the country' (Rimmerfors, 1952, p. 159).

Guides in the 1960s told that no earlier people could farm on the plains since it was an inhospitable region that is now changed, and 'all over the fertile fields with mature crops and newly sown fields. As far as the eye could reach, one saw fertile arable land' (Borgström, 1961, p. 65).

The message sounds very much like Fredrik Franson's but it differs by some 70 years in time, and presents a whole new historiography which is perpetuated in travellers' descriptions until the present time. Any traveller to the Holy Land should be aware that what you see and hear is part of the process of interpretation and re-interpretation. It is part of creating a new history for new inhabitants.

Sacred Places as Political Watersheds

Increasingly, during the 1900s and especially after the establishment of the State of Israel in 1948, a political aspect has been added to visiting Jerusalem and the

Holy Land. In relation to the conflict of names (i.e. Israel/Palestine), present-day pilgrimages or tours visiting Jerusalem express a need to issue some kind of statement on the political situation or simply declare that they do not need to do so. Either way, the modern traveller carries political opinions about what went on in the Ottoman Empire, under the British mandate, under the State of Israel, on the West Bank and so on.

This is exemplified through the records of two travellers from the early 1950s, which are of special interest since their books were published at the same publishing house. Already the titles (in Swedish) indicate a difference: *A People on Their Way Home: Palestine Reports* (1952) and *Israel on Dangerous Roads* (1954). Both authors took time to visit Arab refugee camps with 'great poverty and totally unbearable living conditions' (Ollén, 1954, p. 27) and 'compared to the European refugee camps, the Arab [paid] the price' (Rimmerfors, 1952, p. 140). Regarding the cause of the catastrophe that befell the Arabs there were diverging views: Einar Rimmerfors saw the origins in 'the Arab League's propaganda', while J.M. Ollén spoke of 'Jewish propaganda' which argued that the Arabs fled on the orders of their leaders. Ollén saw the situation as a truth with modifications, established to reduce the debt of the Jews regarding the Arab catastrophe. Both viewpoints are marked by political developments and share a Christian humanist perspective with passion for rights as a driving force. However, they differ – Rimmerfors expresses a committed solidarity with the Jewish state while Ollén's stance is more sceptical because of certain alarming symptoms which he observed.

These two accounts are examples of choices every traveller has to consider in addition to visiting the holy sites. Depending on what you choose to see and then how you interpret what you see, you develop political viewpoints. A trip organized in order to bless Israel and show solidarity with Israel will be different from a trip in order to see the living conditions of the Christians in the West Bank and show solidarity with Palestine. Not even the most pious pilgrim can avoid this – the trip will have political implications whether you like it or not.

Conclusion

This chapter presents a number of themes regarding Swedish Protestant Christian travellers to Jerusalem and the Holy Land. The discussion commences with an exploration of Jerusalem's special place as a sacred connection between heaven and earth. Before the popularization of travel, Christians in Sweden used imagery and maps to develop their conceptualization of this most holy landscape. It is important to recognize that for Christians, Jerusalem (and the Holy Land) is present in the real world while also coexisting as a symbolic expression of faith and hope. As early as the 1000s, Nordic pilgrims were travelling to sites such as Jerusalem and Rome. And while their travels are well documented, it would appear from their writings that their motivations were more to do with curiosity and adventure than pilgrimage. The next generation of travellers discussed in the chapter were those who were interested in building upon their Sunday-school learned concepts of the Holy Land. The manner in which they reported and illustrated what they found, further perpetuated the dominant imagery.

From the beginning of the 20th century, it became apparent that the commercialization and modernization of Bethlehem, Jerusalem and other important Christian sites was challenging travellers' preconceived notions of these historically and spiritually important spaces. Travel writers started to question the established concepts and traditions, and thereby reflected on the importance for their readers of experiencing something new. In more recent times it has become apparent that this 'something new' is heavily influenced by the writer's own viewpoint, and that of the guides who lead them in their own travels. Thus, the chapter concludes with discussions on witnessing radical change in society, and sacred places as political watersheds. Important religious sites such as those visited by Christian Swedish travellers in Jerusalem and the Holy Land are imbued with political gravitas, and it is important to remember that their interpretation is often influenced by the beliefs presented in published guides or guidebooks, which mediate the narrative of the traveller's experience.

Note

[1] All translations from Swedish are made by the author of this chapter.

References

Andrén, G. (1949) *Palestinabilder*. Israelsmissionen, Stockholm.
Andrén, Å. (1999) *Svensk kyrkohistoria 3. Reformationstiden*. Verbum, Stockholm.
Aurelius, E. (1913) *Palestinabilder*. Askerberg, Uppsala, Sweden.
Berggren, J. (1826) *Resor i Europa och Österländerne*. Rumstedt, Stockholm.
Borgström, G. (1961) *Resa till Israel: ett Snabbreportage*. Filadelfia, Stockholm.
Briem, E. (1938) *Det Underbara Palestina.* Natur och kultur, Stockholm.
De Heer, J. (1931) *Folkvärldens Slutkris eller den Stundande Världsdomen vid Harmageddon.* Bibliska förlaget, Skövde, Sweden.
Edberg, R. (2006) Spår Efter en Tidig Jerusalemfärd. *Fornvännen* 101(5), 342–347.
Franson, F. (1889) *Reseskildringar öfver missionär F. Franssons resa genom Italien, Egypten, Palestina, Syrien, Mindre Asien, Europeiska Turkiet och Ryssland*. Falköping, Sweden.
Hasselquist, F. (1969 [1757]) *Iter Palaestinum eller Resa til Heliga Landet: förrättad ifrån år 1749 till 1752*. Rediviva, Stockholm.
Lagerberg, J. (ed.) (1935) *Kronprinsparets Orientresa: En Minnesbok i Bilder: September 1934–Januari 1935*. Saxon & Lindström, Stockholm.
Launis, I. (1950) *Frälsarens fotspår*. Saxon & Lindström, Stockholm.
Lüpsen, F. (1958) *Palestina*. Fosterlands-Stiftelsen, Stockholm.
Montgomery, J.E. (2000) Ibn Faḍlān and the Rūsiyyah. *Journal of Arabic and Islamic Studies* 3, 1–25.
Murray, R. (1973) *Ensam i belägrat Jerusalem*. Verbum, Stockholm.
Nordlander, A. (1899) *Reseminnen från det Heliga Landet, Egypten och Turkiet*. Fritzes, Stockholm.
Ollén, J.M. (1954) *Israel på Farliga Vägar*. Gummessons, Stockholm.
Pernow, B. (1936) *Palestina förr och nu*. Israelsmissionen, Stockholm.
Pernow, B. (1958) *Till Bibelns Län: En Resehandbok*. Diakonistyrelsen, Stockholm.
Pethrus, L. (1922) *Resor och Rön i Palestina*. Filadelfia, Stockholm.

Rangman, Hj. (1923) *Reseminnen från Egypten och Palestina hösten 1922*. Hj. Rangman, Katrineholm, Sweden.

Rimmerfors, E. (1952) *Ett Folk på Hemväg: Palestinareportage*. Gummessons, Stockholm.

Saxon, J.L. (1921) *Det Nya Palestina*. Nutiden, Stockholm.

Searby, D. and Morris, B. (2008) *The Revelations of St. Birgitta of Sweden*. Oxford University Press, Oxford.

St Bridget of Sweden (2015) *Revelations of St. Bridget: On the Life and Passion of Our Lord and the Life of His Blessed Mother*. TAN Books, Charlotte, North Carolina.

Stave, E. (1893) *Genom Palestina. Minnen från en resa våren 1891*. Norstedt, Stockholm.

Tägt, N. (1979) *Från Siljan till Gennesaret*. Gummessons, Stockholm.

Wærn-Bugge, E. (1931) *Det Omstridda Arvet: utblickar över Palestina av i dag*. Norstedt, Stockholm.

Waldenström, P.P. (1896) *Till Österland. Skildringar från en resa i Turkiet, Grekland, Syrien, Palestina, Egypten samt på Sinaihalfön hösten och våren 1894*. Norman, Stockholm.

Walder, A. (1925) *Från Fyris till Damaskus*. Svenska Missionsförbundet, Stockholm.

von Höpken, C.F. and Carlsson, E. (1789) *Twänne stora swenska herrars rese-beskrifning, ifrån Cypern, til Asien, förlofwade landet, Jerusalem och Christi graf, jämte andra märkwärdiga orter och namnkunniga ställen*. Johan Pehr Lindh, Örebro, Sweden.

5 Islam – Contemporary Perspectives

RAZAQ RAJ[1]* AND IRFAN RAJA[2]

[1]Leeds Beckett University, Leeds, UK; [2]University of Huddersfield, Huddersfield, UK

Introduction

In today's secular world the relationship between tourists and their beliefs plays a major part in influencing individuals when visiting religious sites. The patterns of visitation within individuals depend on the strength of religious beliefs. In current literature limited research is available that explores the understanding and motivation of visitation patterns of religious tourists. In the Muslim world from Australia to the USA, the mosque in its many forms is the fundamental pilgrimage destination to visit five times a day. The word mosque is a translation of the Arabic word masjid – meaning the Muslim gathering place for prayer. Mosque simply means 'place of worship'. In reality the five daily prayers set in Islamic practice can take place anywhere, but Muslims are required to gather together at the mosque for the five daily prayers if they are free and able to attend. In the media, the importance of this Muslim concept of mosque visitation for religious worship is being underestimated and undermined.

In recent times, Western societies have begun to view Islam as incompatible with, and a security threat to, secular and liberal ways of life. This is mainly because most often sections of the media, polity and conservative writers present a distasteful view of Islam featuring it as a source of social ills and all sorts of troubles in the world. Several notable studies offer convincing analysis that the media has an important role in building misperceptions and misunderstandings of Islam (these include: Said, 1979, 1997; Mitchell and Marriage, 2003; Saeed, 2007; Asmal, 2008; Bowen, 2012; Gomes, 2014; Kolig, 2014). Accordingly, narratives come into view that suggest Islam is an old-fashioned, authoritarian and outdated religion.

*r.raj@leedsmet.ac.uk

Distortion and Misunderstanding of Islam

Considerable evidence shows that aside from some periods of tension and mutual distrust mainly resulting from the agendas of ruling political elites, Islam and Christendom have a long history of trade, educational and business ties.

Nevertheless, today, Islam is a greatly misunderstood and victimized religion as noted by one of the leading Western scholars John Esposito in his article 'True Islam has been Distorted', published on 19 April 2007. This paper provides a detailed narrative that shows the way Islam has been misrepresented to both non-Muslims as well as Muslim political elites. Esposito writes: 'Throughout history, the sacred scriptures of Judaism, Christianity, and Islam have been used and abused, interpreted and misinterpreted, to justify resistance and liberation struggles, extremism and terrorism, holy and unholy wars' (Esposito, 2007).

Writing further on this concept, Michael Wolfe (2004) finds that perhaps Islam is the most misunderstood of the world's great religions. He notes that, 'We heard anti-American fanatics quote the Qur'an to justify mass murder, and we heard anti-Muslim bigots quote it back – both sides use bad translations and phrases out of context' (Wolfe, 2004). Of course this is a worrying situation because words are 'weapons of mass destruction' that do have an impact on people's minds whether it is positive or negative.

Islamic Tension and the Origins of the Mosque in Britain

According to a BBC archive entitled *History of Islam in the UK* (2009), Britain's first mosque is presumed to have been built in the 1860s at 2 Glyn Rhondda Street, Cardiff. Historical records (throughout the 19th and early 20th centuries) relating to the construction of mosques, reflect a challenging struggle by Muslims who confronted misconceptions, fear and the hostility towards their proposals to build a place of prayer. This may have been fuelled by the ongoing tensions between Turkey and Britain, which in turn gave rise to negative feelings among some sections of the British public. In his edited volume *The Making of East London Mosque, 1910–1951* Humayun Ansari (2011) discusses the building of the East London Mosque in the context of confrontation between the British and Ottoman Empires (from as early as the first decade of the 19th century). Perhaps this encouraged many British politicians, including Prime Minster David Lloyd George and Sir Arthur Hirtzel, to oppose the idea of a mosque (into the 20th century). Ansari quotes Hirtzel who commented: 'I am dead against it – on grounds of both policy and religion [... that] a Christian Government should be party to erecting one [a mosque] in a Christian country is to me unthinkable' (cited by Ansari, 2011).

At the same time Lord Headley (in 1916) acknowledged the 400,000 Muslims who fought for the British Empire, many of whom lost their lives, while 14 received the Victoria Cross for their bravery (Ansari, 2011). Ansari traces a series of vandalism-related incidents and racial attacks on East London Mosque and its surrounding areas throughout the 1960s, 1970s, 1980s and 1990s.

Understanding the Concept of the Mosque

In a study exploring the essence and true meaning of 'mosque', Mahmutćehajić sees it as the 'Station of the spirit' (Mahmutćehajić, 2006). He goes further to explain the significant place which the mosque plays, linking human beings with their 'master' and helping them to earn an eternal happiness and peace through performing prayers (Mahmutćehajić, 2006). On the back cover of his book Mahmutćehajić provides a short passage which further explains the role of the mosque: 'The Mosque is an extended meditation on a dimension of the Muslim intellectual world unfamiliar to most Western readers' (Mahmutćehajić, 2006).

In the same vein, Macaulay sees the mosque as an inspirational place particularly for those who wish to pray or 'simply to find temporary refuge from the chaos' of demanding life, or even want to get a reassuring sense of life (Macaulay, 2008, p. 7).

The mosque holds a central position in Islam because of its vital role in promoting and maintaining community bonds, binding individuals to a central system that helps them not only to practise their religion and live accordingly but to engage with a wider community. Gathering five times a day at the mosque helps attendees to know what is going on in their neighbourhood. Unlike Church, Senegal, Temples and Gurdawara, mosques assist in developing a sense of brotherhood and unity which encourages and propagates good deeds and helps to discourage crime and other bad doings within society.

'Masjid' is an Arabic word meaning 'place of worship' and according to Islamic teaching a Muslim can pray at any place as long as it is clean (pure). Turner states that 'The whole world is a "place of prostration" or masjid – the Arabic word for mosque – and so long as one faces Mecca, one can pray virtually wherever one likes' (Turner, 2006, p.140).

Esposito extensively discusses Islam and Muslims and also discusses that a Muslim can perform prayer facing Mecca anywhere he/she likes – in a mosque, at work, home or on the road side (Esposito, 1998). Robinson (1999), explaining the mosque and its position in Islam, says '[t]he English word mosque is derived from Arabic masjid, which means a place for prostration', and in referencing Prophet Muhammad's (pbuh) hadiths [sayings] he highlights that 'the whole earth is a mosque except for bath-houses and camel pens' (Robinson, 1999, p. 102). Robinson's comprehensive inquiry about the mosques affirms that:

> The wall usually has an ornate convex niche called a mihrab, a feature which was introduced in 706 by the Umayyad Caliph al-Walid I during restorations in the Prophet's mosque in Medina ... minarets were first built by the Abbasids.
>
> (Robinson, 1999, p. 102)

Marwan Ibrahim Al-Kaysi offers a more inclusive idea of mosque, saying that 'The mosque is where Muslims should pray five times every day, where they seek refuge from the troubles of this world, from its everlasting daily demands, its complications and its vanities' (Al-Kaysi, 1986, p.107).

An interesting perspective on the mosque is provided by this author (Al-Kaysi), whose book *Morals and Manners in Islam: A Guide to Islamic Adab* deals with manners, which are extremely important in Islam. His overall conclusion suggests a clear message, that a mosque should be simple (Al-Kaysi, 1986).

Nielsen (2004) offers a substantial account of Muslims in Western Europe through the provision of factual surveys and analyses relating to Muslims' political, social, cultural and religious position in contemporary Europe. Nielsen (2004) points out that the increase in the number of mosques in Britain is the result of a growing Muslim population, and finds that 'In 1963, there was a total of thirteen mosques registered with the Registrar-General ... by June 1985, a total of 314 mosques had been registered, a figure which by 1990 had reached 452' (Nielsen, 2004, p. 45).

On the role of mosques, Nielsen refers to the UK Islamic Mission, an organization that 'works primarily through a network of mosques' and undertakes several remarkable roles in UK mosques such as: (i) welcoming visiting groups of professionals who wish to familiarize themselves with Muslim perspectives and concerns; (ii) making itself available to local officials in government, law, school and church; and (iii) inviting individuals to open celebrations of the major festivals (Nielsen, 2004).

Mosques as Religious Sites for Muslim Pilgrimage

The first obligation of a Muslim is to worship on a regular basis in his or her house, mosque or any suitable place. This means to observe the salaat regularly five times a day at the proper times stated and prescribed in the Qur'an and the manner in which it is performed comes from the Sunnah of Prophet Muhammad (pbuh). One of the essential principles to remember is that the salaat was given to Prophet Muhammad by the Lord of the Worlds (Allah) himself, during the night of Miraaj (journey to heaven). It was a present to Prophet Muhammad (pbuh) from Allah, with a binding duty to complete salaat 50 times a day at the beginning. This was reduced to five times a day, at the begging of the Prophet Muhammad (pbuh) during the night of Miraaj, by the advice of Prophet Moses to Prophet Muhammad in the sky. After the appeal of Holy Prophet Muhammad, Allah showed his mercy and blessing by announcing good news to the Holy Prophet Muhammad, by reducing it to five daily prayers. Ibn Maja, Ikametu's-Salah (Shafi, 1998, p. 194) reports that Allah said: 'O the Prophet (pbuh)! Allah abides by His word. You will get reward of fifty for the five.'

The Holy Prophet Muhammad after returning from Miraaj, announced to his people that Allah had given a gift of five daily prayers. Allah said:

> I enjoined the five daily prayers on your people. There is a pledge by Me. I will surely place those who perform the five daily prayers in time into the paradise. And there is no pledge by Me to those who do not keep these prayers.
>
> (Ibn Maja, Ikametu's-Salah, Topbas, 2006, p. 149)

These five daily prayers consist of recitations from the holy Qu'ran and the glorification of God by undertaking various bodily movements. They are a vital part of Muslim belief. There is very clear wisdom behind the practice of praying at specific times of the day (see Fig. 5.1). These prayers offer benefits for human beings, both spiritual and bodily, providing those who are offering them are serious and prepare themselves before standing to offer the prayer. Allah says in the Qur'an: 'So (give) glory to Allah, when you reach eventide and when you rise in the morning; to him be praise, in the heavens and on earth; and in the late-afternoon and when the day begins to decline' (Surah Al Ar-Rum 30: 17–18) (from Shafi, 1998).

Fig. 5.1. Names and times for daily prayers.

These times correspond to the organization of an individual's life, and the various activities he/she performs during the day. The purpose of salaat is a multi-facetted act of worship, to keep the individual's relationship with their creator very close, by offering the salaat five times a day. This important prayer can be performed anywhere, in a mosque, at home, at one's place of work, outdoors or in any other clean place.

The salaat can be offered either individually or in a congregation. Congregational prayer is preferred to individual salaat because of its obvious aspects of brotherhood and solidarity. Muslims around the world have established mosques for congregational worship. According to the teachings of Islam, the rewards of congregational prayer increase 25–27 times and are most generous if undertaken in a mosque – where the mercy of God descends. The mosque is considered the best of places by the Messenger of Allah (upon him be peace). Ibn 'Abbas (may Allah be pleased with him) relates: 'Mosques are the houses of Allah on the earth. They shine up to the inhabitants of the heavens just as the stars in the sky shine down to the inhabitants of the earth' (Tabarânî) (from Shafi, 1998).

Once a mosque is erected and built by the local community, it will always be a mosque and the property of Allah. It cannot return to being the property of any person or community even those who may have paid for establishing it. Mosques are very special places of worship, which cannot be sold for financial gain by individuals. The Messenger of Allah (upon him be peace) said, 'All the earth will disappear on the Day of Judgment with the exception of the masjids for they will join with one another' (Suyûtî, Jâmi' al-Shaghîr) (from Shafi, 1998).

Concept of Ummah: An Illustration of Community Building

Before Islam, Arabs were mostly known for tribal fighting, burying their daughters alive, bad treatment of women, slavery, ill-manners and social ills so offensive that even the Romans and Persian Empires left them alone (Barakat, 1993; Nicholson, 1998; Hitti, 2002). These Arabs, once famous for their tribal wars and bloodshed, became one community under the banner of Islam. A classic example of this community is the historical bond of brotherhood between the Ansar and Muhajirin in the holy city of Madinah during times of migration and hardship (Ahmed, 2003).

Hunter's (1998) inquiry into early Islamic history and teachings reveals that the concept of 'Ummah', has often been misunderstood in the Western world, because it is regularly taken to refer to a wider 'Muslim community' only. In reality it considers all non-Muslims as part of the Ummah: '[In the] main political document remaining from the Prophets' time in Medina, often called the Constitution of Medina, the concept of the Ummah also included the Jews of the Madinah' (Hunter, 1998).

It is indeed true, however, that Ummah is sometimes used quite widely to refer to a 'unity within a [single] religious community' – as among the Muslims (Hunter, 1998). Hunter (1998) offers evidence to support his viewpoint and says that:

> The term Ummah is not limited to Islam. In the Christian world, the empire of Charlemagne and the Holy Roman Empire were based on the concept of the unity of the Christian community, and the Holy Roman Empire could be interpreted as a Christian Ummah community.
>
> (Hunter, 1998, p. 37)

Here it is important to note that while studying both 'historic and abstract Islam', Hunter dismisses several assumptions which are held by both Muslim and Christian thinkers – for example, he strongly rejects the simplistic 'clash of civilization theory' as espoused by some historians and theologians. Hunter's work helps us to understand one of the most important issues relating to Muslims in non-Muslim countries (using British Muslims as an exemplar) – who are often seen as incompatible with modern society; there is a growing perception that Muslims prefer to stick with their fellow Muslims and hence avoid integration, which puts them 'into a box' or a ghetto. For Hunter, this is not just: 'an inevitable clash between the Islamic world and the West ... based on the specificity of Islam ... its alleged inherent incompatibility with secular, liberal western political ideology' (Hunter, 1998, p. 70).

Clear evidence shows that different religions have lived peacefully and side by side with Muslims in Medina and later in different parts of the world. The historical archives attest that this model was successful in Muslim Spain, Mughal India, in the Ottoman Balkans and in Eastern Europe. There is ample evidence that the world's major faiths such as Christians, Jews, Sikhs, Hindus and Buddhists have all lived together peacefully. Several scholars' historical works support this: for instance Lowney writes: 'Medieval Spain's enterprising, devout, imaginative, ambitious, and adventurous men and women forged a civilization that in many ways far outshone that elsewhere in Europe. They almost built the peaceful, common society that we must learn to build' (Lowney, 2005, p. 3).

Examples run throughout history: such as in the Indian subcontinent during Muslim rule that continued until the late 17th century, various religious groups lived in harmony.

Islam – Compatible with the Modern Way of Life?

Esposito assumes that, 'For many, Islam was seen as incompatible with modernity, in particular with democratization and modernization' (Esposito, 2003, p. 3). Andrew Rippin in his two-part study *Muslims: Their Religious Beliefs and Practices* (2005) looked into the history of early Islam to explore and compare the past and present state of the religion in the contemporary world. A great deal of text in Rippin's inquiry deals with the current crisis that has put Islam and Muslims into the spotlight – particularly in Europe, where the faith is increasingly seen as outdated or incompatible with modernization. Rippin's work deals with the emergence of Islam, the Prophet of Islam and the Qur'an. He then covers the emergence of 'Islamic identity' and its various forms. In his second volume, the main discussion revolves around Muslims in the contemporary world and this 'modernity' which has become a central point of modern discussions about Islam and Muslims. Considering wider definitions of the terms 'modernity' and 'tradition', Rippin attempts to untie the complications involved in understanding both concepts in reference to Europe and Islam in scholarly texts. He writes:

> Modernity is that which has created fundamental changes in behaviour (*sic*) and belief about economics, politics, social organisation and intellectual discourse ... modern era enlightened, secular, rational, disenchanted (i.e. the loss of magic), scientific.
>
> (Rippin, 2005, p. 178)

Opposing this are the concepts of 'traditional' or 'traditionalists' which are often applied to Islam and Muslims, and in most such texts, Rippin suggests that change is highly valued over tradition (Rippin, 2005).

From Rippin's point of view it is important to realize that 'modernity' is a worldwide phenomenon, which is not exclusively 'Western'. There are also many problematic characteristics of 'modernity' which writers overlook. Modernity involves conceptual linkage to ideas such as 'colonial, imperialist, missionary ... [and] ... invasion' which are commonly seen (by those suggesting that Islam rejects modernity) to be traits which are evident in the Muslim world (Rippin, 2005).

Rippin goes on to explore various Islamic authorities in the long history of Islam and finds that modernity is not restricted in Islam but, in reality, has been embraced by many reformers including: Al-Gazali (1058–1111), Ibn Taymiyya (1263–1328), Shah Wali Ullah (1702–1762), Ibn 'Abd al-Wahhab (1703–1787), Sayyid Ahmed Khan (1817–1898), Jamal-ud-Din Afghani (1839–1897), Muhammad 'Abduh (1849–1905), Rashid Rida (1865–1935), Muhammad Iqbal (1876–1938) and Sayyid Qutb (1906–1966). This illustrates, first, that these were all reformers, and secondly, the essence of change exists in Islam (and can be understood by the terms 'Mujaddid'or 'Ijtihad') (Rippin, 2005).

According to Edward Said, both Islam and the West have failed to understand each other, ironically, despite both recognizing the need for knowledge and understanding. For Muslims '[to] seek knowledge even you have to travel as far as to China', is a prophetic teaching; while in Europe since the Greek period the thirst for knowledge remains a popular tradition. However, in the present arena, regardless of technological advancements, both seem disturbingly ignorant of each other's cultures. This has fuelled the view that Islam is a threat in Europe and America. Largely, the media is responsible for the fact that most people in America and the West only link 'unpleasant news' such as individual acts of violence and extremism to Islam (Said, 1997).

Ways of Life – Similarities and Differences between 'the West' and 'Islam'

Dick Douwes (2000) quoting al-Makki, discusses the following passage: 'And they imposed a reign of injustice which was beyond description; even the rains stopped because of the injustice done' (Douwes, 2000).

Douwes tells us that this injustice lay in the sultan's absolute and unchallenged authority which did not follow the Islamic concept of Sharia (Douwes, 2000). Under Sharia law, or the rule of God, every individual is the same so the needs of both rich and poor are catered for equally.

This desire for equality is also mentioned in the Qur'an where Allah SWT says:

> Let there be no compulsion in religion. Truth has made clear from error. Whoever rejects false and worship and believes in Allah has grasped the most trustworthy handhold that never breaks. And Allah hears and knows all things.
>
> (Surah al-Baqarah: 256)

Here 'no compulsion' means that no one is forced to adopt, practise and worship God, reinforcing the elements of individual choice and freedom.

To further enhance our knowledge and understanding of Sharia, let's take a look at examples from everyday life in Europe and particularly Britain, to explore the roots of the problem which lie in the press and some political minds, but not the literature. Take the case of Siesta in Spain which is an Islamic practice developed from Sharia (see study on sleeping by BaHammam, 2011). Similar practices developed from Islamic guidelines include: customer rights, product exchange, wages, queuing, banking, charity, benefits, child milk vouchers, 6 month break from work after giving birth and animal rights. There are many other social practices in the West which originated in Muslim Spain. These are all mentioned in the Sunna (the acts/sayings of Prophet Muhammad (pbuh) and the teachings of holy Qur'an.

Sharia is the combined directions included in the Qur'an and Sunnah, meaning the law of the creator for the benefits of humanity. In other words it is a way of life according to certain principles. Take for example, guidelines with regard to drinking water and eating food – various recommendations are outlined in the Qur'an and in the Hadith. One states: begin in the name of God, look into the pot, sit down and drink three sips with the right hand, and then thank God. It is prohibited to drink water after food but recommended that you drink water before eating lunch, dinner or supper. While directives such as this are discredited by some, it is worth pointing out that this one aspect of Sharia could help millions of people improve their health – as the Western world is fighting a battle against rising cancer rates. A Royal College of Nursing, National Health Service (NHS) report, *Water for Health: Hydration Best Practice Toolkit for Hospitals and Healthcare* which is part of its wider 'nutrition now campaign' says 'Drink a glass of water before and during each meal' (Royal College of Nursing, 2007, p. 25). This matches what is described in the Hadith and Sunnah part of Sharia law.

Waldron *et al.* (1993) in their edited volume, *Food and Cancer Prevention: Chemical and Biological Aspects* recommend that food is eaten in three parts. This means that you divide your appetite into three parts: for example, water, food and leave an empty space. This advice is also given in the Sunnah.

Also one has to be generous and think of one's neighbours. For example, according to a hadith: 'The believer is not he who eats his fill while his neighbour is hungry' (Bukhari, Muslim). Similarly, going to the toilet and having Gusal – meaning bathing in a prescribed manner – is hygienic and scientifically beneficial for human beings. This was common Islamic practice centuries before the Western world developed hygienic practices. Several other British customs, traditions and laws such as walking on the right-hand side, cleaning streets, maintaining food quality and the right for customers to return and exchange products are all mentioned in Hadiths which are part of Sharia law.

Conclusion

This chapter has examined various contemporary perspectives of Islam and in particular has addressed an under-researched aspect of religious pilgrimage – the motivation to attend mosques on a daily basis. It is not easy to define the concept of Muslim pilgrimage motivations in simple terms. This is added to by the problem of quantifying religious pilgrimage visitation to mosques throughout the week for prayer, study or simply as a place for rest and reflection. Muslim pilgrimage follows the Sunnah of Holy Prophet Muhammad (pbuh) and claims that doing so is an emulation of the Prophet's Sunnah. Therefore, performing salaat prayer at a religious site is one of the pilgrim's fundamental beliefs when visiting religious sites. Pilgrims enjoy a sense of purification, repentance and spiritual renewal during their journey to pilgrimage sites.

Also the chapter highlights a Muslim's need to worship on a regular basis in his or her house, mosque or any suitable place. This means that they observe the salaat five times a day at the proper times stated and prescribed in the Qur'an, and the manner in which it is performed comes to us from the Sunnah of Prophet Muhammad. The Mosque holds a central position in Islam because of its vital role in promoting and keeping the community bonded, connecting individuals to a central system that helps them not only to practise their religion and live accordingly but to engage with a wider community.

Bibliography

Abaid, N. (2008) *Sharia, Muslim States and International Human Rights Treaty Obligations: A Comparative Case Study.* British Institute of International Comparative Law, London.

Abdo, G. (2000) *No God but God: Egypt and the Triumph of Islam.* Oxford University Press, New York.

Ahmed, S.A. (2003) *Islam under Siege.* Polity Press, Cambridge.

Akbar, M.J. (2002) *The Shade of Swords: Jihad and the Conflict between Islam and Christianity.* Routledge, London.

Al-Kaysi, M.I. (1986) *Morals and Manners in Islam: a Guide to Islamic Adab.* The Islamic Foundation, Kube Publishing, Markfield, Leicestershire, UK.

Allen, C. (2007) *God's Terrorists: the Wahhabi Cult and the Hidden Roots of Modern Jihad.* Abacus, London.

Andar, R. and Aroney, N. (2010) *Shaira in the West*. Unity Press, Oxford.

An-Na'im, A.A. (2008) *Islam and the Secular State*. Harvard University Press, London.

Ansari, H. (2011) *The Making of East London Mosque, 1910–1951*. Minutes of the London Mosque Fund and East London Mosque Trust Ltd, Cambridge University Press, Cambridge.

Armstrong, K. (2002) *Islam: a Short History*. Modern Library Chronicles, London.

Asmal, F. (2008) Islamophobi and the media: the portrayal of Islam since 9/11 and an analysis of Danish cartoon controversy in South Africa. PhD thesis. Available at: www.2008-media-asmal.pdf (accessed 22 May 2016).

Backer, K. (2012) *From MTV to Mecca: How Islam Inspired My Life*. Arcade Books, London.

Baderin, A.M. (2003) *International Human Rights and Islamic Law*. Oxford University Press, Oxford.

BaHammam, A.S. (2011) Sleep from an Islamic perspective. *Annals of Thoracic Medicine*. Available at: http://www.ncbi.nlm.nih.gov/pmc/articles/PMC3183634/ (accessed 11 October 2015).

Barakat, H. (1993) *The Arab World: Society, Culture, and State*. University of California Press, Berkeley, California.

Baran, Z. and Tuohy, E. (2011) *Citizen Islam: the Future of Muslim Integration in the West*. The Continuum International Publishing Group, London.

Barber, R.B. (2003) *Jihad vs. McWorld*. Corgi Books, London.

BBC (2009) *History of Islam in the UK*. Available at: http://www.bbc.co.uk/religion/religions/islam/history/uk_1.shtml (accessed 12 October 2015).

Blankinship, Y.K. (1994) *The End of the Jihad State: the Reign of Hisham Ibn 'Abd Al-Malik and the Collapse of the Umayyads*. State University of New York Press, New York.

Bloom, M. (2005) *Dying to Kill: the Allure of Suicide Terror*. Columbia University Press, New York.

Bowen, J.R. (2012) *Blaming Islam*. MIT Press, Cambridge.

Brachman, M.J. (2008) *Global Jihadism: Theory and Practice*. Routledge, London.

Bruce, S. (2008) *Fundamentalism*. Polity Press, Cambridge.

Buchler, A. (2011) *Islamic Law in Europe? Legal Pluralism and its Limits in European Family Laws*. Ashgate, London.

Burke, J. (2004) *Al-Qaeda: the True Story of Radical Islam*. Penguin Books, London.

Cateura, L. (2005) *Voices of American Muslims*. Hippocrene Books, New York.

Cole, J. and Cole, B. (2009) *Martyrdom*. Pennant Publishing, London.

Douwes, D. (2000) *The Ottomans in Syria: a History of Justice and Oppression*. I.B. Tauris, London.

Elgamri, E. (2010) *Islam in the British Broadsheets: the Impact of Orientalism on Representations of Islam in the British Press*. Garnet Publishing Limited, Reading.

Esposito, J. (1998) *Islam: the Straight Path*. Oxford University Press, Oxford.

Esposito, J. (2003) Introduction: modernizing Islam and re-Islamization in global perspective. In: Esposito, J. and Burgat, F. (eds) *Modernizing Islam: Religion in the Public Sphere in the Middle East and Europe*. Rutgers University Press, New Jersey.

Esposito, J. (2007) True Islam has been Distorted. *FaithStreet* 17 April 2007. Available at: http://www.faithstreet.com/onfaith/2007/04/19/islam/7720 (accessed 11 October 2015).

Fetzer, S.J. and Soper, C.J. (2005) *Muslims and the State in Britain, France, and Germany*. Cambridge University Press, Cambridge.

Gabriel, A.R. (2007) *Muhammad: Islam's First Great General*. University of Oklahoma Press, Norman, Oklahoma.

Gellhorn, M. (1998) *The Face of War: Wars in Central America*. Granta Publications, London.

Gomes, I. (2014) The coverage of Islam – marginalized and moralizing narratives. *Intercom – RBCC São Paulo* 37(1), 71–89. Available at: http://www.scielo.br/pdf/interc/v37n1/en_a04v37n1.pdf (accessed 22 May 2016).

Hafez, M. (2003) *Why Muslims Rebel: Repression and Resistance in the Islamic World*. Lynne Rienner Publishers, London.

Hargreaves, I. (2005) *Journalism: a Very Short Introduction*. Oxford University Press, Oxford.

Hitti, K.P. (2002) *History of the Arabs*. Palgrave Macmillan, London.

Hunter, S. (1998) *The Future of Islam and the West: Clash of Civilizations of Peaceful Co-existence?* Greenwood Publishing Group, Westport, Connecticut.

Husain, E.D. (2007) *The Islamist*. Penguin Books, London.

Ibn Maja, Ikametu's-Salah, Topbas (2006) Available at: http://www.namazzamani.net/english/the_five_compulsory_daily_prayers.htm (accessed 30 October 2015).

Kolig, E. (2014) Muslim sensitivities and the West. In: Kolig, E. (ed.) *Freedom of Speech and Islam*. Dorset Press, Dorchester.

Laughey, D. (2009) *Media Studies: Theories and Approaches*. Kamera Books, Harpenden, UK.

Lawrence, B.B. (1998) *Shattering the Myth: Islam Beyond Violence*. Princeton University Press, Princeton, New Jersey.

Liddell, R. (1956) *Byzantium and Istanbul*. Jonathan Cape, London.

Lowney, C. (2005) *A Vanished World: Medieval Spain's Golden Age of Enlightenment*. Free Press, New York.

Lowney, C. (2006) *A Vanished World: Muslims, Christians, and Jews in Medieval Spain*. Oxford University Press, Oxford.

Macaulay, D. (2008) *Mosque*. Houghton Mifflin, Boston.

Mahmutćehajić, R. (2006) *The Mosque: the Heart of Submission*. Fordham University Press, New York.

Marshall, P. (2005) *Radical Islam's Rules: the Worldwide Spread of Extreme Sharia Law*. Rowman and Littlefield Publishers, Oxford.

Masud, M.K. (1990) The obligation to migrate: the doctrine of *hijra* in Islamic law. In: Eickelman, F.D. and Piscatori, J. (eds) *Muslim Travellers: Pilgrimage, Migration and the Religious Imagination*. Routledge, London, pp. 29–49.

Mitchell, P.J. and Marriage, S. (2003) Introduction: In: Mitchell, P.J. and Marriage, S. (eds) *Mediating Religion: Studies in Media, Religion, and Culture*. T & T Clark Ltd, London.

Nicholson, A.R. (1998) *A Literary History of the Arabs*. Kegan Paul International, London.

Nielsen, J.S. (2004) *Muslims in Western Europe*, 3rd edn. Edinburgh University Press, Edinburgh, UK.

Price, J. (2012) *The End of America: the Role of Islam in the End Times and Biblical Warnings to Flee America*. Christian House Publishers, Cambridge, Ohio.

Rehman, A. and Afsar, A. (2008) *Shariah: the Islamic Law*. Ta-Ha, London.

Rippin, A. (2005) *Muslims: Their Religious Beliefs and Practices*, 3rd edn. Routledge, London.

Robin, C. (2004) *Fear: the History of a Political Idea*. Oxford University Press, New York.

Robinson, N. (1999) *Islam: a Concise Introduction*. Routledge, London.

Rodgers, R. (2012) *The Generalship of Muhammad: Battles and Campaigns of the Prophet of Allah*. University Press of Florida, Miami, Florida.

Rogers, P. (2008) *Why We're Losing the War on Terror*. Polity Press, Cambridge.

Royal College of Nursing (2007) *Water for Health: Hydration Best Practice Toolkit for Hospitals and Healthcare*. Royal College of Nursing and National Patient Safety Agency, London. Available at: http://www2.rcn.org.uk/newsevents/campaigns/nutritionnow/tools_and_resources/hydration (accessed 19 May 2016).

Saeed, A. (2007) Media, racism and Islamophobia: the representation of Islam and Muslims in the media. *Sociology Compass* 1(2), 443–462.

Said, E. (1979) *Orientalism*. Vintage Books, New York.

Said, E. (1997) *Covering Islam: How the Media and the Experts Determine How We See the Rest of the World*. Vintage Books, London.

Schiffer, S. (2010) Demonising Islam before and after 9/11: Anti-Islamic spin. An important factor in pro-war PR? Institute of Media Responsibility, 14 September 2010. Available at: http://www.medienverantwortung.de/wp-content/uploads/2009/07/20100914_IMV-Schiffer_Media-Terror_antiislamic-spins_fin.pdf (accessed 31 October 2015).

Scruton, R. (2002) *The West and the Rest: Globalization and the Terrorist Threat*. Continuum, London.

Selbourne, D. (2005) *The Losing Battle with Islam*. Prometheus Books, New York.

Shafi, M. (1998) *Maariful Qur'an*. Maktaba Darul-Uloom Publishers, Karachi, Pakistan.

Snow, J. (2005) *Shooting History*. Harper Perennial, London.

Southern, R.W. (1962) *Western Views of Islam in the Middle Ages*. Harvard University Press, London.

Turner, C. (2006) *Islam: the Basics*. Routledge, London.

Waldron, K., Johnson, I.T. and Fenwick, G.R. (1993) *Food and Cancer Prevention: Chemical and Biological Aspects*. Woodhead Publishing Ltd, Cambridge.

Watt, W.M. (1961) *Muhammad: Prophet and Statesman*. Oxford University Press, Oxford.

Wolfe, M. (2004) Introduction. In: Wolfe, M. (ed.) *Taking Back Islam: American Muslims Reclaim Their Faith*. Rodale Inc. and Beliefnet Inc., Emmaus, Pennsylvania, pp. xi–xiv.

Yasin, A.I. (1996) *Islamicizing America*. J.C. Winston Publications, Philadelphia.

6 Islam – Spiritual Journey in Islam: The Qur'anic Cognitive Model

TARIQ ELHADARY*

Ministry of Presidential Affairs, Abu Dhabi, United Arab Emirates

Introduction

This chapter has been written with two objectives: first, to acquaint the reader with certain matters which they should grasp before embarking on an Islamic-related religious journey, or more specifically visiting Muslim religious historical places, if they wish to reach a more than superficial understanding of the Qur'an; and secondly, to illuminate the major tenets of faith referred to in the Qur'an. Thus, the chapter attempts to clarify the concept of pilgrimage in Islam and to address questions about Islam that commonly arise in the mind of the non-Muslim tourist. These notions are drawn out and explored by utilizing the *Qur'anic Cognitive Model* (QCM) and thus present the basic claims of the Qur'an, and thereby minimize the degree of deviation from mainstream Islam.

The chapter focuses on Islamic monotheism, on the essential comprehensive characteristics of Islamic doctrine and its primary bases. It also illustrates the relationship between God's omnipotence and monotheism. The theme of prophethood and the message of the Qur'an will be discussed in some detail and linked to an investigation of the human mission on earth – particularly exploring the search to achieve and maintain balance.

The Qur'anic Cognitive Model (QCM)

In this introductory section, the pillars (tenets of faith) of Islam are introduced and investigated. We have employed QCM as a descriptive tool that can be employed effectively for the analysis of problematic features in Qur'anic discourse,

*tariqelhadary@yahoo.com

and other controversial issues. The QCM is a 'frame' which can be used to explore knowledge structure or structured sets of elements drawn from Qur'anic conceptual domains and consists of encyclopaedic knowledge associated with the Qur'an's linguistic form (Dirven *et al.*, 2001a, b). Lack of an in-depth knowledge of the Qur'an hinders true understanding, since this holy text illuminates the Islamic profession of faith. Understanding the Qur'an necessitates detailed examination of its chapters and verses. The QCM provides an interpretation of the text which makes possible a deeper understanding of the pillars on which the message of the Qur'an is based. Abu al-A'la Maududi holds:

> Whether one ultimately decides to believe in the Qur'an or not, one must recognize the fundamental statements made by the Qur'an and by the man to whom it was revealed, the Prophet Muhammad, to be the starting point of one's study.
>
> (Maududi, 1988, p. 9)

A meaningful account of these claims – which are reinforced by the QCM – cannot be arrived at without looking deep into the literature of the QCM which reflects Muslim religious and social thought at its best. Moreover, QCM draws out the textual components that outline the Qur'anic knowledge system.

The cognitive concept presented here – QCM – is proposed to be understood in line with Lakoff's ICM (Idealized Cognitive Models). QCM helps the reader to explore the Qur'an to find religious directions for their life. From here arises the need to understand the QCM as a tool to expound the way the Qur'an is read and the way it is understood. Muslim readers of the Qur'an have always been referred to further readings which expand their understanding of the cultural domain within which this holy text was developed and further recapitulation of the Qur'an's aims and cultural background. The QCM constitutes a frame whereby transferable cultural material of Qur'anic discourse can be utilized to assist religious tourists in reaching unambiguous interpretation of the Qur'an.

Time and again it is emphasized for Muslims, that the Qur'an is the Holy Book of Islam. It embodies and symbolizes the true essence of their faith. For them, the Qur'an is the book of guidance and inspiration for the fashioning of their socio-economic and political life. Musa (2002) maintains that in the Islamic profession of faith, the Qur'an promotes the themes of religious unity, political unity and social unity; it is the religion of the mind and intellect, of instinct and clarity, of liberty and equality as well as of humanity. For all this, it can be said that Islam is a religion and a state of being, and it is this religion which proclaims the rights of humans. For Muslim scholars the Qur'an, with its 114 chapters, contains between its covers the complete message from God: 'This day, I have perfected your religion for you, completed My favour upon you, and have chosen for you Islam as your religion.' (Q5: 3).

Islam holds that only through the guidance of the Qur'an does the individual learn where she/he came from, where she/he is going, why the universe exists, and what her/his role is in the universe. This understanding can be deepened by use of methods of investigation such as the QCM. To the faithful Muslim there is a great difference between those who know and those who do not know: 'Is he who walks without seeing on his face, more rightly guided, or he who (sees and) walks on a straight way' (Q67: 22).

Irving *et al.* (2002) hold that the Qur'an was revealed to be realized and to show that the ideas and values that inspire humans to establish the Kingdom of God on earth are characterized in the basic teachings of the Qur'an. QCM promotes the realization of the optimal vision of God-fearing beings living in a just society fulfilling His mission here and seeking His rewards in the hereafter; this optimal vision can only come into effect through the ideal of humans living at peace with themselves and with the creation around them, and thus, by living at peace with the Creator. This concept is epitomized in the following verse which reiterates that the Qur'an is the source of divine guidance for mankind. This often repeated reference is to humankind in general and not just to Muslims, Arabs or any other ethnic group – it emphasizes the Qur'an's eternal and universal message.

> This Qur'an does indeed show the straightest way. It gives the faithful who do right the good news that they will have a great reward and warns that We have prepared an agonizing punishment for those who do not believe in the world to come.
>
> (Q17: 9–10)

An intrinsic element of a QCM interpretation of this text is that the Qur'an is the Word of God. The Qur'an articulates truth and the necessary attributes to live by. Irving *et al.* (2002) have elaborated the theme:

> The Book contains the Divine Word, uncreated, unaltered and intact. The Book reveals those aspects of Divine Reality whose knowledge is required to develop a correct relationship with God and His creation, even though the totality of the Divine Reality remains beyond human comprehension. As such the real intent of the Revelation is not the disclosure of God's Person, but of His Will.
>
> (Irving *et al.*, 2002, pp. 5–6)

The Qur'an itself reinforces this by stating: 'We have neglected nothing in the Book' (Q6: 38).

It must also be observed that the Qur'an, for Muslim scholars, contains the Divine constitution that is – according to analysis by the QCM – applicable anywhere at any time, as it is the Book of guidance for the whole of humanity. An interesting and important observation by Abu al-A'la Maududi (1976) which reinforces the importance of a QCM approach is that the Qur'an is not a literary work of the common conventional type that develops its central theme in a logical order; nor does it conform to the style of such work. The Qur'an adopts its own style to suit the guidance of the Islamic movement that was started by God's Messenger under His direct command (Maududi, 1976).

Abu al-A'la Maududi (1976) contends that all the chapters of the Qur'an contain reference to the basic creed: monotheism (the Unity of God, His attributes), the hereafter and accountability, punishment and reward, Prophethood, and belief in the Book. Abdul-Raof (2003) states that monotheism, prophethood, eschatology and reward and punishment are the 'four Qur'anic notions', they are also the 'roots of Islam', and thus, the 'tenets of faith' at the same time.

Islamic Monotheism

While monotheism is the essential comprehensive characteristic of Islamic doctrine and its primary basis, it is also one of its components. Monotheism is the
foundation of all the 'revealed' religions given to the prophets by God. However, it
is unique to Islam when viewed in the context of the Qur'an. Abdul-Raof (2003)
defines monotheism in light of the Qur'anic verses that refer to monotheism (Q7:
59, Q16: 36, Q17: 23, Q21: 25, Q47: 19 and Q51: 56) as:

> the relationship with the only One (i.e. God) that excludes a similar relationship with
> anyone else. It is [hu]man's genuine commitment to God, the focus of all his
> reverence and gratitude, the only source of value.
>
> (Abdul-Raof, 2003, p. 238)

The Qur'an affirms that there is one God to whom alone divinity can be attributed
and no one has the right to be worshipped but God. No one has the right to rule
but God – no legislator, no organizer of human life or of human relationships in
the world – no living things or human beings, but God. From Him alone is received
all guidance and legislation, all systems of life, norms governing relationships and
the measure of values. That is why Islamic monotheism symbolized by *la ilaha illa
Allah* (none has the right to be worshipped but God) constitutes a core notion of
QCM: 'This is God, your Lord, there is no God but Him, the Creator of all things, so
worship Him; He is in charge of everything' (Q6: 102).

Faith in a single God is deeply rooted in the theological literature of the Qur'an,
which is centred round this fact. More importantly, God is the source of everything seen and unseen, known and unknown, and the source of all knowledge.
In fact, it was essential for Islam to explicitly promote monotheism in a society of
idolaters and pagans where the idea of one God was not favoured. Therefore, it is
logical that the Meccan chapters concentrate on the theme of monotheism as a
means of uprooting the idea of associating with multiple Gods, from the minds
and hearts of the believers. Abdul-Raof (2003) is of the belief that the priority
was for the faith over any other economic or sociopolitical issues. The stress then
was on establishing a strong foundation based on the oneness of God.

The belief in *la ilaha illa Allah* (none has the right to be worshipped but God) is
the keystone of the Qur'an. That is why it is common to find great emphasis on the
theme of monotheism in the Qur'an and Hadith (Prophetic traditions). Within
QCM, the belief in *la ilaha illa Allah* is not just muttering throw-away words but it
needs tremendous and strenuous work to be implemented in the minds and the
hearts of believers. Consequently, followers have to execute all their actions, deeds
and behaviours accordingly.

It goes without saying that QCM elaborates the meaning of worshipping
One God and attributes Divinity, Creatorship and Omnipotence to God. By worshipping One God, people derive their conceptions, values and standards, institutions, legislature and laws, orientation ethics and morals from Him alone. In the
Islamic profession of faith *la ilaha illa Allah, Muhammad rasul-Allah* (none has the
right to be worshipped but God, and Muhammad is the Messenger of God) can be
expounded as follows: the first part defines the unconditional surrender to One
God who is one at all times. The second half reflects Muhammad, 'the Seal of the

Prophets', being chosen for the last message to mankind: 'Luqman counselled his son, "My son, do not attribute any partners to God: attributing partners to Him is a terrible wrong"' (Q31: 13).

The first pillar of Islam is that we bear witness that there is no god other than God and that Muhammad is the Prophet of God. The approximate meaning of bearing such witness is that God is the exclusive possessor of divinity, and none of His creation shares in any of the aspects or properties of divinity. The first aspect of divinity is an absolute rule, whence arises the right to legislate for His worshippers, to ordain paths for their lives, to prescribe values on which their lives should be based. It is not possible that there is no god other than God without recognizing that God alone has the right to ordain the path which human life should follow. Bearing witness that Muhammad is the Prophet of God means approximately admitting that this path has been conveyed to people from God; that it is truly God's path for the life of mankind; and that it is the only path humans are obliged to follow and implement in life.

Islam pays special attention to the intellect. When it calls for the worship of One Single God the Qur'an provides the QCM reader with the necessary proofs:

> Who spread out the earth for you, and built the sky; who sent down water from it and with that water produced things for your sustenance. Do not, knowing this, set up rivals to God.
>
> (Q2: 22)

> It is God who splits open the seed and the fruit stone: He brings out the living from the dead and the dead from the living – that is God – so how can you turn away from the truth?
>
> (Q6: 95)

> He makes the dawn break; He makes the night for rest; and He made the sun and the moon to a precise measure. That is the design of the Almighty, the All Knowing.
>
> (Q6: 96)

> It is He who first produced you from a single soul, then gave you a place to stay (in life) and a resting place (after death). We made our revelations clear to those who understand.
>
> (Q6: 98)

The Qur'an provides full evidence for the existence of God, the Creator. The Qur'an as the last message from God, for Muslim scholars, should demonstrate all possible means to promote the theme of One Single God. The Qur'an emphasizes God's lordship and ultimate power in all of His creation when it addresses the intellect and the intellectual faculties of humans.

Thus, QCM instils into the minds and the hearts of Muslims the fact that believing in monotheism truly means observing and consequently implementing the 'straightway' predestined by God. Therefore, the spiritual capabilities of Muslims are elevated as a result of the fear of God and the establishment of relations consequently between the rulers and the ruled and between different categories of Islamic society on the basis of a communal support for the benefit of justice and virtue. The QCM addresses human nature – implemented in the person – which by instinct, worships one true God. Consequently it identifies itself with the true God and holds Islamic monotheism as a cornerstone of its message and all consequences thereof:

> Say, 'Shall I take for myself a protector other than God, the Creator of the heavens
> and the earth, who feeds but is not fed?' Say, 'I am commanded to be the first of (you)
> to devote myself to (Him).' Do not be one of the polytheists.
>
> (Q6: 14)

The notion of the unity of God in Islam is repeatedly emphasized in the Qur'an.
This builds enthusiasm in the hearts and minds of believers, to lovingly adhere
to the message of God throughout all circumstances. A celebrated description of
the thorough and dramatic change in behaviour once a Muslim declares their
submission to God is found where Arnold (1935) discusses the spread of the faith
as follows:

> [Islam] was a revolt against empty theological polemics; it was a masculine protest
> against the exaltation of celibacy as a crown of piety. It brought out the fundamental
> dogmas of religion – the unity and greatness of God, that He is merciful and
> righteous, that He claims obedience to His will, resignation and faith. It proclaimed
> the responsibility of man, a future life, a day of judgment, and stern retribution to
> fall upon the wicked; and enforced the duties of prayer, almsgiving, fasting and
> benevolence. It thrust aside the artificial virtues, the religious frauds and follies, the
> perverted moral sentiments, and the verbal subtleties of theological disputes. It
> replaced monkishness by manliness ... and recognition to the fundamental facts of
> human nature.
>
> (Canon Taylor cited in Arnold, 1935, p. 62)

The theme of unity of God in the Qur'anic message also advocates that all scriptures were sent down from God to mankind on earth. It also calls for belief in all the
prophets of God because they represent the very same message, the complete whole
as embodied in the Qur'an. Let us consider the following Qur'anic verse:

> In matters of faith, He has laid down for you (people) the same commandment that
> He gave Noah, which We have revealed to you (Muhammad) and which We
> enjoined on Abraham and Moses and Jesus: 'Uphold the faith and do not divide into
> factions within it' – what you (Prophet) call upon the idolaters to do is hard for
> them; God chooses whoever He pleases for Himself and guides towards Himself those
> who turn to Him.
>
> (Q42: 13)

God's Omnipotence and Monotheism

The Qur'an links two major concepts – God's omnipotence and monotheism.
In other words, the Qur'an, in order to drive the message of monotheism to the
reader, offers details about the power of God which is referred to as God's omnipotence – this entails reference to rain, mountains, the sun, the moon, the womb,
the creation of humans, etc. In the same vein, Abdul-Raof (2005) emphasizes
that monotheism is echoed by God's omnipotence and that He alone has provided everything for our interests and needs. It is understood in Islam, that as
long as a person submits in worship to God the only one God, their submission
needs to be activated in terms of obedience to whatever God or His Prophets have
commanded.

Examining the *Shahadah* – the Muslim profession of faith – via QCM, leads the argument to the importance of monotheism in Islam, which is represented in the Islamic concept of God, that can be highlighted in the following Qur'anic verses, and which show God's omnipotence as a link to monotheism:

> The Creator of the heavens and the earth. He made mates for you among yourselves – and for the animals too – so that you may multiply. There is nothing like Him: He is the All hearing, the All Seeing.
>
> (Q42: 11)

The Qur'an provides evidence which affirms the oneness of God. In this regard, QCM assists in understanding the Qur'anic proposal that rational proofs are needed to urge people to believe in the one God. In this way the Qur'an respects the intellectual faculties God has bestowed on people and reminds the faithful of God's presence:

> It is He who sends down water for you from the sky. Some of it you drink, and the shrubs that you feed to your animals come from it.
>
> (Q16: 10)

> With it He grows for you corn [maize], olives, palms, vines, and all kinds of fruit. There truly is a sign in this for those who reflect.
>
> (Q16: 11)

In this regard, the spiritual capabilities of humans are elevated as a result of the respect for God, and the development of relations between the rulers and the ruled and between different categories of Islamic society on the basis of a communal support for the benefit of justice and virtue. Thus, a person is elevated to the position of a conscious member of society with a will of their own, choosing their own job as well as freely selecting the place they would like to work. They enjoy freedom to comply with the orders of the ruler, or refuse to obey him, if the ruler should happen to transgress the bounds set by God's obedience and Islam. In QCM, every individual is understood to be a guardian of the community's morals, besides holding them responsible for the eradication of all forms of evils.

It is crucial to remember that humans are the only ones among all creatures who have been given the power of choice, whereas the rest were left with no choice. This is understood to be a call for humans to use their mind to know their God. The Qur'an claims that the signs that point to the direction of God's unity and activity in the universe are multifarious and countless:

> Say (Prophet), 'Who owns the earth and all who live in it, if you know (so much)?' and they will reply, 'God.' Say, 'Will you not take heed?' Say, 'Who is the Lord of the seven heavens? Who is the Lord of the Mighty Throne?' and they will reply, 'God.' Say, 'Will you be mindful?' Say, 'Who holds control of everything in His hand? Who protects, while there is no protection against Him, if you know (so much)?' and they will reply, 'God.' Say, 'Then how can you be so deluded?'
>
> (Q23: 84–89)

Irving *et al.* (2002) emphasize that mankind does not stand alone in the firmament of Creation. In this perspective, human existence is not a fortuitous accident of history and therefore the world around us is not unrelated to us and our purpose in life. According to Irving *et al.* (2002) everything is part of the Divine

Plan – the overall scheme of Providence. In this line of reasoning, He who has created mankind has also provided for all that people need for the good life: whether that be in the nature of physical providence ensuring existence and growth, or of moral and social guidance for the full flowering of the human personality and culture (Irving *et al.*, 2002). The following verses embody the unity of creation and its impact on humans as explored via QCM:

> There truly are signs in the creation of the heavens and the earth, and in the alternation of night and day, for those with understanding, who remember God standing, sitting, and lying down, who reflect on the creation of the heavens and earth: 'our Lord! You have not created (all) this without purpose, glory to You! Give us salvation from the torment of fire.'

> (Q3: 190–191)

As a revelation to the Prophet Muhammad and to believers, the Qur'an was determined in emphasizing God's lordship and ultimate power in all of creation. The Qur'an speaks of God's sustenance and provision for creation, particularly for human beings and of recreating of new forms of creations – which brings an ecological dimension to the QCM:

> Say (Prophet), 'Praise be to God and peace on the servants He has chosen. Who is better: God, or those they set up as partners with Him?
> Who created the heavens and earth? Who sends down water from the sky for you – with which We cause gardens of delight to grow: you have no power to make the trees grow in them – is it another god beside God? No! But they are people who take others to be equal with God.
> Who is it that made earth a stable place to live? Who made rivers flow through it? Who set immovable mountains on it and created a barrier between the fresh and the salt water? Is it another god beside God? No! But most of them do not know.
> Who is it that answers the distressed when they call upon him? Who removes their suffering? Who makes you successors in the earth? Is it another god beside God? Little notice you take!
> Who sends the wind as heralds of good news before His mercy? Is it another god beside God? God is far above the partners they put beside Him!
> Who is it that creates life and reproduces it? Who is it that gives you provision from the heavens and earth? Is it another god beside God?' Say, Show me your evidence then, if what you say is true.

> (Q27: 59–64)

The reminders of God's signs are then meant to indicate that everything is dependent on God; that God, with all His might and glory, is essentially the Lord of Mercy and the Giver of Mercy; this in turn establishes a relationship between human beings and God, where humans are made to love Him through surrendering their entire self to Him. The QCM reveals an important idea of God's centrality in all the themes of the Qur'an. Time and again the Qur'an reiterates that man carries the ethos of Islam in himself. For the sake of teaching and education God has grandly and repeatedly emphasized the faith of monotheism in order to establish belief in the recesses of the hearts and minds of the believers. To make the faith of monotheism more comprehensible in the QCM, God has given examples, set parables and told stories of past generations to highlight truth and falsehood (i.e. belief and disbelief).

At this juncture, Musa (2002) signals that a belief in the oneness of God also leaves a great imprint on the hearts and souls of people, and consequently upon their deeds. According to Musa, if man is faithful to God alone, and if he fears and pleads to none but Him, soliciting Him alone to bestow upon him whatever is good and to save him from ills – if man does that, he is consequently rendered strong in himself, becomes capable of upholding truth and would in all that which concerns him, depend on God alone (Musa, 2002).

> Who is it that answers the distressed when they call upon him? Who removes their suffering? Who makes you successors in the earth? Is it another god beside God? Little notice you take!
>
> (Q27: 62)

Prophethood and the Universal Message of the Qur'an

Muslim scholars claim that the Qur'an is the final Scripture to be sent down to earth and the Prophet Muhammad is the 'Seal of all the Prophets'. The Qur'an repeatedly attempts to communicate this to all mankind, and this is precisely what makes the Qur'anic message universal – as clarified utilizing the QCM. The universality of Islam is envisaged as inevitable because Islam is the last of all divine messages sent from heaven to earth, and as such, it has to be a universal religion for all people (Musa, 2002). For Muslim scholars, the nature of this message must be of a kind that makes it fit for humanity in every age, generation and time. The personality, character and nature of the Prophet must, according to the QCM, be of the ideal type befitting his being the elect Messenger for all God's slaves so that every person can in him find his/her ideal and the light which will guide him/her throughout his/her life:

> Who follow the Messenger – the unlettered prophet they find described in the Torah that is with them, and in the Gospel – who commands them to do right and forbids them to do wrong, who makes good things lawful to them and bad things unlawful, and relieves them of their burdens, and the iron collars that were with them. So it is those who believe him, honour and help him, and who follow the light which has been sent down with him, who will succeed.
>
> (Q7: 157)

Qamar Ul-Huda holds that the noble message of the Qur'an is meant to guide followers to God's will so that they may implement the provided guidance in their lives (Ul-Huda, 2003). The Qur'an is revelation for humankind and is aimed at redirecting human beings toward God. Consider Q2: 185 when it defines the mission of the Qur'an regarding people's lives:

> The month of Ramadan in which was revealed the Qur'an, a guidance for mankind and clear proofs for the guidance and the criterion (between right and wrong).
>
> (Q2: 185)

Ul-Huda adds that 'this often repeated reference to humankind and not to Muslims, Arabs, Chinese or the Quraishi tribe' underscores the Qur'an's eternal and universal message (Ul-Huda, 2003). Furthermore:

[And] We have not sent you (O Muhammad) except as a giver of glad tidings and a
warner to all mankind, but most of men know not.

(Q34: 28)

Say (Muhammad), 'People, I am the Messenger of God to you all, from Him who has
control over the heavens and the earth. There is no God but Him; He gives life and
death, so believe in God and His messenger, the unlettered prophet who believes in
God and His words, and follow him so that you may find guidance.'

(Q7: 158)

We should not go without emphasizing the human nature of the Prophet. Ul-Huda
(2003) stresses this point and is of the view that 'the Prophet in Islam is purely a
human being that was divinely selected to serve as a messenger of Allah's message to humanity' (Ul-Huda, 2003). The Qur'an also places an emphasis on the
human element in the Prophet:

Say (Prophet), 'I am only a mortal like you, (but) it has been revealed to me that your
God is one.'

(Q41: 6)

Irving *et al.* (2002) hold that the Qur'an spells out the Message which was revealed to Muhammad and that it therefore represents the permanent and ultimate
source of guidance for mankind. Arnold reiterates that the message of Islam was
not exclusively for Arabia; the whole world was to share in it. As there was but one
God, so there was to be but one religion into which all humans are to be invited. The
claim to be universal, to hold sway over all men and all nations, found a practical illus-
tration in the letters which Muhammad is said to have sent in the year AD 628 (AH 6) to
the great sovereigns and monarchs of that time. Invitations to embrace Islam was
sent that same year to the Emperor Heraclius, the king of Persia, the governor of
Yemen, the governor of Egypt and the king of Abyssinia (Arnold, 1935).

This shows that the Prophet wasted no time in launching a campaign to
convey his message to the whole world and that is why he sent delegations to
kings and governors of the neighbouring countries to deliver to them the Word
of God as revealed in the Qur'an. It should be noted that the Prophet did not start
his mission before he witnessed the emergence of the Islamic State and the ap-
plicability of Islamic teachings. Abu al-A'la Maududi states that the only right
method to start an international movement is in the country of the movement's
origin. Further, according to Mududi, exponents should impress the mind-set of
their own people who have a common language, common habits and common
customs. In other words, they should first of all put these principles into practice
in their own country and prove their worth by evolving a happy and successful
system of life before moving on (Maududi, 1976). This is the strategic plan which
the Prophet and his companions implemented successfully as they attempted to
establish the universality of the message of the Qur'an.

The Role of Individuals in Achieving Balance

The meaning of *Islam* underlies the ethos of the message of the Qur'an: complete submission to God, and in this particular context, complete submission to

the Word of God – the Qur'an. When the Qur'anic approach of *do* and *not do* is realized in Muslims themselves, only then do Muslims achieve harmony with the unity of God, and become capable of implementing the ethos of Islam. In the QCM the clearly evident guidance and light from God is indispensable for mankind, to achieve and then to maintain balance.

A significant theme related to this, which has not so far been investigated, is how Chapter 1 (Q1) of the Qur'an symbolizes the mission of people on earth. al-Zarkashi (1988) states that Q1 is the mother of the Book because it entails the three main pillars of the Qur'an: (i) monotheism; (ii) reminder; and (iii) rulings. He further elaborates that monotheism is present from the beginning of Q1 until Q1: 4 ('the day of Resurrection') 'It is You we worship; it is You we ask for help'. In this sense Q1 symbolizes the mission of humans when it outlines their duties and sets them up for testing.

> In the name of God, the Lord of Mercy, the Giver of Mercy! Praise belongs to God, Lord of the Worlds, the Lord of Mercy, the Giver of mercy, Master of Judgement. It is You we worship; it is You we ask for help. Guide us to the straight path: the path of those You have blessed, those who incur no anger and who have not gone astray.
>
> (Q1: 1–7)

Abdel Haleem (1999) holds this impact passage, an independent chapter of the Qur'an consisting of seven verses divided into three groups (invocation, affirmation and petition) in a sequential progression that exemplifies the conclusively convincing logic of Qur'anic material. According to Abdel Haleem, the passage embodies the essence of Islam, which is monotheism. In the QCM then, if a follower considers Q1 thoughtfully and through meditation, they will realize the meaning of the Oneness, Supremacy, Sustenance, Beneficence and Sovereignty. Taken together, people should strive to become more in harmony with the Creator and His creation; consequently for the individual, she/he must act in this life accordingly. People cannot do without guidance from God, for God is the All-Knowing, the All-Mighty, the All-Wise, the All-Sufficient, and the owner of Great Bounty. As presented in Q1: 'It is You we worship; it is You we ask for help. Guide us to the straight path'.

The mission of mankind on earth is well presented in the previous verses, namely, worshipping God, populating the earth and following the straight way. Endeavouring to accomplish all the aforementioned assignments requires guidance and support from God. Abu al-A'la Maududi (1988) proposes that God bestowed upon people, a kind of autonomy and appointed them as His vicegerent on earth. In this way it was made clear to people that life in this world, for which they have been placed and invested with a certain honour and authority, is in fact a temporary term, and is meant to test them. After the end of this earthly life man and woman must return to God, who will judge them on the basis of their performance, declaring who has succeeded and who has failed (Maududi, 1988). Hence, it can be argued that Islamic ideology looks upon humans as a being that aspires to soar high in the realms of spirit and thought, although they walk on earth and possess a physical body. Humans' needs are not limited to food, shelter and sexual gratification; Islam attaches great significance to the individual, and relies more on them than on society for the realization of its ends. QCM investigation illustrates that Islam civilizes man/woman from within, so that they would willingly discharge all their responsibilities as members of a community. Moreover, they carry the responsibility of guiding others, as is clear from the mission of the Prophet who is a model for the individual character:

> Just as We have sent among you a messenger of your own to recite Our revelations to you, purify you and teach you the Scripture, wisdom, and (other) things you did not know.
>
> (Q2: 151)

In this regard, it is worthwhile classifying Q1 (using QCM) as a code for unity. Rephrased, Q1 proves the unity of God, the unity of the message and the unity of mankind. In fact these three types of unity harmonize with *Shahadah* – the profession of a Muslim: *la ilaha illa Allah, Muhammad rasul-Allah* (none has the right to be worshipped but God, and Muhammad is the Messenger of God). Verse Q42: 13 emphasizes the unity of the message, Q16: 22 the unity of God, and Q6: 98 the unity of mankind:

> In matters of faith, He has laid down for you (people) the same commandment that He gave Noah, which We have revealed to you (Muhammad) and which We enjoined on Abraham and Moses and Jesus.
>
> (Q42: 13)

> Your God is the One God.
>
> (Q16: 22)

> It is He who first produced you from a single soul, then gave you a place to stay (in life) and a resting place (after death).
>
> (Q6: 98)

Divine Guidance should be the greatest moral and social need of mankind. According to Irving *et al.*, who state that if man needs air and water for his physical existence and growth, he needs Divine Guidance for his moral and social existence and development. This explains why the central quest of mankind is not just physical survival or economic advancement, but for guidance. This becomes evident in the QCM through invocation in Q1, which a Muslim recites in every prayer. It is crucial to understanding the spirit of Islam (Irving *et al.*, 2002).

Ibrahim Stokes writes that a person contains within him or herself something of their Creator (Stokes writing in the Foreword to Haeri, 1985). Man/woman was born to worship their Creator, in order to return from this outward-bound journey of separation to a state of conscious awareness. In Stokes' words, the gate to worship is through submission to the unseen and the reward for complete abandonment is perfect freedom (Haeri, 1985). In such a perspective, all knowledge that moves a person to unity with the Creator is useful, and that which separates people from this goal is to be avoided as it is considered evil and off the well-defined path. There is no way in which man/woman can find this royal road by their own efforts, no matter how hard they try. The 'way' is in the message of those guides who were sent in times past and who have left a record and an example for us to follow. QCM articulates that mankind has been cherished and honoured by the Creator to the extent that they are even preferred over the heavenly angels.

> We have honoured the children of Adam and carried them by land and sea. We have provided good sustenance for them and favoured them specially above many of those we have created.
>
> (Q17: 70)

The reason for this preference is due to the child of Adam accepting all the duties which God has ordained upon him/her. A crucial element here is that humans are the only ones among all creatures who have been given the power of choice, whereas the rest were left with no choice. Haeri (1985) stresses when a person's inner memory becomes a looking glass, the follower of monotheism, the lover of God will receive all the surrounding manifestations as emanating from God. The Qur'an becomes the key which can unlock divinity within a person's heart by its most glorious discriminating and divine light (Haeri, 1985). It must be stressed that the Qur'an (as epitomized in its essence, drawn out via QCM) stands for wisdom beyond the creation and life cycle of mankind – it is the beginning and the end of our journey on earth: 'I created jinn and mankind only to worship Me' (Q51: 56).

Therefore *worship* is the purpose of existence and the key to excellence through abandonment and submission to the Creator God. The notion of QCM revolves around: لا إله إلا الله محمد رسول الله *la ilaha illa Allah, Muhammad rasul-Allah* (None has the right to be worshipped but God, and Muhammad is the Messenger of God).

Abu al-A'la Maududi (1988) holds that the Qur'an is a book of broad general principles rather than of legal minutiae. It can be understood as a method of guidance for practical Islamic life. It does not consist of laying down minutely detailed laws and regulations. According to Maududi, it prefers to outline the basic framework for each aspect of human activity, and lays down certain guidelines within which a person can order their life in keeping with the Will of God (Maududi, 1988). The QCM can be utilized to fully appreciate this, and to realize that humans have a degree of freedom and opportunity of manoeuvring, to do what they have to do with an air of freedom. Yet, for a good Muslim following the straight way, this will exist within the frame of general guidelines articulated in the Qur'an.

Conclusion

To summarize, in a spiritual interpretation people metaphorically walk on earth and God is their destination. The Qur'an shows man/woman the way, and worship is the means to get there. As understood in the QCM, God is both the starting point and the destination of the spiritual journey of a Muslim. As narrated by Anas:

> I heard the Messenger of Allah say: Allah the Almighty has said: O Son of Adam, as long as you invoke Me and ask of me, I shall forgive you for what you have done, and I shall not mind. O Son of Adam, were your sins to reach the clouds of the sky and you then asked forgiveness from Me, I would forgive you. O Son of Adam, were you to come to Me with sins nearly as great as the Earth, and were you then to face Me, ascribing no partner to Me, I would bring you forgiveness nearly as great as it [too].
>
> (Hadith no. 34: Ibrahim and Johnson-Davis, 1997)

In this chapter the need is presented for QCM to be established as a basic background for exploring and understanding the Qur'an. In most studies of Muslim travel or pilgrimage, a lack of interpretation can be observed, and furthermore, results are not authenticated by Muslim scholars. That absence of rigour can be tackled via the QCM, which represents the Islamic religion as believed and performed by mainstream Muslims. The chapter draws our attention to the need for QCM to present the basic claims of the Qur'an and to minimize the degree of deviation from mainstream Islam. It is then essential that the basic beliefs and principles on which QCM is based should be taken into account when studying religiously motivated tourists and pilgrims. Focusing on the basic Islamic concepts which QCM presents, as exemplified in this chapter, religious tourists can reach a profoundly solid understanding of Qur'anic discourse. More importantly, the QCM aids us to understand the cultural moral of Islam and can help to spread peace and to instil tranquillity into the hearts and minds of religious tourists visiting Muslim holy cities.

References

Abdel Haleem, M.A.S. (1999) *Understanding the Qur'an: Themes and Style*. I.B. Tauris, London.
Abdul-Raof, H. (2003) *Exploring the Qur'an*. al-Maktoum Institute Academic Press, Dundee, UK.
Abdul-Raof, H. (2005) *Consonance in the Qur'an: a Conceptual, Intertextual and Linguistic Analysis*. Lincom Europa, Munich, Germany.
al-Zarkashi, B.D. (1988) *Al-Burhan fi Ulum al-Qur'an*. Four volumes. Dar al-Kutub al-Ilmiyyah, Beirut.
Arnold, T.W. (1935) *The Preaching of Islam: a History of the Propagation of the Muslim Faith*. Luzac, London.
Dirven R., Hawkins, B. and Sandikcioglu, E. (eds) (2001a) *Language and Ideology*, vol. 1: *Theoretical Cognitive Approach*. John Benjamins, Amsterdam.
Dirven R., Frank, R. and Ilie, C. (eds) (2001b) *Language and Ideology*, vol. 2: *Descriptive Cognitive Approaches*. John Benjamins, Amsterdam.
Haeri, S.F. (1985) *Journey of the Universe as Expounded in the Qur'an*. KPI, London.
Ibrahim, E. and Johnson-Davis, D. (1997) *Forty Hadith Qudsi*. The Islamic Texts Society, Cambridge.
Irving T.B., Ahmad, K. and Ahsan M.M. (eds) (2002) *The Qur'an: Basic Teachings*. The Islamic Foundation, Leicester, UK.
Maududi, A.-A. (1976) *The Meaning of the Qur'an*, vol.1. Islamic Publication, Lahore, Pakistan.
Maududi, A.-A. (1988) *Towards Understanding the Qur'an*, vol.1. English version of *Tafhim al-Qur'an* edited by Zafar Ishaq Ansari. The Islamic Foundation, Leicester, UK.
Musa, M.Y. (2002) *Islam and Humanity's Need of it*. Commercial Press, Cairo.
Ul-Huda, Q. (2003) Knowledge of Allah and the Islamic view of other religions. *Theological Studies* 64, 278–305.

Part II Managing Pilgrimage Sites in Holy Cities

Pilgrimage Policy Management: Between Shrine Strategy and Ritual Improvisation

SIMON COLEMAN*

University of Toronto, Toronto, Canada

Introduction: Managing Space

In the introduction to his book *Coping with Tourists* (1996, p. 8), the anthropologist Jeremy Boissevain tells a story about some Maltese friends of his who were celebrating the annual *festa* or 'celebration' of St Leonard on the island, and who made a rather surprising discovery in their house during the event. Two tourists who had come on a commercial *festa* trip had actually opened the glass inner door to Boissevain's friends' home and had started to look around, eventually walking into the front room, where they encountered the surprised residents. Boissevain reports that his friends politely ushered their unwanted guests out into the street, before doing something they had never done before: they went to the wooden outer door of their house – which would normally be left open during the event in order 'to display festive furnishings and decorations to passers-by' (Boissevain, 1996, p. 8) – and then they closed it, effectively shutting off the outside world from their personal space.

What are we to make of such an incident of tourists straying off the beaten track into territory that should have been off-limits to them? Boissevain remarks that 'such blatant infringements of privacy in Malta are increasing' (1996, p. 8), and indeed on other occasions they may provoke more violent reactions in Malta as tourists, encouraged by government brochures to explore the countryside, are menaced by local hunters who feel that their domain is being threatened (Boissevain, 1996, p. 20). He attributes these changes and worries over infringement of local areas to the development and marketing of mass cultural tourism in Europe (see also Griffin, 2007). Boissevain may well be right, and the transformations he describes seem to have accelerated further in the two decades since

*simon.coleman@utoronto.ca

he edited his book. But perhaps there is still more to be made of the story that he tells; and in reflecting on these further dimensions I hope to introduce the themes I cover in this chapter on the management of religious tourism, and especially pilgrimage, in urban contexts of Europe. I think the following kinds of questions are prompted by Boissevain's example:

- Where do the boundaries of a 'site' – of a shrine, a *festa* or a cultural event – end, and are they marked in ways that can easily be read and understood by visitors as well as locals?
- Might such signals as an open door be perceived as not just a display but also an invitation, and if so to whom?
- Who actually 'manages' a site? Is it only those people officially designated and paid to do so, or are numerous other informal and possibly unseen processes of management likely to occur?

These questions are made more complex by the ways in which places of touristic significance, whether religious or not, are frequently located adjacent to contexts that have very different functions, especially in urban situations. Furthermore, shrines in major cities, for instance the Vatican, are especially likely to be visited by people who come for cultural rather than explicitly religious reasons (Nolan and Nolan, 1992, p. 72). Various forms of administration, surveillance, display and so on, are inevitably juxtaposed, so that what the sociologist Erving Goffman (1959) would have called different 'dramaturgical models' or performances might be operating and even overlapping simultaneously, as individuals and groups enact various roles within culturally heterogeneous but physically proximate publics. In other words, diverse groups with different social and cultural expectations are forced to occupy the same space, with sometimes unexpected consequences. This kind of situation is both an opportunity and a problem for administrators as well as local residents generally.

The story of a door that is closed indicates what is presumably an unwelcome development in the interactions between domestic ritual and mass tourism, involving a literal firming of boundaries, a transformation of cultural display in the public or civic realm into a cultural protectionism that develops new practices of privacy in response to unwelcome intruders. But it may also reveal two other latent dimensions of such interaction that suggest the possibility of more optimistic outcomes:

- One is the prompting not of alienation and annoyance, but of new forms of *reflexivity* in relation to tourism management among local inhabitants who are likely to serve a double role as 'the people who both service tourists' needs and are the object of their attention' (Boissevain, 1996, p. 1; compare with Abram, 1996). By reflexivity I mean the ways in which hosts become aware of the assumptions they make about others, and also how such others are likely to perceive them. This awareness may clearly be defensive in character and intention but it also has the potential to indicate a more positive sense of what can, and cannot, be presented without offence or likely disruption.
- Another dimension is associated with visitors themselves: what if we view their actions as revealing not so much ignorance and insensitivity (or not only these), but also initiative – at least a willingness to experiment?

And so, if we accept the possibility of these two dimensions being in play in any given encounter, how might we combine the growing reflexivity of hosts with the adventurous explorations of visitors in ways that might be satisfactory to both parties? This question leads me to my next section.

Loosening Up

At the heart of my discussion on the management of religious sites is an interest in ways in which such sites can be opened up, rather than closed down, as contexts for the reception of tourists. By 'opening up' I mean not only that religious sites can be made available, but also that management itself involves positive, and not merely annoyed, recognition that the boundaries of a site and the behaviours of tourists can be more flexible and indeed unpredictable than first appears likely or even desirable. I argue that such openness, under the right circumstances, can add to the long-term sustainability of a site in relation to its urban context.

The metaphor of openness has parallels with the recent work of urban geographers Karen Franck and Quentin Stevens (2007), who have recently discussed the varieties of what in their volume's title they call 'loose space' in the manifestation of 'possibility and diversity in urban life'. Noting that cities are obviously composed of a large variety of spaces, they contrast more constraining contexts for action such as office towers or shops, where choices of appropriate or possible behaviour are relatively restricted and levels of surveillance are high, to those contexts, often outdoors, where expectations and systems of control are more fluid. So what are the consequences of thinking about space in this way, especially in relation to management of movement and activity? Drawing on Franck and Stevens, three points can initially be made:

- Loose space ideally provides 'the breathing space of city life, offering opportunities for exploration and discovery, for the unexpected, the unregulated, the spontaneous and the risky' (Franck and Stevens, 2007, p. 3). This is an argument that can be made about both locals and visitors.
- Many of the activities that loose space generates are not associated with production or reproduction as such, but are instead often temporary and 'a matter of leisure, entertainment, self-expression or political expression, reflection and social interaction – all outside the daily routine and world of fixed functions and fixed schedules' (Franck and Stevens, 2007, p. 3).
- Cities are especially good at providing loose space because they grant free access to many public open areas, while drawing on the possibilities inherent in the presence of anonymity among strangers.

Franck and Stevens are interested in the tensions between public and private uses of space in urban contexts, but also in how areas of a city may be used in ways that were not originally planned or expected. The loose use of a context designed for other purposes can have deeply political and unsettling implications – as when a riot erupts in a parliament building, or a protest is staged in a shopping mall – as well as reflecting contrasts between different understandings of how space might relate to local and transnational economic imperatives, including global tourism. Thus it is not surprising that administrative authorities sometimes become nervous. None the less, 'tightness' of design ensures order but looseness provides vitality – sometimes illicit, often liminal.

These themes relating to the juxtaposition of different frames of action, the relationships between 'loose' and 'tight' space, and the connections or frictions between the local and the transnational, will be relevant to later sections as I examine sites of religious tourism. They are also anticipated by the story with which I began this chapter, as we saw how visitors to a local *festa* in Malta assumed that they could simply continue their browsing activities, appropriate for the relatively loose, public space of a *festa* in a town square, inside a private home. In the following, I begin by briefly considering what might be particular to religious sites as places to visit and relate this issue to questions of legitimacy and authority, before reflecting on Europe as a changing and heterogeneous context for religious tourism. I then move to cases drawn from my own research on pilgrimage shrines and cathedrals in the UK. For the purpose of this chapter, I am particularly interested in seeing such places as contexts where debates over the management of 'openness' and 'looseness' can be discerned and enacted.

There is a further dimension to my argument. While it is often assumed – at least by many scholars of religion – that the area of primary interest and focus in a shrine is at its religious and liturgical centre, where the core of visitors/pilgrims tends to be concentrated and also where they act in relatively more predictable ways, I think we also gain much by seeking to relocate – or at least to recognize – key points of engagement away from apparent liturgical and aesthetic 'hot spots'. One implication of such an approach is to blur the boundaries between sacred and secular, but also between shrine and wider environment.

Religious Hosting

In what ways might religious sites such as shrines be different from other, more obviously secular attractions in terms of the management of visitors? We should be wary of drawing sharp distinctions as we need to bear in mind that religious tourism is often embedded within other forms of travel (Stausberg, 2011, p. 13). In addition, motivations for travel may change during a journey, or shift according to time and specific location, even within the same site. Some shrines may even see it as their duty to try – however subtly – to convert tourists into pilgrims. Overall, religion retains a particular legitimacy, even at times of secularization. It is true that tourists often assume that they possess considerable social and cultural, as well as monetary, influence as they travel around Europe, especially when richer Northern Europeans visit other parts of the continent. None the less, religious shrines often possess an authority that trumps conventional, secular forms of prestige and influence. Such authority may not constitute 'authenticity' as such (compare with MacCannell, 1976), in the ways that a remote and rural destination might, but even non-religious visitors are likely to be aware that sites of spiritual significance may demand a certain etiquette, even if they are not quite sure what such etiquette might be.

As cathedrals, temples and mosques attract increasing numbers of visitors for any combination of spiritual, recreational, educational and cultural purposes, administrators of such institutions not only have to establish priorities among the activities offered, but are also likely to indicate that at key points of the calendar or in particular spatial domains, religious demands and expectations must be assumed to be of primary importance (Hughes *et al.*, 2013, p. 210). Specific techniques to manage visitor flows typically include (following Nolan and Nolan, 1992, p. 73; Shackley, 2001, p. 90; Stausberg, 2011, p. 92):

- zoning of space to demarcate special areas or separate secular from religious visitors;
- reserving parts of a pilgrimage season for the visits of special interest groups, such as youth groups or the sick and infirm;
- charging of entrance fees or fees to gain access to certain areas or activities, such as climbing bell towers or visiting treasures;
- management of transport and vehicles;
- queue controls;
- temporary closures at sensitive times, such as during worship services;
- forcing or strongly encouraging people to go on guided tours;
- rules concerning appropriate dress;
- restrictions on photography; and
- provision of general information at entrances, ranging from offering postcards to running book stores.

These methods may also be applied differentially in relation to visitors. For instance, experienced tour guides tend to discern early on how religious or secular are the interests of any given group of visitors, and design their presentations accordingly. In this sense, they act as cultural brokers, mediating between hosts and guests (as discussed in Hughes *et al.*, 2013, p. 212).

The decision to charge an entrance fee to those who come as cultural visitors, but not those who come to pray, signals very powerfully how the symbolic character of different journeys may differ, although donations – in other words money *voluntarily* given – may discreetly be requested from both categories of visitor. Of course, the drawing of such distinctions is sometimes difficult and sensitive to carry out, and it may also transform the expectations of the secular visitor who comes to see him- or herself as a customer with certain rights and raised expectations as to what the fee will provide. Furthermore, it may lead to a cultural and marketing paradox: as Stausberg suggests (2011, p. 93), under some circumstances the less commercialized a religious place may appear, the greater the potential for its commercial success, given the desire of some tourists to encounter places ostensibly *divorced* from market relations.

The balance between these demands and expectations is clearly difficult to strike in the context of competition between cities and their religious sites for visitors, as religion becomes part of a wider 'symbolic economy' pitched at attracting seekers for memorable experiences (Raj and Morpeth, 2007, p. 8, drawing on Richards, 2001, p. 58). Reader (2014, p. 8) – writing mainly but not exclusively of Japan – argues indeed that pilgrimages must be seen as operating not just *in* the marketplace, but *through* it, with commercialization potentially adding to the vibrancy of a shrine, and also providing a distant echo of how markets in medieval Europe developed close to churches, frequently being held on a church's feast days. Intriguingly, Mary Lee Nolan and Sidney Nolan (1992, p. 71) suggest that it is often the secular or Protestant tourist, rather than the devout pilgrim, who is shocked by the apparent commercialization of pilgrimage shrines such as Knock, Lourdes and Fatima. For more pious visitors, the ability to purchase religious goods may contribute powerfully to the spiritual experience of the shrine, as well as providing the opportunity to bring back spiritually charged souvenirs to friends and relatives at home.

Questions relating to who has the ultimate say in shrine administration become more complex as we step back to consider how the authority of shrines may relate to, or clash with, that of municipal or national government, or indeed other interested parties. One theme of Franck and Stevens' book (2007) is that state regulation may interfere in public spaces in order to maintain social order or create a sense of unified national identity, and these kinds of actions can lead to some striking debates over competing interests. Thus Malory Nye (2001) provides an extensive account of the controversial conversion of a large, rambling house on the outskirts of London into a shrine renamed Bhaktivedanta Manor. Debates over the 'orderly' management of the space involved complex negotiations between neighbours annoyed at the presence of a busy, 'foreign' shrine in a peaceful suburb, the local council, national government and ultimately the European Court of Human Rights in Strasbourg. Once the Manor was finally permitted to function as a place of public worship it became a major pilgrimage site for Hindus across Britain (Nye, 2001, p. 4), but the granting of such permission raised powerful questions relating to the role and rights of religion in general – and not just Hinduism – in a Western state.

The scale of control may also shift as a result of the success of a religious location. Vitor Ambrósio and Margarida Pereira (2007) draw on the work of Richard Butler (1980) as they reflect on the shifting trajectories of 'sanctuary' towns such as Banneux in Belgium, Fátima in Portugal, Knock in Ireland and Lourdes in France – all of them attractive to pious visitors given their status as locations of apparitions of the Virgin Mary, but also subject to very different forms of urban development and planning. One of Butler's points (Ambrósio and Pereira, 2007, p. 147) is that as larger numbers of people come to a site, the character and location of tourist administration may easily change, passing out of local hands as commercial bodies from elsewhere move in. Once again, we encounter a recurrent dilemma associated with heritage tourism, religious or not: how to balance success and growth with the need to avoid destroying the very site that is the centre-point of most people's travels.

At the same time, there are at least two further complications associated with the religious character of such sites:

• One is that religious destinations may not be subject to quite the same marketing pressures as secular sites, since believers' motivations to travel are not dictated by fashion – though admittedly this claim is disputed by writers who claim that little difference can be discerned between religious and secular fashions (Stausberg, 2011, p. 93; Reader, 2014).

- Another relates to how to interpret the significance of the public present at a religious site: whereas mass tourism is often avoided by certain tourists who seek apparently authentic and exclusive experiences associated with removing themselves from common tastes and crowds, the very authority of a religious site may in fact be constituted by the size of the assemblies that it can attract. Thus, under some circumstances the denigration of 'the mass' in secular terms may be converted into its opposite – a positive valuing of the impressive gathering of believers who have chosen to visit a site in order to celebrate common religious aims.

This section has focused largely on the character of shrines themselves, and the authority that they may exercise in controlling and classifying visitors. Clearly, the assertion of such control is important in determining, at any given point, the 'looseness' or 'tightness' of the spaces through which visitors of different motivations and backgrounds move. In the next section, I expand my perspective further to consider the European continent as a host context for pilgrims and other visitors.

Europe as a Religious Landscape

Europe provides a varied landscape for religiously motivated travellers. Many of its inhabitants proclaim a Judaeo-Christian heritage, but such heritage is hardly all-encompassing, and is currently challenged by secular impulses, especially in the north and east of the continent, as well as immigration and tourism from populations professing other religious affiliations, including Islam, Hinduism and Buddhism. Over the past quarter of a century, the opening up of Orthodox religious shrines in post-Soviet contexts has added to the array of destinations on offer. In addition, links between real places and popular fiction have been developed through the considerable success of such works as the Harry Potter novels of J.K. Rowling or Dan Brown's *The Da Vinci Code*, which have sparked pilgrimage-like journeys by readers keen to retrace the landscapes of these authors' narrative imaginations (Badone, 2008).

Some of the most influential survey work on sites in Europe – and particularly Christians ones – has been carried out by Nolan and Nolan. Besides emphasizing the variety of visitors to shrines (Nolan and Nolan, 1992, p. 69), they note the variety of destinations themselves:

> Europe's religious tourism system consists of pilgrimage shrines, sacred places of artistic and/or historic significance without pilgrimage associations, religious festivals, and various blends of these basic components.
>
> (Nolan and Nolan, 1992, p. 77)

Some shrines or activities hold little or no interest for tourists, of course, and appeal instead to community or devotional groups or pious individuals. In this category, Nolan and Nolan place the sites of reported visions of the Virgin Mary at San Sebastián de Garabandal in northern Spain and San Damiano in Italy's Po Valley. In contrast, some of Europe's best-known religious tourist attractions are also important pilgrimage shrines, such as Chartres Cathedral and the island abbey of Le Mont-Saint-Michel in France (Nolan and Nolan, 1992, p. 72).

Interestingly, Nolan and Nolan (1992, p. 76) note that 'the tourist promotional literature from Spain, Portugal and Italy lists many more pilgrimages and religious festivals than does literature from other European countries'. This difference seems to reflect the fact that large numbers of festivals are indeed held in Mediterranean countries, but also points to a conscious strategy on the part of many folkloric pilgrimages in Catholic regions of southern Germany, Austria and Switzerland to avoid publicity. Thus, the desirability of attracting secular visitors varies regionally, with a tendency towards greater tolerance of non-devotional spectators in Mediterranean Europe's 'festive pilgrimages' (Nolan and Nolan, 1992, p. 77).

One important point not made by the Nolans, but more evident in the work of scholars such as Boissevain, is the link between patterns of migration within Europe and the timing or staging of festivals. In the introduction to a volume on ritual in Europe, Boissevain (1992, p. 1) observes that, contrary to predictions that secularization, industrialization and the presence of alternative forms of entertainment would undermine the celebration of public rituals on the continent, in fact such celebrations have been increasing since the 1970s. One factor here, as highlighted by Margaret Kenna (1992; see also Boissevain, 1992, p. 6) in her work on the Cycladic island of Nisos, is that the festive dimension of the island's annual patronal celebration is boosted by the island's blue-collar emigrants, who live abroad for much of the year but come back for their summer holidays to re-engage with local life.

Migration has had other effects on European shrines. John Eade and David Garbin (2007) examine ways in which global flows of population that have produced multicultural urban contexts in Britain have also transformed the country's pilgrimage landscape. They see religious pilgrimage as having been 'ethnicized' by the arrival and settlement of Hindu, Sikh, Muslim and Buddhist minorities as well as Catholics from Africa, Latin America, South and South-east Asia and Eastern Europe. Such developments raise an important question that warrants more discussion in the literatures on tourism and religion: How are we to view visitors to a holy shrine who come from another religion to that ostensibly celebrated by the shrine? Are they to be classified as tourists or as pilgrims? No single answer can be provided, but we see here a trend that is only likely to increase in coming decades, as migrants not only create new shrines in their countries of settlement (such as Bhaktivedanta Manor, mentioned above) but seek to find connections with already existing holy places.

The points made in this section reinforce the idea that the role of shrines has changed as people's mobility – expressed in migration, tourism, pilgrimage or some combination of these activities – has increased. Kevin Griffin (2007, p. 28) reinforces this conclusion in observing that in recent years newly affluent Irish people have welcomed the opportunity to go on international pilgrimages to such well-known places as Lourdes, Rome and the Holy Land, but also Medjugorje (in Herzegovina), Fátima (in Portugal) and San Giovanni (in Italy). None the less, he adds that local and national pilgrimages are still valued, so that a widening of perspectives has proved complementary to the valuing of the local religious landscape.

In thinking of the changing pilgrimage context of Europe, it is hard to ignore one of the oldest traditions of religious travel, and yet also one that has had a remarkable new lease of life in recent decades. The *Camino de Santiago* or Way of St James refers to the pilgrimage routes across Europe leading to the cathedral at Santiago de Compostela, in northern Spain. The remains of St James are said to have been in what is now the city, and the site was an important part of the European pilgrimage landscape in the Middle Ages. By the mid-1980s, just a few hundred pilgrims a year were making the trip, indicating a considerable fall in popularity from the prime years of the historical pilgrimage. Nowadays, however, perhaps 200,000 people make the trip annually to the cathedral by following various routes, and indeed the 'camino' model is copied by pilgrimages elsewhere in the world. Such success seems to have come about through a mixture of the planned and the unplanned. At the end of the 1980s in Spain difficult economic circumstances prompted people to seek alternative forms of income to industry or indeed 'sun and beach' tourism, and at the same time the country entered the European Union (Santos and Cabrera, 2014, p. 722). The marking of culture and history became important in urban economies across the country, and Santiago de Compostela provided a fine venue for such a shift in tastes, not least when the Camino was declared a European Cultural Route by the Council of Europe in October 1987, and also a UNESCO (United Nations Educational, Scientific and Cultural Organization) World Heritage Site.

Inevitably, the cathedral and surrounding city have faced the usual challenges and opportunities associated with attracting tens of thousands of people into a dense and compact area. What I want to emphasize, however, is that part of the European – indeed global – success of this form of religious tourism has come from what I call its 'looseness' – embodied most notably in the *camino*, made up of routes across the continent. In other words, travellers can choose if they wish to walk all the way, toiling for days or weeks across hundreds of kilometres; others prefer to cycle or even take the car, although the latter is not a highly valued means of transport along the *camino*. While some people self-identify as Christian pilgrims, others see themselves as more broadly spiritual, or perhaps as belonging to another religion, or even as possessing no faith at all. Thus, the routes – multiple in themselves – provide a fine example of a stretched-out space, permitting numerous forms of improvisation as people travel on their own, form bonds with friends and family as they travel, or go with religious groups. Such flexibility celebrates the journey as much as the arrival, and also allows for diverse forms of engagement that are none the less often deeply felt. And in the light of such observations, I want finally to turn to some of my own work, on pilgrimage and cathedrals in England.

Shrines as Tight and Loose Spaces: English Case Studies

Since the 1990s, I have been carrying out fieldwork at the English Christian pilgrimage shrine of Walsingham, in North Norfolk in the eastern part of England. The shrine was an important one in the Middle Ages as it was associated with a vision of the Virgin Mary (Coleman, 2014), but was largely destroyed at the time of the Reformation, before being restored in the early part of the 20th century by separate groups of both Anglicans and Roman Catholics. It is now a flourishing place of pilgrimage, which attracts both devout pilgrims and visitors who come for daytrips from nearby coastal resorts.

What I want to emphasize here is how Walsingham functions as a space that manages diversity of movement and motivation among visitors. When I began my work there I expected to find intense engagement on the part of pilgrims at the Anglo- and Roman Catholic shrines, and I was not disappointed. Many devoted pilgrims would come on annual visits from parishes located across the country, and the Anglican shrine administration estimated that around 10,000 residential visitors attended its formally organized pilgrimages every year (Walsingham, 2012). However, the Anglican shrine provides another striking statistic, which is that perhaps 300,000 people in total 'visit' the small village of Walsingham each year – a much greater figure. So, what does 'visit' mean for those non-residential pilgrims who make up over 90% of people who are present? If anything is clear, it is that they represent a huge range of people, many of whom have little idea what a pilgrimage shrine actually entails. Indeed, here is what one shrine administrator told me about such visitors:

> I think I can sometimes tell people who are definitely not pilgrims ... there's a group of, there's a kind of ... class of people, category of people, who have no sense of the numinous, or, of place, of boundaries ... This ... came home to me earlier on in the summer when I was sitting in the shrine saying the office or something, and watching one of Father Andrew's cats that caught my eye. And it walked *through* the sanctuary ... it just walked right through ... I thought why has the cat crossed those boundaries and not gone round in the way that everybody else does, and of course it's because the cat doesn't *see* the boundaries ... but actually there are lots of boundaries which are unmarked, physically, but which are marked mentally, emotionally, in the minds of people who know. You can tell those who don't know because, they actually, like the cat, cross the boundaries.

The image of the wandering cat perhaps reminds us of the tourists wandering into Jeremy Boissevain's friends' house in Malta. Both examples indicate that some visitors simply do not 'see' certain boundaries. But what I want to emphasize is that this administrator was not telling me this story in order to suggest that the doors to the shrine should be closed, or that stern notices should be erected telling people to follow certain pathways. In fact, I took his comments to be as much a celebration of the flexibility and openness of the shrine as it was a wry comment on the lack of awareness of some visitors. Indeed, my own fieldwork at Walsingham has revealed a wealth of responses and behaviours in the village, including deliberate attempts to stage rituals not in churches but in surrounding roads and fields. Some visitors are *only* willing to come to Walsingham because they know they will not be forced to engage directly in conventional ritual, but will be allowed to perform rites that are adjacent to official liturgies, within the general orbit of Walsingham but not directly controlled by clergy. Whatever one might think of these rituals, they contribute to the flourishing of a site that has moved from relative obscurity in mid-20th-century Britain to a major part of the contemporary British pilgrimage landscape.

In many ways, a site such as Walsingham belongs to the same part of the contemporary British Christian landscape as cathedrals. As the sociologist Grace

Davie (2012) suggests, visits to cathedral spaces bring together a range of possible experiences – heritage, aesthetics and the possibility of anonymous worship away from regular rituals of the parish church. But arguably they also belong to a still wider constellation of contexts, also including multi-faith rooms, hospital and university chaplaincies, and indeed pilgrimages, that are both gaining in salience and providing spaces of encounter between religions, religious and secular practices, even the public and the private. Davie (2012, p. 486) notes that 'in the 1970s these iconic buildings were frequently referred to as dinosaurs, large and useless'. What is striking, however, is that current evidence tells us that the constituencies for cathedrals are now growing rapidly, consisting of both regular and less regular worshippers, as well as 'more transient communities of pilgrims and tourists' (Davie, 2012, p. 486).

Davie's claims are backed up by the work of other scholars. The statistician Peter Brierley's 2005 English Church Census revealed a 21% rise in attendance at Anglican cathedral services between 2000 and 2004 (Brierley, 2006, p. 198; quoted in Guest *et al.*, 2012, p. 67). In reflecting on such popularity, Davie (2012) suggests that cathedrals appeal to the senses as much as to the intellect: they are 'places that pay attention to aesthetics of worship, to music, to art, to liturgy, to worship', while they are 'places where the individual can find space to reflect' in contexts of relative anonymity, thus avoiding the sometimes overly warm embrace of a parish church.

My own work on English cathedrals (Canterbury, Durham, York and Westminster, as part of a team based at the University of York) is just beginning at the time of writing. However, it is already clear that they are powerful receptacles for the variety of experience described by Davie. In a given day, a cathedral may play host to hundreds of unplanned and unpredictable visitors of many or no religions, before switching quite suddenly towards the 'tight' liturgical frame required by a mass or a prayer service, before accommodating a pilgrimage group whose members may range from the devout to the deeply sceptical. Looseness and tightness may thus be occurring simultaneously, but then the whole cathedral may shift serially from one to the other, once a worship service starts. Pilgrimage to this kind of space is not isolated from other activities; nor is the pilgrimage–tourism spectrum the only relevant behavioural and motivational index along which it should be measured. Like cathedrals themselves, pilgrimage is implicated in chains and adjacencies of movement and other activity that indicate how cathedrals, as well as places such as Walsingham, can thrive through providing flexible spaces of action in the 21st century, where the boundaries between tourism and religion may not always be clear to visitors themselves. It is this very flexibility that can provide a model of sustainability for such sites, which a few decades ago might have been written off as part of a dying Christian landscape in a secularizing country.

Concluding Remarks

My argument in this chapter has been that the boundaries between religious and cultural or secular tourism, especially in contemporary urban contexts, is complex and shifting. Allied to that, the apparent secularization of large parts of the European continent has not led to a lessening interest in shrines, but has contributed to a diversification of interest. One model of sustainability in relation to increased numbers of visitors at such sites and shrines can be seen as a 'defensive' one, attempting to protect holy places from large numbers of people, many of whom are ignorant of appropriate ways to act. However, an alternative model of sustainability is one that emphasizes how sites might encourage flexibility of movement and interpretation, thus responding to shifting understandings and engagements, often in ways unexpected by both hosts and visitors. In exploring this alternative model, this chapter has discussed the relationship between 'loose' and 'tight' space in contexts of tourism and religious practice.

References

Abram, S. (1996) Reactions to tourism: a view from the deep green heart of France. In: Boissevain, J. (ed.) *Coping with Tourists: European Reactions to Mass Tourism.* Berghahn, Oxford, pp. 174–203.

Ambrósio, V. and Pereira, M. (2007) Case study 2: Christian/Catholic pilgrimage – studies and analyses. In: Raj, R. and Morpeth, N.D. (eds) *Religious Tourism and Pilgrimage Management: an International Perspective.* CAB International, Wallingford, UK, pp. 140–152.

Badone, E. (2008) Pilgrimage, tourism and *The Da Vinci Code* at Les Saintes-Maries-de-la-Mer, France. *Culture and Religion* 9, 23–44.

Boissevain, J. (1992) Introduction: revitalizing European rituals. In: Boissevain, J. (ed.) *Revitalizing European Rituals.* London: Routledge, pp. 1–19.

Boissevain, J. (1996) Introduction. In: Boissevain, J. (ed.) *Coping with Tourists: European Reactions to Mass Tourism.* Berghahn, Oxford, pp. 1–26.

Brierley, P. (2006) *Pulling Out of the Nosedive: a Contemporary Picture of Churchgoing.* Christian Research, London.

Butler, R.W. (1980) The concept of a tourist area cycle of evolution: implications for management. *Canadian Geographer* 24, 5–12.

Coleman, S. (2014) Pilgrimage as trope for an anthropology of Christianity. *Current Anthropology* 55, 281–291.

Davie, G. (2012) A short afterword: thinking spatially about religion. *Culture and Religion* 13, 485–489.

Eade, J. and Garbin, D. (2007) Reinterpreting the relationship between centre and periphery: pilgrimage and sacred spatialisation among Polish and Congolese communities in Britain. *Mobilities* 2, 413–424.

Franck, K.A. and Stevens, Q. (2007) Tying down loose space. In: Franck, K.A. and Stevens, Q. (eds) *Loose Space: Possibility and Diversity in Urban Life.* Routledge, London, pp. 1–33.

Goffman, E. (1959) *The Presentation of Self in Everyday Life.* Doubleday Anchor, New York.

Griffin, K.A. (2007) The globalization of pilgrimage tourism? Some thoughts from Ireland. In: Raj, R. and Morpeth, N.D. (eds) *Religious Tourism and Pilgrimage Management.* CAB International, Wallingford, UK, pp. 15–34.

Guest, M., Olson, E. and Wolffe, J. (2012) Christianity: loss of monopoly. In: Woodhead, L. and Catto, R. (eds) *Religion and Change in Modern Britain.* Routledge, London, pp. 57–78.

Hughes, K., Bond, N. and Ballantyne, R. (2013) Designing and managing interpretive experiences at religious sites: visitors' perceptions of Canterbury Cathedral. *Tourism Management* 36, 210–220.

Kenna, M.E. (1992) Mattresses and migrants: a patron saint's festival on a small Greek island over two decades. In: Boissevain, J. (ed.) *Revitalizing European Rituals.* Routledge, London, pp. 155–172.

MacCannell, D. (1976) *The Tourist: a New Theory of the Leisure Class*. University of California Press, Berkeley, California.

Nolan, M.L. and Nolan, S. (1992) Religious sites as tourism attractions in Europe. *Annals of Tourism Research* 19, 68–68.

Nye, M. (2001) *Multiculturalism and Minority Religions in Britain*. Curzon, Richmond, UK.

Raj, R. and Morpeth, N. (2007) Introduction: establishing linkages between religious travel and tourism. In: Raj, R. and Morpeth, N. (eds) *Religious Tourism and Pilgrimage Management: an International Perspective*. CAB International, Wallingford, UK, pp. 1–14.

Reader, I. (2014) *Pilgrimage in the Marketplace*. Routledge, London.

Richards, G. (ed.) (2001) *Cultural Attractions and European Tourism*. CAB International, Wallingford, UK.

Santos, X. and Cabrera, L. (2014) Management of tourist flows: the Cathedral of Santiago de Compostela. *Pasos* 12, 719–735.

Shackley, M. (2001) *Managing Sacred Sites: Service Provision and Visitor Experience*. Thomson Learning, London.

Stausberg, M. (2011) *Religion and Tourism: Crossroads, Destinations and Encounters* Routledge, London.

Walsingham (2012) Welcome: The Anglican Shrine of our Lady of Walsingham. Available at: http://www.walsinghamanglican.org.uk/welcome/index.htm (accessed 17 May 2012).

8 The Management of Pilgrims with Malevolent Behaviour in a Holy Space: A Study of Jerusalem Syndrome

MOSHE KALIAN* AND ELIEZER WITZTUM

Ben-Gurion University of the Negev, Beer-Sheva, Israel

Introduction

Cohen (1979) suggested that different kinds of people may desire different modes of touristic experiences; hence 'the tourist' does not exist as a single prototype. He described a phenomenological typology of tourist experiences based upon the concept of the 'centre' and 'the quest for the centre' introduced by Eliade (1971). Eliade pointed out that every religious 'cosmos' possesses a 'centre' which is pre-eminently the zone of the sacred – the zone of absolute reality. The 'centre' is considered to be the location 'where the *axis mundi* penetrates the earthly sphere' (Eliade, 1971, p. 971). However, the 'centre' is not necessarily geographically central in the daily life space of the community of believers. According to Turner the *ex-centris* location of the 'centre' creates a meaningful content for believers by giving directions and structure to the act of pilgrimage – a sacred journey of spiritual ascension to 'The Centre Out There' (Turner, 1973). A relatively new development in this regard concerns psychopathology observed in certain types of tourists and pilgrims (Witztum *et al.*, 1994; Kalian and Witztum, 1998). The dramatic malevolent behaviour, at times observed in certain tourists and pilgrims arriving in Jerusalem has been called 'Jerusalem syndrome' (Witztum and Kalian, 1999). The syndrome is clearly related, both in content and actions, to the cultural–religious background of the pilgrim and to the geographical space where it is overtly demonstrated. Pathological behaviour of such nature, conducted in a place as holy as Jerusalem, may breach the fragile delicate equilibrium maintained for generations by the three major monotheistic religions, and yield catastrophic results.

The most famous example is the case of Michael Dennis Rohan, an Australian Christian tourist, a schizophrenic who believed he was destined for a special

*kalian@netvision.net.il

Messianic mission, who in 1969 set fire to Al-Aqsa mosque, so that the Jewish temple could be built on its ruins. The incident raised a tremendous uproar all over the Muslim world, still echoed until today. In light of such events one can understand the extreme caution taken by the authorities, as reflected for example by the act of expelling a group of eccentric 'Concerned Christians' – members of a sect with vague apocalyptic intentions, who suddenly disappeared from America and were discovered residing on the outskirts of Jerusalem (Leppäkari, 2014a). In some cases, action by afflicted individuals with poor judgement slide into a criminal category. Nevertheless, it seems that pilgrims afflicted in this manner require emergency psychiatric intervention.

Tourism and Pilgrimage

Modern pilgrimage is often indistinguishable from tourism and people who are travelling mostly look the same. Still, by analysing their motivation we can see the differences between 'pilgrim-tourists', who travel towards the religious or cultural centres of their spiritual life and 'traveller-tourists' who travel away from them to the periphery of the world. Pearce (1982) suggests five different modes of tourist experience. The fifth form – the 'existential mode' – is characterized by travel to an elective spiritual centre and is analogous to pilgrimage. Cohen (1984) concludes that tourism is principally a modern metamorphosis of pilgrimage, yet secularization has destroyed their deep structural themes and much of their symbolic significance and mystical powers. This has transformed sacred loci to 'places of attraction' or mere tourist destinations.

Traditionally, pilgrimage has been a significant aspect of major religions. According to the Jewish faith, believers are obliged to make pilgrimage to Jerusalem three times a year. Christians travel to holy places in the footsteps of their master, worshipping places connected to the life of Jesus and to his gospels. Muhammad commanded Muslim pilgrims 'to experience God'. This has resulted in millions of Muslims undertaking pilgrimage (which is one of the five pillars of Islam) to Mecca and Medina every year. The followers of Hinduism make pilgrimage to the Ganges – the holy river – an act which cleanses their sins. Buddhists make pilgrimage to places Buddha consecrated by his life. Shintoists go into deep forests and meditate in silence. These multiple forms of pilgrimage result in a myriad of pilgrimage experiences, which influence and impact on adherents of the various faiths in many ways, in their search for 'centre'. In Jerusalem, a specific yet rare type of pilgrim-tourist has been detected, mainly with a psychiatric background; these are afflicted by the so-called 'Jerusalem syndrome'. A small yet noticeable subgroup among these are 'apocalyptic' individuals who believe they have a special mission in the end-of-times process.

Psychogeography: The Role of 'a Significant Place'

One of the earliest professional observations, relating to the impact of a significant earthly site on specific mental symptomatology was documented by Sigmund

Freud. Being an enthusiastic admirer of the Hellenistic culture and a keen self-observant, Freud documented his personal experience of derealization upon arriving at a unique place, referring to his visit to the Acropolis in 1904. Writing home he related that the experience there had surpassed anything he had ever seen or could imagine (Jones, 1955). The emotional impact of that single incident was so deep, that more than 30 years later, in a letter to Romain Rolland (Freud, 1962) Freud still remembers in detail his overwhelming psychological experience. It was a peculiar disbelief in the reality of what was before his eyes. He puzzled his brother by asking him if it was true that they were on the Acropolis. He felt himself being divided into two persons, one who was in fact on the Acropolis and the other who could not believe that it was so. Another skilled self-observant traveller was the famous 19th-century French writer Stendhal (Marie-Henri Beyle) who gave a vivid description of his sudden 'fainting' upon observing the frescoes by Giotto at the church of Santa Croce in Florence (Stendhal, 1957).

In recent years, apart from our observations regarding the so-called 'Jerusalem syndrome' (Witztum *et al.*, 1994), there have been several psychiatric reports relating to similar phenomena at other sites of significance. Shapiro (1976, 1977, 1982), working at a department of Queen's New York Psychiatric Hospital, studied 359 patients referred from the nearby Kennedy Airport, whom he diagnosed as 'airport wanderers'. Contrary to the findings of others, who stressed the importance of phobic anxiety relating to flight or of culture shock, he found that the airport settings gave a specific 'colour' to pre-existing problems. The airport had a symbolic value. Separation and reunion, as major areas of disturbance, may be important issues in the explanation of the phenomenon of 'airport wanderers'. In addition, for certain groups of people, 'the airport can also serve to disorganize by generating degrees of overwhelming anxiety stimulated by feelings related to separation, abandonment, and hostile impulses' (Shapiro, 1977, p. 557).

Magherini and Zanobini (1987) describe a particular form of an acute mental reaction arising in art-loving tourists while confronting the overwhelming renaissance paintings upon visiting Florence. The so-called 'Stendhal syndrome' (named after the famous French writer), was observed in 107 visitors who required psychiatric hospitalization between the years 1978 and 1986. From the analysis of data it is clear that there were no relevant differences between males and females; most of them came from European countries; the most affected age was between 20 and 40, mainly single people who have undertaken an individual journey, not an organized one. Hospitalization was short, the prognosis was benign and the holiday was only temporarily interrupted.

Another striking phenomenon is the so-called 'White House syndrome', seen in Washington DC. This relates to psychotic tourists, mainly schizophrenics, who demand to meet the American president or claim they are presidents themselves. About 100 of these individuals are hospitalized each year (Sebastiani and Foy, 1965; Shore *et al.*, 1985, 1989).

There is a noticeable difference between the four 'syndromes', derived from the symbolic significance of these sites. Florence is perceived as the ultimate shrine of renaissance art, exhibiting an overwhelming wealth of colossal classical works, which symbolize a turning point in the history of Christian humanism. The 15th century renaissance works reflect a religious philosophy, viewing life no longer as a vale of tears but as a quest for enlarging human powers, and thus a greater awareness of God. Thus the Florentine art treasures, apart from their overwhelming physical dimensions, symbolize the adherence of pagan antiquity and unorthodox thinking to the spirit of Christian faith. As for the 'airport wanderers', the gigantic airport arena symbolizes technology's edge as well as paces and stressors of global society. The White House is regarded as a symbol of the mightiest of modern powers. It symbolizes a modern philosophical political thought, where a mortal is elected by the people for the people, and is granted the power to influence global affairs. It is a symbol of human superpower. However, the significance of Jerusalem as a unique symbol is entirely a spiritual one. It is embedded in the history of both Jewish and Christian Messianic tradition, and its uniqueness is derived from being perceived as 'the centre of the world', 'a place where the last episode of doomsday will occur at the end of times'. The so-called 'Jerusalem syndrome' is thus considered to be related to the spiritual significance of the city.

Pilgrimage to Jerusalem

The Judeo-Christian tradition is constructed around Messianic aspirations in which the Holy City – Jerusalem – the *axis mundi* of faith, is perceived as the arena where great dramatic events are about to occur. This eschatological core element is at times exploited in a broader sense in the service of a public or an individual, to the extent where boundaries between reality and imagination are blurred. Bowman discusses the spiritual magnetism of Jerusalem from an anthropological point of view, stressing that 'the visions of pilgrims, as presented in the massive body of their writings, provide a glass through which we can see the transformations of European beliefs and perceptions as clearly' (Bowman, 1992, p. 164).

Jerusalem, the Holy City, is regarded as a sacred space for the three main monotheistic religions. The custom of Jewish pilgrimage to Jerusalem goes back to the days of the first temple, and exists in Christianity since its early days of foundation. Pilgrimage became an established model of worship by Christians in the 4th century. Turner defines this phenomenon as a 'prototypical' pilgrimage, in which the spiritual content of the act is directly related to the life of the founder of the faith and to geographical sites where major events in the history of the religion took place (Turner, 1978).

The Messianic Idea and Millennialism

The origin of the Messianic idea is derived from the Jewish faith. It is based on the belief that the Messiah – a descendent of King David – will be revealed and shall break the regime of foreigners, will revive the kingdom of Israel and gather its children from the Diaspora, the temple will be rebuilt and the work of sacrifice will be re-established. Messianism was born during the post-biblical era, and it reappears repeatedly throughout history with each generation developing a new set of ideas. The original definition of the Messiah as an eschatological figure originates from the apocalyptic literature of the second temple contemporaries. There is no unified relation to the Messiah in the Talmud and the Midrash, and references regarding his appearance are varied (Licht, 1968). Calculations and speculations on the date of redemption have become an unseparated part of Jewish culture since the Middle Ages, as well as in modern times.

The central theme in Christian eschatology is the expectation of the Second Advent of Christ and the establishment of the Kingdom of God on earth. This belief is based on interpretations of the book of Daniel and the book of the vision of John. According to the Christian faith, due to the evil rule of the Antichrist, the world will suffer a set of disasters, at the end of which, redemption will occur, with its climax in the fall of the Great Babel, and the overthrow of Satan and his aids, who will be doomed to incarceration in Hell for a thousand years (the millennium). At the end of the millennium there shall be the war of Gog and Magog with the triumph of Good over Evil. The results shall lead to the resurrection of the dead and the establishment of the New Jerusalem (Witztum, 1987). Millennialistic movements are known to exist since the Middle Ages (Cohn, 1970), with Millennialiasts tending to adopt the 'method' of applying biblical quotations to contemporary events, thus 'proving' current events to be significant 'markers' of the soon-coming redemption. As noted in Chapter 10 by Ariel, 19th century Jerusalem became an active arena for such believers (Witztum, 1987).

Malevolent Behaviour in a Holy Space – 'Jerusalem Syndrome'

In recent years attention has been focused upon a relatively uncommon condition, labelled as 'Jerusalem syndrome'. This so-called 'syndrome' is an outcome of deep individual psychological needs, at times reflecting a production of psychopathology coloured by the individuals' cultural background. The benign forms of exhilaration are quite a common phenomenon among overseas visitors to Jerusalem. In its extreme and uncommon forms, the overwhelming experience may lead to fantastic behaviours, and even to mental breakdown and psychiatric hospitalization. However, studying individual cases throughout history reveals that the overwhelming unique experience of facing a holy space does not necessarily yield a malevolent outcome. A journey to Jerusalem could become significantly benevolent, utilized as a force for enhancing recovery and for materialization of positive endeavours. Still, psychiatric intervention is required for those 'apocalyptic emissaries' being afflicted by the syndrome, since some individuals may slide into dangerous actions that might be harmful for themselves or others, as well as jeopardizing the delicate equilibrium between the three monotheistic religions in the holy place.

Our Study of Jerusalem Syndrome

Approximately four decades after the first psychiatric observations of the so-called 'syndrome' were published by Dr Heintz Herman (1937), who was a pioneer psychiatrist in the Holy Land, Kfar Shaul Psychiatric Hospital started to admit foreign tourists to the Jerusalem region in need of psychiatric hospitalization. This was an administrative arrangement ordered by the Ministry of Health in 1979, since residents of Jerusalem at that time were referred to the other three local psychiatric hospitals in their vicinity. In the first year only 25 tourist-patients were admitted. However, with the increased influx of tourists, the average number rose to 50 patients per annum. For several years comprehensive statistical data have been gathered regarding the hospitalized tourists. The most extensive data, on which our findings are based, were collected between 1986 and 1987 from a group of 89 tourists (Bar-El *et al.*, 1991). The data of this group were compared with the demographic data of an earlier study of 177 tourists hospitalized in the same facility between 1979 and 1984 (Kalian *et al.*, 1985). No significant differences were found regarding age, gender, marital status, religion, country of origin, method of referral and number of previous visits to Israel. The group studied in 1986–1987 comprised 32 women and 57 men whose mean age was 32.4 years, 74% were single, 15% divorced and only a minority – 11% – were married, 52% had received 13 or more years of education, 36% had between 8 and 12 years of education, while 7% had an education of fewer than 5 years. Most tourists came from North America (40%) and Western Europe (44%); the remainder were from Eastern Europe, South America, South Africa or elsewhere. Recreational tourism was the mode for 38% of our group while 26% came for reasons of a mystical-religious nature. About 15% were visiting relatives and 7% came to do volunteer work. The experiential mode (i.e. trying out a new lifestyle) provided the chief impetus for 11% of our group. These people came to learn and considered staying. Table 8.1 shows the religious affiliation of the patients and their level of religious involvement. There was no difference in distribution of the religious involvement of the patients across the religions.

Table 8.1. Religion and level of religious involvement in a group of tourist-patients with Jerusalem syndrome.

Religion	Level of religious involvement			Total
	Observant	Strict	Non-observant	
Jewish	22	10	13	45
Catholic	8	5	5	18
Protestant	3	2	9	14
Other	1	0	1	2
Unknown				10
Total	34	17	28	89

Examination of the behaviour of the patients before admission shows that deviant behaviour, including excessive preaching and vagrancy, was found in 33%. Manifestations of aggression, such as physically attacking people or threatening them with a weapon, led to the admission of 11%; another 11% were walking around naked when apprehended and referred to hospital; and 13% were admitted after attempting suicide.

The psychiatric diagnoses (as presented in Table 8.2) were: (i) schizophrenia – 49 cases; (ii) acute psychosis – 14 cases; (iii) affective psychosis – 11 cases;

(iv) personality disorder – seven cases; (v) dementia – two cases; and (vi) 'other' – six cases (some patients had more than one psychiatric diagnosis) (Bar-El *et al.*, 1991).

Table 8.2. Diagnosis compatible with the 10th revision of the International Statistical Classification of Diseases and Related Health Problems (ICD-10).

Diagnosis	Number of cases
Schizophrenia	49
Acute psychosis	14
Affective psychosis	11
Personality disorder	7
Dementia	2
Other	6

To bring the nexus between religion and their illness into a sharper focus, patients were asked to describe the nature of their experience at the time of their admission. Of these 40% reported mystical experiences and the majority of them believed they were a mystical/religious figure. Twenty patients (22.5%) thought they were the Messiah, three felt they were God, two identified with Satan and another six patients identified with biblical figures (Table 8.3).

Table 8.3. Patients reporting religious delusions and mystical experiences.

Identification with	Mystical experiences[a]	
	Yes	No
Messiah	20	2
God	3	1
Satan	2	1
Other (mostly a biblical figure)	6	1
No identification	5	29
Unknown		19
Total	36	53

[a]Of the 89 tourists admitted for short hospitalizations in a period of 2 years, while visiting Jerusalem 36 demonstrated symptomatology related to 'Jerusalem syndrome'. All in that group reported having mystical experiences and delusions.

An interesting observation is that mystical experiences were more frequent in patients with a Roman Catholic background than in Jewish or Protestant patients.

Our assumption that people suffering an acute psychotic episode during a journey had previous psychiatric problems was confirmed: 82% of the patients in our survey had a psychiatric history dated and documented before they set out on their journey to Jerusalem. However, there was no clear previous documentation regarding 18% of the patients dating before their odd behaviour emerged in Jerusalem. Still, no differences appeared in the demographic variables, purpose of their journey, religious involvement or the nature of their religious delusions.

A brief interjection needs to be made regarding the year 2000 and 'apocalyptic emissaries' – individuals who come to Jerusalem with a 'mission' to enhance the process of 'The End of Times'. Perhaps somewhat surprisingly, no significant increase in the number of 'emissaries' was detected.

Regardless of their small number, the afflicted individuals set a challenge to the authorities and this is exemplified in the following case.

The case of 'Patrick the emissary'

The wounded 'Patrick the emissary' couldn't believe what was really happening to him, and that his extraordinary mission to the Holy City ended up with a serious accusation regarding an attempted attack on police officers. The bad news was given to him by a representative of his consulate and the lawyer that was hired to defend him, while still being hospitalized in a surgical ward, recuperating from gunshot injuries by the police. It turned out that he had been shot while running towards policemen guarding the church of the Holy Sepulchre, waving a large knife as if he was going to attack them, ignoring their warnings when they ordered him to stop. Being well aware of the sensitivities derived from the religious significance of the church, the guards automatically perceived his endangering behaviour as the actions of a fanatic terrorist attempting a lethal provocation in a most sacred and sensitive place. Patrick's reaction to the situation was as follows:

> How could it be that such an important mission would go astray? All I wanted was to get killed at the church of the Holy Sepulchre, dying the way an emissary should, announcing to the world that 'The End of Days' has come ... It seems that Satan tricked me again ... I should have realized that.

A mixture of Satanic and Messianic content preoccupied the thoughts of this strange single 40-year-old male since his early adulthood. However, Patrick's peculiar history begins in his childhood, where he exhibited emotional difficulties in the maintenance of relationships with peers before and during schooldays. He was the younger son in an upper-middle class yet disharmonious family. His father held a senior position and used to travel a lot in the service of the organization that employed him. At times the family joined him. Actually, the parents were separated for years and finally got divorced when he was 20. Though economically privileged, he grew up in an atmosphere of somewhat emotional deprivation. People described Patrick as timid, solitary, at times bizarre and with learning difficulties. Being self-disappointed with his academic failures, he went into a handwork apprenticeship; however, he soon quit because he could not concentrate in his job and was unable to hold logical conversations. A few years later he suffered a full-blown paranoid psychotic episode, but refused any treatment. He gradually indulged himself in a mission he perceived as 'destined' to him, to combat satanic forces wherever they existed. One night he called a friend of the family and told him of signs he saw on a television show revealing that a famous rock singer was involved in a plot to assassinate Tony Blair and urged him to deliver an urgent warning to Downing Street. He was sure that he saw signs indicating that the singer was a modern personification of 'Nero' – the representation of Satan along the ages. In spite of recurrent attempts by family members to convince him to get professional help, he refused any treatment. He tried twice to establish meaningful relations with women but both attempts ended with great disappointment and distress. Soon he became over-indulged with religious scripts, living in solitude and becoming more estranged. At times he threw articles and pieces of furniture out of the window, claiming that they had been used by hostile entities to spy on him and other family members. He managed to gather some financial resources to travel abroad and went to China, Turkey, South Africa and Israel, usually carrying with him pamphlets of missionary content. While in Jerusalem for his third time he gradually became immersed in his own interpretation of the theology of dispensationalism. (Dispensationalism is a Christian evangelical, futurist, biblical interpretation that believes God has related to human beings in different ways under different biblical covenants in a series of 'dispensations' or periods in history. Dispensationalists believe that the nation of Israel is distinct from the Christian Church, and that God has yet to fulfil his promises to Israel. Some dispensationalists interpret elements of the Book of Revelation not as an account of past events, with specific reference to the destruction of Jerusalem, but as predictions of the future.)

Soon Patrick felt elated, being convinced that he was 'one of the four emissaries' who would bring tidings of redemption to mankind. However, by that time he ran out of financial resources and was forced to return to his country to gather more money, 'waiting for his day to come'. A chain of global events – of which the last was a dramatic eruption of a volcanic mountain in Iceland, convinced him that 'the end of days' was approaching and that he was chosen to be the emissary to announce the fantastic news in the Holy City. According to his myth, once he would reach the church of the Holy Sepulchre and make his announcement he would be killed by Satan, and the killing of the emissary by Satan would initiate an apocalyptic chain of events, at the end of which evil powers would be defeated, Satan would then be thrown to hell for a thousand years and good would prevail.

Although there was still havoc caused by the cloud of volcanic ash over Europe, he managed to catch a flight to Israel, and return to Jerusalem in spite of various obstacles and delays. He was determined to combat Satan and sacrifice his life for the sake of mankind, thus initiating the millennial apocalyptic process. Yet, when he finally reached the holy site, the gates of the church were closed for further visits that afternoon. Patrick was sure that the closure of doors was simply another trick by Satan to prevent him from fulfilling his mission. Determined to fulfil his mission and overcome Satan's tricks he rushed to a shop in the old city and bought an impressive big knife. His improvised plan was to get killed at the doorsteps of the church by the armed policemen guarding the place, and deliver his tidings just before he died. He was convinced that the guards would cooperate in assisting him to overcome Satan. He then ran towards the guards waving his knife dramatically, as if he was going to stab one of them, ignoring their shouts of warning, and eventually got shot. However, the guards deliberately aimed at only wounding him and he was not killed. Later on, while being interviewed in the surgical ward and being confronted with the outcome of his deeds, he expressed remorse for his violent act. Still, he remarked: 'It was a foolish act; I should have known that Satan was cunning and tricky enough to avoid the death of the emissary, since he knew that such act would eventually lead to his own defeat'.

In court the defence lawyer pleaded for insanity. Observations in the hospital as well as recurrent psychiatric interviews confirmed the diagnosis of paranoid schizophrenia. Patrick was declared not responsible for his deeds due to mental illness. He was expelled back to his country with an obligation by the local authorities that his mental illness would be treated under court order.

Psychological commentary

Patrick's early and formative years of childhood were characterized by deep subjective experiences of emotional deprivation and insecurity. He grew up in an atmosphere of tension and disharmony between his parents, with a frequently missing father who took jobs abroad. He also had to cope with symptoms of suspected attention deficit disorder since his early childhood. It seems that there weren't any good-enough parenting figures to support and contain him during these crucial years of social isolation and poor academic and vocational achievements. Apart from that, signs of mental illness emerged during his early adulthood. In his painful and isolated world the most meaningful and stable source of solace was God – an imagined, ideal, parenting figure. Side by side with deep feelings of enduring agony and the emergence of his mental illness, his religiousness took an extreme and mystic turn, afflicted by his impaired sense of judgement, and he perceived himself as a unique fighter against satanic forces and 'a chosen emissary with special missions', a favourite son in the service of God. This mode of self-perception on personal backgrounds of deep individual emotional distress is characteristic of those demonstrating 'Jerusalem syndrome' (Kalian and Witztum, 2002). In his early twenties, Patrick was diagnosed as suffering from paranoid schizophrenia and was demonstrating typical symptoms of his mental disease. Concerning the role of religious experience in the psychotic process, we assume that religious experience and its practices serve as an idiom of distress. These patients tie religious experience to some sort of reality and offer a means of coping with their disorder or at the very least confronting it, on both the existential and the practical level. They either construct or explain their disorder in terms which construct a narrative that integrates the 'experience' into their religious lives (Witztum and Goodman, 1999). These patients can integrate the disorder into their life in such a way that they do not have to look at themselves as being insane. In effect, the use of the religious idiom of distress enables them to remain within the framework of the world in which they feel a part, in spite of the disruptions of their disorder (Heilman and Witztum, 2000). Leppäkari (2014b) points out that for many Christians, Jerusalem is vitally important because of the apocalyptic promise Jesus left his followers with: I'll be back! Therefore, the position of Jerusalem in the religious end-time play is crucial. Thus being convinced in the reality of his mission, Patrick found himself hospitalized and treated as a mental patient. The psychiatric management of such cases does not differ at large from the standard best possible treatment delivered to any hospitalized psychotic patient. Patrick was offered both medications and brief verbal therapy, aiming at helping him to gain some insight into what happened to him and urging him to continue treatment once he is back at his homeland.

Conclusion

Pilgrimage is a major and significant act in the spiritual life of the believer, at times being the peak of their religious experience. The vast majority of pilgrims who fulfil a mission of pilgrimage, experience a unique and deeper spiritual connection with their belief. This profound and benevolent experience is at times commonly and normally associated with feelings of excitement and exhilaration. However, at the outskirts of a common and normal phenomenon shared by the vast majority of pilgrims, are rare and extreme forms of behaviour. These unusual phenomena attract attention due to their theatrical characteristics, and at times require hospitalization in cases of endangering behaviour.

It should be remembered that in the delicate and fragile equilibrium maintained in Jerusalem, it is essential to distinguish between fanatics driven by radical tendencies and the mentally ill. The former should be neutralized by law-enforcement agencies. The latter should be brought to treatment. In the so-called 'Jerusalem syndrome', pilgrims identify themselves as biblical or Messianic figures and utilize Jerusalem as a stage upon which they should perform their mission. Some of them perceive themselves as apocalyptic emissaries destined to fulfil a special role in the end of times. Studies of 'Jerusalem syndrome' reveal that on the grounds of their cultural–religious background, which colours the content of their performance, these tourists are characterized by a personal history of significant emotional distress and at times by a full-blown mental illness. Their personal agony has a crucial role in blurring borders between the concrete and the spiritual. Their imagined 'unique role' is perceived as a source of solace. They act out their personal distress by adopting fantastic behaviour, compatible with their imagined unique role, trying to resolve suffering, yet this is often incompatible with reality and even with the spiritual meaning of their religion. Management and treatment of these conditions is aimed at regaining some insight into their malevolent behaviour and its concrete unfortunate outcome. Compassion and awareness is required, since hospitalization by itself is perceived by the patient, at least initially, as a tragedy. In cases of extreme psychotic behaviour, psychiatric medications are inevitable. In cases of good verbal rapport, treatment is aimed at helping the patient understand, at least logically, the chain of events that eventually lead to hospitalization. During the whole procedure of treatment, awareness of the patient's religious affiliation is required. Benevolent experiences attached to their belief are illuminated and stressed. Personal malevolent conducts and their undesired outcomes are at times clarified. The aim of treatment, in the short term, is helping the patient gain some control of their undesirable dangerous behaviour, thus avoiding unfavourable or tragic outcomes.

In our opinion, no believer should be deprived of experiencing pilgrimage to sacred places of their religion. However, considering the emotional impact of the tour, special precautions should be taken prior to travelling. Such an approach is relevant to any medical or vulnerable condition, as it also is to mentally fragile individuals. It is advised that people with formal psychiatric history should travel only in periods of good remission of their illness, and not solitarily. They should be furnished with medical insurance, a letter from their doctor and with pre-scribed medications to maintain their good psychiatric remission. Long-distance flights, as well as quick time-zone changes, should be minimized if not avoided. An accompanying responsible adult is essential. If travelling in a group, the leader should be aware of their condition. It is also advised that the leader of the group would be supplied with pertinent local medical and psychiatric ser-vices. The utilization of a local psychiatrist is recommended once exhilaration is spotted, particularly if it is accompanied by clear disturbance of sleep, odd be-haviour or odd verbal content. In such cases psychiatric consultation is never too early and could avoid further deterioration and undesirable hospitalization, which is always perceived to be traumatic by the patient. Once hospitalized, it is essential to maintain contact with the hospital staff, to inform the local consulate and to establish contact with the patient's family and their psychiatrist (if there is any). In accordance with the staff, visits are advised to reduce feelings of es-trangement and isolation.

All in all, once they have gained some initial insight, patients are encouraged to continue therapy on their return home. We believe that in the long run, com-bating unfavourable ideation that may lead to undesirable conduct, side by side with understanding the patient's religiousness and beliefs, require interference by skilled professionals who share a profound knowledge of the patient's language and cultural–religious background.

References

Bar-El, I., Witztum, E., Kalian, M. and Brom, D. (1991) Psychiatric hospitalization of tourists in Jerusalem. *Comprehensive Psychiatry* 32, 238–244.

Bowman, G. (1992) Pilgrim narrative of Jerusalem and the Holy Land: a study in ideological dis-tortion. In: Morinis, A. (ed.) *Sacred Journeys: the Anthropology of Pilgrimages*. Greenwood Press, Westport, Connecticut, pp. 149–168.

Cohen, E.A. (1979) Phenomenology of tourist experiences. *Sociology* 12, 179–201.

Cohen, E. (1984) The sociology of tourism: approaches, issues, and findings. *Annual Review of Sociology* 10, 373–392.

Cohn, N. (1970) *The Pursuit of the Millenium*. Oxford University Press, Oxford.

Eliade, E. (1971) *The Myth of Eternal Return*. Princeton University Press, Princeton, New Jersey.

Freud, S. (1962) A disturbance of memory on the Acropolis. In: *The Standard Edition of the Complete Psychological Works of Sigmund Freud*, Vol. 22. Hogarth Press, London, pp. 237–248.

Heilman, S.C. and Witztum, E. (2000) All in faith: religion as the idiom and means of coping with distress. *Mental Health, Religion and Culture* 3(2), 115–124.

Herman, H. (1937) Psychiatrisches aus Palastina. *Folia Clinica Orientalia* 1, 232–237.

Jones, E. (1955) *The Life and Work of Sigmund Freud*, Vol. 2. Basic Books, New York.

Kalian, M. and Witztum, E. (1998) Facing a holy space: psychiatric hospitalization of tourists in Jerusalem. In: Kedar, B.Z. and Werblowsky, R.J.Z. (eds) *Sacred Space: Shrine, City, Land*. Macmillan, London, pp. 316–330.

Kalian, M. and Witztum, E. (2002) Jerusalem syndrome as reflected in the pilgrimage and biographies of four extraordinary women from the 14th century to the end of the 2nd millennium. *Mental Health, Religion and Culture* 5, 1–6.

Kalian, M., Eisenberg, M. and Bar-El, I. (1985) Tourists who need psychiatric hospitalization: population characteristics and treatment principles. Paper presented at the *First International Congress on Hospital Laws*, Tel Aviv.

Leppäkari, M. (2014a) Apocalyptic management by Monte Kim Miller. *Journal of Religion and Violence* 2, 122–133.

Leppäkari, M. (2014b) Protestant pilgrimage to Jerusalem. Preparations for the Kingdom of God in apocalyptic rhetoric strategy. *Scripta Instituti Donneriani Aboensis* 18, 131–138.

Licht, J. (1968) Messiah. In: *Encyclopaedia Judaica*, Vol. 11. Bialik Institute, Jerusalem, pp. 1407–1417.

Magherini, G. and Zanobini, A. (1987) Eventi e psicopatologia:Il perturbante turistico: nota preleminare. *Rassegna di Studi Psichiatrici* 74, 1–14.

Pearce, P. (1982) *The Social Psychology of Tourist Behaviour*. Pergamon, Oxford.

Sebastiani, J.A. and Foy, J.I. (1965) Psychotic visitors to the White House. *American Journal of Psychiatry* 122, 679–686.

Shapiro, S. (1976) A study of psychiatric syndromes manifested at an international airport. *Comprehensive Psychiatry* 17, 453–456.

Shapiro, S. (1977) Psychiatric symptoms and the airport. *Aviation, Space and Environmental Medicine* 158, 555–557.

Shapiro, S. (1982) Airport wandering as a psychotic symptom. *Psychiatria Clinica* 15, 173–176.

Shore, D., Filson, C.R., Davis, T.S., Olivos, G., Delisi, L. and Wyat, G.R. (1985) White House cases: psychiatric patients and the Secret Service. *American Journal of Psychiatry* 142, 308–312.

Shore, D., Filson, C.R., Johnson, W.E., Rae, D.S., Meuhrer, P., Kelley, D.J., Davis, T.S., Waldman, I.N. and Wyatt, G.R. (1989) Murder and assault arrest of White House cases: clinical and demographic correlates of violence subsequent to civil commitment. *American Journal of Psychiatry* 146, 645–651.

Stendhal (Marie-Henri Beyle) (1957) *Impressions d'Italie, Rome, Naples, et Florence*. Germaine Raoult, Paris.

Turner, V. (1973) The center out there: the pilgrim's goal. *History of Religion* 12, 191–210.

Turner, V. (1978) *Image and Pilgrimage in Christian Culture*. Blackwell, Oxford.

Witztum, E. (1987) Doomsday prophets, millennialists and Messiahs in Jerusalem of the 19th and early 20th century. *Teva va Aretz* 30, 36–39.

Witztum, E. and Goodman, Y. (1999) Narrative construction of distress and therapy: a model based on work with ultra-Orthodox Jews. *Transcultural Psychiatry* 36, 403–436.

Witztum, E. and Kalian, M. (1999) Jerusalem syndrome – fantasy and reality, a survey of accounts from the 19th century to the end of the second millennium. *Israel Journal of Psychiatry* 36, 260–271.

Witztum, E., Kalian, M. and Brom, D. (1994) Pilgrims' perils: breakdown in Jerusalem. *Medical and Health Annual, Encyclopedia Britannica*. Encyclopedia Britannica Inc., Chicago, pp. 124–133.

9 Logistics at Holy Sites

ANNA TRONO*

University of Salento, Lecce, Italy

Introduction

The rapid transformation of modern society has led to radical developments in the ancient practice of pilgrimage. While conserving distinctive characteristics of a religious nature concerning visits to holy places and the experience of pilgrimage itself (Belhassen *et al.*, 2008), pilgrimage is now undertaken for a new set of reasons linked to the search for authenticity, spirituality and cultural enrichment. However, this also means that destinations require complex organization in the provision of structures, infrastructure and services, and the active involvement of public and private sectors, as well as secular and religious authorities.

These changes, which partly reflect the parallel sociocultural transformation of the average visitor, have led to a profound reorganization of the places involved, with consequent socio-economic and environmental impacts. While conserving the spiritual meaning of pilgrimage, sites of religious interest have adapted to the new visitors' needs by acquiring infrastructure and structures for providing transport (car parks, low-cost flights, coach lines), catering and accommodation for the pilgrims/tourists. The latter also generate demand for tourist goods (religious souvenirs, local food and craft products) and services (travel agencies, specialized tour operators). There is a proliferation of promotional activities (creation of foundations, tourism bourses) and complementary initiatives of a cultural nature (concerts, festivals, shows). These generate interest while consolidating and strengthening the image of the place, diversifying tourist demand with potential socio-economic effects on the region (Herrero *et al.*, 2009).

After briefly analysing the characteristics of visitors to holy places, this chapter explores the identity and role of large and small operators, both secular

*anna.trono@unisalento.it

© CAB International 2017. *Pilgrimage and Tourism to Holy Cities:*
Ideological and Management Perspectives (eds M. Leppäkari and K. Griffin)

and religious, in the organization of pilgrimages and the management of certain holy places in the Western world. It considers the benefits and the limits of the work they do, as well as the risks and opportunities that 'modern' pilgrimage offers the host regions, with reference to some of the most famous and popular European places of pilgrimage such as Pompeii and San Giovanni Rotondo, but also some smaller and less popular sites.

The 'Pious' Contemporary Pilgrim

The physiognomy and motivation of those who set off towards places of worship today are somewhat different from those of the Christian pilgrim who was such a significant figure in medieval culture.

The term *peregrinus* derives from the Latin verb *peragere* (i.e. *ire per agros*) meaning 'move restlessly, without pause' or 'bring to a conclusion'. Therefore the pilgrim is a foreigner or an exile. German and Spanish both use different terms – *Pilgerfahrt/ Wallfahrt* and *peregrinación/romería*, respectively – the difference between the terms lying in the distance to the destination, for example *wallfahrt* and *romería* refer to pilgrimage linked to local devotion and to sanctuaries reachable in a day's journey on foot (Vantaggiato, 2012). In the 11th and 12th centuries simple wandering gave way to journeys with a fixed destination (Caucci von Saucken, 1996), for reasons of asceticism, penitence or criminal justice (Lavarini, 1997; Vantaggiato, 2010). This reached its apogee in the 12th and 13th centuries, involving masses of believers, many of whom saw it as a means to gain social prestige.

The great epoch of Christian pilgrimage lasted until the end of the 14th century, by which time religious motives began to be accompanied by cultural ones. As European society began a process of secularization, pilgrims became simple travellers, thereby becoming, more or less unwittingly, the targets of commercial strategies in a market characterized by growing demand and public and private intervention with a view to fulfilling the potential of religious items as a resource for regional development.

Faith and the fascination with travel towards a holy place are as strong as ever and continue to move millions of people all over the world, devout and otherwise, who decide to set off in search of God or themselves or even out of simple curiosity. The motivations, like the methods, change over time, being closely linked to the subjective conditions of the pilgrim/tourist. They include the search for strong emotions or a feeling of ideological belonging, the desire to be together with others or to meet a charismatic religious leader, or the need to perform an act of faith or penitence. However, they also include the wish to learn about the region they are visiting.

In addition, a 'day-trip' approach to religious tourism is becoming increasingly popular. This combines religious aspects with recreational motives, sharing many features of organized tours, including more 'consumerist' behaviours on the part of the visitors, and a more limited commitment to religious rites (Rizzello, 2014). This is a mass-market form of journey, of a devotional nature, that takes the form of a short- or medium-range excursion, quick and simple, that may last a weekend or a day, undertaken by car or, more frequently, by coach. Composed of singles and families, animated by religious fervour, but also by a desire to get away from their daily routines (Cohen, 1979), these groups of pilgrims are organized and managed above all by religious bodies but also by a large number of private companies. With reference to the increasingly abundant literature on the differences between religious tourism and pilgrimage (Cohen, 1992; Smith, 1992; Rizzello and Trono, 2013; Damari and Mansfeld, 2014; Trono, 2014), this type of pilgrimage has not been extensively studied. However, it deserves attention, especially to its underlying intentions, the practices that distinguish it, and – crucially – the economic impact it has on holy places. A growing number of localities appear to be affected by this type of journey, which is often seen as a form of 'fast tourism' or 'hit-and-run tourism', always of brief duration and producing limited gains for the local community.

The Religious Tourism Market

While the modern pilgrim's reasons for travelling remain generally of a religious or spiritual nature, the objectives of those who organize and manage the journey are often more concrete and financial. Demand for visits to holy places is increasing but so are the possibilities on offer, provided by a broad and varied range of operators. Indeed, there is now a whole universe of companies attuned to the latest developments in the international tourism market, many characterized by exceptional competitiveness and ability to form strategic alliances with the key players in the sector, both public and private.

The ecclesiastical world is also becoming more able and effective, managing to perfectly combine Christian values and managerial needs, ideal principles and commercial practice. In line with the rules of the market, it efficiently organizes guides, travel reps and promoters. It has set up bodies (agencies, associations, co-operatives) that operate in the context of institutional relations, using tools that make it possible to act in the national and international tourism market. These organizations have an active presence in negotiation and marketing contexts such as trade fairs (i.e. Josp Fest, the pilgrimage festival), forums and tour operator bourses, which successfully conduct regional marketing, heighten information and communication and improve the efficiency and flexibility of services.

An Italian example of this is the leading role played by the CEI (the Italian Bishops Conference), whose national office, responsible for leisure, tourism and pilgrimage, operates on a regional level via the CER (Regional Bishops Conference) and on a local level via the dioceses and in some cases parishes, churches, oratories and sanctuaries. Another key player is the *Opera Romana Pellegrinaggi* (ORP), the Roman Pilgrimage Board, run by the Rome Vicariate, an organ of the Holy See, which depends directly on the Vicar General of Rome, appointed by the Pope. The ORP has been operating for 80 years with the declared aim of 'promoting and organizing pilgrimages and other initiatives of Christian piety towards the most famous places of religious, spiritual, ecumenical and cultural interest'. It provides accommodation services in Rome and elsewhere in Italy and assistance in Italy and abroad with religious and cultural itineraries and pilgrimages, supporting dioceses, parishes, public bodies, associations and religious institutes. By means of this specific 'pastoral service', the ORP operates as a significant tour operator in its own right, with its own commercial network. The organization of its religious journeys has been transformed over the years from an occasional activity to a regular service, from an improvised and modest cottage-industry operation to a fully-fledged service provider employing skilled professionals, just like a successful private company. It has begun a structural transformation in line with the new demand for travel; becoming specialized, adopting a quality tourism model that focuses on assistance, safety, tour guides, public relations and the negotiation of deals with hoteliers and all players involved in the success of the journey. In doing this, the ORP has succeeded in creating a very special combination of the sacred (pilgrimage) and the profane (professional, competitive, competent organization).

A myriad of players interact more or less directly with the religious world (confraternities, associations, foundations, etc.), offering complete services to pilgrims. Among others, worthy of particular mention here is UNITALSI (National Italian Union for the Transport of the Sick to Lourdes and International Sanctuaries), a Catholic association founded in 1903, dedicated to helping the sick, that works throughout Italy. With the contribution of volunteers, and benefiting from the cooperation of organizations specialized in religious journeys for the sick, it plans trips to the most famous holy places, paying careful attention to logistic details (accommodation in its own structures, high-quality services to pilgrims and medical assistance to the disabled).

There are many travel agencies and secular associations that cooperate with ecclesiastical bodies, from which they obtain operational and other indications enabling them to make sure that the product reflects the requirements of the individual parishes. They seek to interpret the fundamental features of the destination understood as a place of prayer and reflection that is not, however, cut off from modern, high-quality tourism designed to ensure the highest levels of comfort. The sector boasts numerous tour operators who are experts at intermediation, organization and consultancy in terms of holidays and pilgrimages. A broad range of visits to holy places of high artistic and cultural value (sanctuaries, convents, abbeys, hermitages, spiritual itineraries) is accompanied by a specialized offer linked to Christian saints' names (journeys to Marian, Franciscan, Pauline destinations, etc.). They offer fully-fledged package tours that can satisfy all types of demand and every client's request in accordance with the traditional formula of 'all inclusive': from guided excursions in the areas surrounding the site being visited to food and accommodation.

The market positioning of religious locations has adopted the same approach as regular tourist destinations, justified by the market and an effective demand which arises partly from their emotional appeal, linked to the place's reputation and the capacity for communicating the services offered (Ejarque, 2003; Shinde, 2007).

Indeed, along with the commercial opportunities and business that derive from it, religious tourism has enabled the creation of large-scale infrastructure while encouraging the use of commercial means of transport and accommodation structures. The billions of dollars' worth of business generated by the hundreds of millions of people who travel each year for religious motives benefits first and foremost hotels, which have shown great interest in a sector that is able to generate not only wealth but tourist flows even in the low season. Their number has grown significantly. In France, the number of hotels and hostels in Lourdes is second only to the capital, Paris. In Italy, where religious tourism has enjoyed growing success, with a total of 5.6 million visits (according to recent studies by the Istituto Nazionale Ricerche Turistiche (ISNART), the National Institute for Tourism Research), there are more than 800 religious accommodation structures (hotels, religious institutes, hostelries, holiday homes, monasteries and convents) (ISNART, 2012). These are found throughout the country but the highest concentrations are seen in the most famous holy places (Padova in the Veneto region, Assisi and Perugia in Umbria, Arezzo in Tuscany and Catania in Sicily), with the highest values in Rome (see Fig. 9.1).

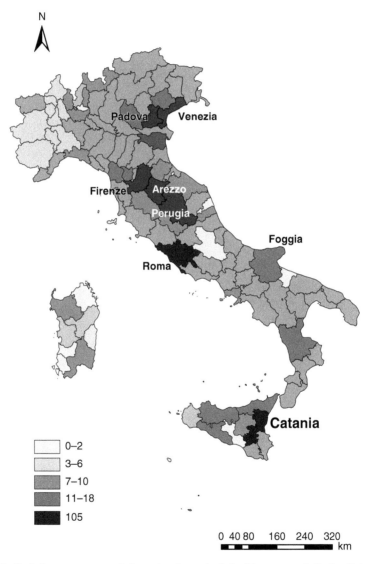

Fig. 9.1. Religious accommodation structures in Italy. (From www.istituti-religiosi.org. Presentation of data by Anna Trono.)

Business Factors in Holy Places

The focus on shrines and places of worship provides an opportunity to shed some light on the works of art, parks and other regional items of interest that transform the religious journey into cultural tourism[1] of interest to the traveller and a source of income for traders and anybody working in the field of tourism (guides, museums) as well as social and health services. In the cultural sector, the 'spirituality' associated with a holy place matches perfectly with the high symbolic density of the surrounding landscape, in which the well-informed traveller can read the complex stratification of regional and social history. For example, the evocative landscapes of Athos and Meteora, the two main holy sites of the Orthodox Christian world in Greece where the largest monastic communities still live, are a powerful magnet for thousands of pilgrims. However, they are also drawn by the uncontaminated and unique landscape, so spectacular that it has been included in UNESCO's list of World Heritage sites. The morphology of the terrain, the gorges, the images of immutability of a landscape still anchored to the historic moments of its geomorphological history, all provide a magnificent panorama of temporal scales. Indeed, they form a spectacle so exciting that travellers interviewed by Veronica Della Dora considered themselves to be '"tourists" as opposed to "pilgrims", because, they claimed, they were there "for the scenery", rather than to pray' (Della Dora, 2012, p. 967). Local tourist operators emphasize this factor above all others:

> Athos and (especially) Meteora's landscapes are commodities available for sale: one can 'consume' Athos' coastal landscape from the boat on organized trips around the peninsula, find Meteora's landscape for sale in souvenir shops, or simply as a hotel room extra – yes, because we do attach a price to landscape. The main attraction of Meteora's landscape is its unique monoliths. On Athos, by contrast, landscape is usually defined more in terms of pristinity than wonder. 'The landscape of Meteora is unique, you don't find it anywhere else', an Athonite monk said. 'That's why it gets mass tourism. By contrast, you can find Athos-like sceneries elsewhere in Greece.'
> (Della Dora, 2012, p. 964)

The situation is similar regarding pilgrimages to the Holy Land and Jerusalem, a place of faith, where tourism promotion emphasizes the historical legacy of its archaeological sites, its architecture and its cultural values. Tour operators often combine spiritual visits to the city with a tour of Israel, with stops in Tel Aviv, Jaffa, Caesarea, Haifa, Mount Carmel, Akko, Tiberias, Nazareth, Mount Tabor, Cana, the Sea of Galilee, Capernaum, the Valley of the Jordan, Bethlehem and the Dead Sea. Even Fatima (Portugal), one of the most highly developed European religious tourism sites and contemporary Christianity's main Marian pilgrimage destinations, represents an opportunity to promote nearby towns such as Nazaré, a typical fishing village, and Obidos, a splendid medieval city, known for its characteristic white and blue houses and its almost intact circuit of walls. The same may said of Santiago de Compostela (Spain), which has 16 tours in the Galicia region and the parks of Alamedam and Santo Domingo de Bonaval. In Pompeii (Italy) a visit to the Sanctuary of the Rosary (Fig. 9.2) is part of a larger itinerary that includes a visit to the archaeological site and the modern city.

Around the holy place other motives of an ethical, social and above all health character are also created, which enhance its attractiveness. An exemplary case is that of the Sanctuary of the Rosary of Pompeii, visited by about 2 million worshippers a year, who come on pilgrimage, especially in the Marian months (May and October), from the South of Italy and abroad (America, France, the UK, Germany, China, Poland). Most of the pilgrims (above all those who come on a week day) come from nearby municipalities, or in any case from the province of Naples, and on average they stay at the Sanctuary for 1 day, sometimes just a few hours, without having a strong economic impact on the local community. Pompeii, however, is known not just for being a Marian city but also and above all, ever since its origins, as a 'place of human promotion and social redemption, a laboratory of peace and a crossroads of cultures' (Mocerino, 2012, p. 3). Built in the second half of the 19th century (started in 1876 and inaugurated in 1887) on the initiative of a lay person of deep faith and generous ecclesiastical and social commitment (the blessed lawyer Bartolo Longo and his wife Countess Marianna Farnaro, the widow of De Fusco), the Sanctuary gave rise to the modern city of Pompeii, forming its original and initial urban segment.

Thanks to the couple's generous commitment, at the end of the 19th century, the Female Orphanage and the Hospice for the Children of Prisoners were opened. In addition to Marian devotion, today the Sanctuary of Pompeii is known for its extensive range of social and educational services for the weakest members of society. It provides accommodation for women in difficulty and minors from poor families or families affected by separation and divorce or problems of

Fig. 9.2. The Sanctuary of the Rosary in Pompeii. (From Anna Trono.)

Fig. 9.2. Continued.

drug addiction and alcoholism. Their accommodation is organized in accordance with a modern approach with an extensive range of social services (see Fig. 9.3). The Sanctuary also pays close attention to the needs of pilgrims: it does not offer them catering services, but areas they can use for eating their packed lunches. For example, the pilgrims are allowed to enter the *Casa del Pellegrino* (a few metres from the Sanctuary) to eat their meals. Medical assistance is usually provided by the

CISOM (Corpo Italiano di Soccorso dell'Ordine di Malta), the 'San Giuseppe Moscati' doctors association, the Italian Red Cross Pompeii committee, the Unitalsi – Pompeii section, and by the Confraternita di Misericordia di Pompeii, a confraternity.

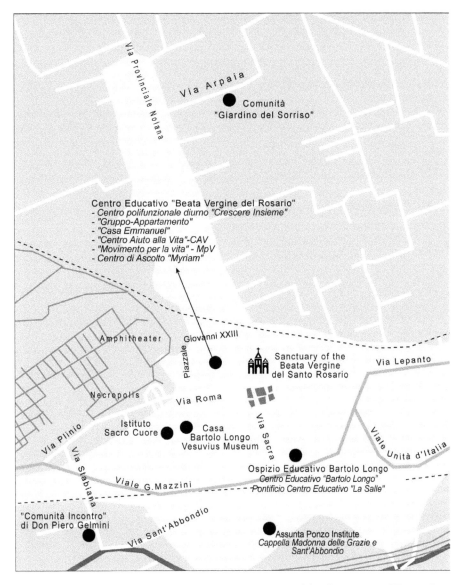

Fig. 9.3. Charity services in the pastoral commitment of the Sanctuary of Pompeii. (From Anna Trono.)

A considerable network of social and health activities is also based around the Church of San Giovanni Rotondo, a town on the Gargano peninsula in the Puglia region in southern Italy. It was here that San Pio da Pietrelcina, a Catholic priest of the Order of Friars Minor Capuchin lived and worked. San Pio (or Padre Pio as he is still widely known) is a striking example of a person who, while still alive, succeeded in attracting millions of followers due to his healing powers. The church is now the destination of an unceasing stream of pilgrims, making it one of the most frequently visited holy places not just in Italy but in the whole of Europe. Prayer groups inspired by Padre Pio have been formed throughout the world. The poor village of San Giovanni Rotondo, to whose tiny monastery the young Capuchin was sent during the First World War, has become a flourishing pilgrimage site. With millions of pilgrims a year, it competes with Jerusalem, Lourdes, Santiago de Compostela and the popular Bosnian sanctuary of Medjugorje, dedicated to the Madonna.

Linked to the monastery of the Capuchin Friars is the hospital called 'Casa Sollievo della Sofferenza' (Fig. 9.4), which Padre Pio hoped would alleviate the suffering of the sick and provide relief and hospitality to those in need of treatment. Conceived by Padre Pio in 1940 and inaugurated by him in 1956 with 250 beds, today it has 1200 beds and wards of all types, and is the best equipped hospital in the Italian Mezzogiorno. Offering a complete range of health services, the Centre has highly qualified personnel and modern and efficient equipment, guaranteeing its patients services of excellent quality. A few metres from the Convento di San Pio, the Casa Sollievo della Sofferenza and Nuova Chiesa (New Church) designed by Renzo Piano on the occasion of the Jubilee of 2000, is a centre for welcoming pilgrims, a structure managed by Capuchin Friars of the Monastic Province of 'Sant'Angelo e Padre Pio', which provides accommodation to families, organized groups and people with special needs.

Fig. 9.4. 'Casa Sollievo della Sofferenza' in San Giovanni Rotondo. (From Anna Trono.)

There is a wide range of alternative, non-religious attractions, including sport (golf, hiking, bicycle tours and other outdoor activities) and wellness activities. Spas, for example, are present in Spain in Santiago de Compostela and in Italy in Lanciano, a town in Abruzzo noted for the first recorded Eucharistic miracle in the history of the Catholic Church. This extraordinary miracle, which occurred in the 8th century in response to the doubts of a Basilian monk, involved the transformation of the Sacred Host into flesh and wine into blood. Every year it draws thousands of worshippers to the church of San Francesco, which conserves the relics in a monstrance of the Neapolitan school. In Oria, a small farming town in the province of Brindisi in southern Italy, next to the sanctuary of Saints Cosimo and Damiano, the object of mainly day-trip-type pilgrimage, there is even a zoo, built as a place of recreation for families and children.

Religious tourism is associated with many complementary activities of a cultural nature: from organized conferences and seminars to archives, libraries and museums, the latter housing not only the various *ex voto* donations (gold, silver, liturgical furnishings, tapestries, etc.), but also items of historic, artistic and scientific interest (natural history, medicine). In addition there are exhibitions, theatrical productions, concerts and festivals, all designed to consolidate and strengthen the image of the locality and enhance tourist flows (among others, for the rich cultural opportunities provided by Santiago de Compostela, see: http://www.santiagodicompostela.it; for Lourdes, see: http://www.francia.be/lourdes.html).

Last but not least, around the holy places a trade in all kinds of religious souvenirs and local products develops. This is driven not only by the pilgrim's awareness that he or she may not get another chance in the future to repeat the journey to the holy place, but also by the 'gifting culture', which induces travellers to purchase souvenirs for relatives and friends, who often have special requests to fulfil, which significantly amplifies the economic impact of each individual pilgrim. Often these are objects of symbolic value, but they can also be high-quality goods, such as the tapestries of Canterbury or the icons of the Pontifical Basilica of San Nicola in Bari, where one of the most popular souvenirs purchased from the Dominican fathers by the large numbers of Russian pilgrims who visit the basilica every year is the miraculous liquid of the 'Manna'. This is an 'almost pure water' that purportedly seeps from the bones of the saint. It is collected annually on the feast of the translation of the saint's relics, and is sold to the pilgrims in diluted form in small flasks (Rizzello, 2014, p. 334).

In small rural towns, devotional pilgrimage to a place of worship often involves a whole series of initiatives on the feast of the patron saint (religious rites, lights, food festivals, markets, brass band and folk music concerts). These activate a media circus (television, social networks, etc.), generating flows of visitors but also attracting public and private funding in the certainty that the feast of the saint enhances overall tourist flows and boosts regional development. Puglia Regional Administration, for example, allocates generous funding to the feast of Sant'Antonio Abate (Saint Anthony Abbot), which is celebrated annually on 17 January in Novoli, a small town in the Salento in Puglia, southern Italy. The celebrations actually last several days, involving a number of initiatives, including (in addition to the religious rite) the lighting of a monumental bonfire made of vine prunings, known as *La Fòcara*, and numerous cultural and recreational activities (a market, shows, conferences, brass band concerts and a popular music festival).

The Management of Holy Places

The spirit of pilgrimage has changed but so has the management of holy places, which must meet the pilgrims' new requirements without trivializing the religious motive or subordinating it to secular interests, considering that, as Myra Shackley points out:

> Visiting a sacred site should be an essentially spiritual experience, uncontaminated (as far as possible) by technical and commercial realities. Sacred sites should offer the attendee a window on infinity ... It is the task of sacred sites to manage the mysterious and reach for the sublime, while coping with the prosaic.
>
> (Shackley, 2001, p. xvii)

However, running the logistics of a holy place is no simple matter. The problem is that the discovery of religious tourism and the flow of public funding that promotes and fuels it have whetted a lot of appetites. The organization of pilgrimages to the most popular places of worship has activated a huge volume of business, sweetened by subliminal messages of peace and serenity of the spirit.

The Catholic Church itself discovered the benefits long ago! As early as the 1930s it understood the value of pilgrimage as a source of earnings, with the foundation of the Comitato Romano Pellegrinaggi, better known as the ORP (Opera Romana Pellegrinaggi meaning Roman Pilgrimage Board), which has also stipulated agreements with the Italian government and major economic players (Alitalia, Trenitalia, Meridiana and Confindustria). On the occasion of the Jubilee year of 2000, the ORP launched its own urban transport company (the yellow and white buses of Roma Cristiana) and signed commercial agreements with the City Council of Rome. One result of this was the Vatican Card, the first 'all inclusive' card that allowed pilgrims or simply tourists to use all means of public transport in the capital (buses, the metro, trams and the Roma-Ostia train line).

The increase in the number of pilgrims and tourists shows how the presence of a shrine can be a key factor in the promotion of tourism in the affected area, sometimes involving significant financial resources. For example, the tourism department of Abruzzo Regional Administration is currently allocating resources for the promotion of religious itineraries, places and events, both traditional and innovative, as are the Regional Administrations of Sicily and Calabria, where religious tourism, for which the turnover has risen in recent years to €180 million (Rutigliano, 2012) has received €7.2 million in funding for the creation of thematic religious tourist itineraries. Other examples include the institutional agreement stipulated between the Province of Benevento, the Municipality of Pietrelcina and Unitalsi (the main Catholic voluntary association in the shrines), which aims to promote the birthplace of San Pio da Pietrelcina in order to boost the flow of religious tourists, especially those who wish to stay for longer periods. The agreement also aims to: (i) increase and improve the accommodation for pilgrims, especially the disabled; (ii) design and build infrastructure that will improve the logistics and usability of the sites so as to enable disabled persons to stay there and move around freely; and (iii) design infrastructure that can facilitate the creation of pilgrimages via the use of trains.

In a society in which radical and arrogant secularism derides every instance of the sacred, in which money slowly but inexorably acquires ever more influence and everything is put on sale, the planning and management of holy places in accordance with a pragmatic and utilitarian logic seems perfectly legitimate and is permitted and/or accepted by both the secular and the religious worlds.

This point is clearly demonstrated by the incredible volume of business linked to the image and memory of Padre Pio in San Giovanni Rotondo, a town that has transformed its very modest local economy, mainly based on grazing and agriculture, into a major centre of services based on the image of the saint. The various forms of commercialization (including all sorts of goods purchasable online) described by reports and documentaries (including the docufiction film *Fan Pio*) and the various methods used to obtain donations even inside the religious structure itself represent an unpleasant blend of religion and marketing in which the sacred place plays a commercial rather than a spiritual role (Fig. 9.5).

Among the plethora of players and 'fixers', some of whom have close alliances with the world of politics, there are many who show great skill in intercepting lines of public funding and investment in the sector that will guarantee them a profit. The greed of those who seek only to make money while remaining indifferent to the supposedly spiritual character of pilgrimage is not improved by public-sector initiatives that are not based on rational regional marketing policies and are thus useless – if not actually damaging – for the community. An example is the 'Plan for measures regarding historical and religious destinations linked to the celebration of the Great Jubilee of 2000 in and outside Rome' (Law 270 of 7 August 1997), which led to a series of initiatives in San Giovanni Rotondo designed to increase the number of primary structures, such as hotels and hostels for pilgrims, in some cases even granting exemptions to the town planning rules. The consequence was a large amount of private investment and a huge increase in the number of accommodation structures (from five to six units in the 1960s to the current 166, with almost 8000 beds). Intended to host a projected multimillion population of pilgrims, by the time Padre Pio was canonized it was clear to all, not least the hotel operators, that such numbers would never be reached.

Conclusion

Undoubtedly, pilgrimage to holy places has many positive aspects but it also generates many negative impacts. Not only does it have substantial implications in sociological and anthropological terms due to its associated religious motivations, but it also goes some way to meeting the new needs of society, increasingly anxious to combine the equilibrium and serenity of the spirit with the need for physical and personal well-being. In addition, thanks to the tourist flows it attracts, it can have a strong economic impact in the regions involved, especially in the accommodation and trade sectors. It combines well with other tourist activities and is thus complementary to new types of tourism (for example linked to health and food-and-wine tourism) whose popularity is currently growing rapidly.

Religious tourism favours the creation of the organizational and communicative networks that are necessary if religious and cultural initiatives, commercial

Fig. 9.5. Advertising and fundraising inside the religious complex of San Giovanni Rotondo. (From Anna Trono.)

and craft activities, places of local culture, ethnographic museums and historic evidence are to be managed in a rational way. It involves not only famous places of worship but also less popular religious sites, 'slow regions' and marginal areas that have become depopulated, even though such places are frequently blessed with spectacular landscapes and networks of small ancient villages where there is still a strong emphasis on traditions, the environment and local culture. It is precisely these areas, however, that run the risk of becoming the object of speculative operations that have nothing to do with ethical/religious or cultural objectives and have little respect for local communities.

Pilgrimage to holy places represents an important source of income for many institutions and organizations, both secular and religious; it generates funding useful for the maintenance and restoration of the heritage items that are found in religious sites. Many such sites are not, however, able to host a large number of visitors and cannot meet the demand from those who seek to access the holy place for purely cultural reasons (e.g. Meteora and Mount Athos).

This intensifies the relationship between tourism and the location's actual conditions of environmental sustainability, mobility, accessibility and hospitality. It is a kind of tourism that conserves and values local diversity while using creative spaces and new technologies, but also raises issues of sustainability, since it poses the problem of the personalization of the tourist offer, considering both the culture of the visitor and the culture of the local population.

It is clear, however, that the 'added value' of a holy place needs to be identified and preserved, organically recovering and rethinking the local culture in terms of its specificity and its capacity for engagement with new cultures. Learning how to manage resources linked to religious tourism in a truly sustainable way is obviously in the interest of all. What is needed therefore is the participation of all local stakeholders, both secular and religious, in accordance with an intelligent and harmonious approach to planning and management. As Lo Presti points out, 'it is not about inventing new sales or religious marketing formulae but about providing new opportunities for experience, knowledge and popular religiosity on the ancient paths of faith and tradition' (Lo Presti, 2011, p. 666).

Those responsible for planning and managing a holy place have set themselves a serious task: that of tackling the needs of the various market segments, considering that they are dealing with a holy place and not a simple tourist site, and that the spiritual experience is fundamental for those who visit it.

Note

[1] There is considerable difficulty in obtaining reliable data on this subject, considering the variety of motives for visiting a place, which may be either essentially cultural or essentially religious, or cultural and religious in equal measure. A recent survey of religious tourism in Italy by ISNART found religious motive to be the main reason for travelling for the vast majority of religious tourists (71.9%), with 37% saying they also intended to participate in events of a spiritual nature, and 42.4% saying they were also drawn by cultural heritage, often associated with religious sites (ISNART, 2012).

References

Belhassen, Y., Caton, K. and Stewart, W.P. (2008) The search for authenticity in the pilgrim experience. *Annals of Tourism Research* 35(3), 668–689.

Caucci von Saucken, P. (1996) Le distanze del pellegrinaggio medievale. Spazi, tempi, misure e percorsi nell'Europa del Basso medioevo. In: *Atti del XXXII Convegno Storico Internazionale* (Todi, 8–11 ottobre 1995). Centro Italiano di Studi sul Basso Medioevo, Spoleto, Italy, pp. 297–315.

Cohen, E. (1979) A phenomenology of tourist experiences. *Sociology* 132, 179–201.

Cohen, E. (1992) Pilgrimage centres: concentric and excentric. *Annals of Tourism Research* 19(1), 33–50.

Damari, C. and Mansfeld, Y. (2014) Reflections on pilgrims' identity, role and interplay with the pilgrimage environment. *Current Issues in Tourism* 2014, 1–24.

Della Dora, V. (2012) Setting and blurring boundaries: pilgrims, tourists and landscape in Mount Athos and Meteora. *Annals of Tourism Research* 39(2), 951–974.

Ejarque, J. (2003) *La Destinazione Turistica di Successo*. Hoepli, Milano, Italy.

Herrero, L.C., Sanz, J.A. and Devesa, M. (2009) Who pays more for a cultural religious festival? A case study in Santiago De Compostela. In: Trono, A. (ed.) *Tourism, Religion and Culture: Regional Development through Meaningful Tourism Experiences*. Proceedings of the International Conference, Lecce, Poggiardo 27–29 October 2009. Mario Congedo Editore, Galatina (Le), Italy, pp. 443–464.

Istituto Nazionale Ricerche Turistiche (ISNART) (2012) Tutti i numeri del turismo religioso: chi sono e come spendono i Pellegrini. *Impresa Turismo*, November 2012. Available at: http://www.impresaturismo.it (accessed 15 May 2016).

Lavarini, R. (1997) *Il Pellegrinaggio Cristiano. Dalle Sue Origini al Turismo Religioso del XX Secolo*, 1st edn. Casa Editrice Marietti S.p.a., Genova, Italy.

Lo Presti, O. (2011) Il turismo fattore attrattivo dello sviluppo locale. In: Becheri, E. and Magiore, G. (eds) *Rapporto sul Turismo Italiano 2010–2011*. Franco Angeli, Milano, Italy, pp. 661–671.

Mocerino, P. (2012) *Beato Bartolo Longo. L'uomo della Madonna*. Editrice VELAR, Torino, Italy.

Rizzello, K. (2014) Pellegrinaggio e turismo spirituale: occasione di sviluppo per la città di Bari. In: Trono, A., Leo Imperiale, M. and Marella, G. (eds) *In Viaggio verso Gerusalemme. Culture, Economie e Territori (Walking Towards Jerusalem. Cultures, Economies and Territories)*. Mario Congedo, Galatina, Italy, pp. 327–337.

Rizzello, K. and Trono, A. (2013) The pilgrimage to the San Nicola shrine in Bari and its impact. *International Journal of Religious Tourism and Pilgrimage* 1(1), 24–40.

Rutigliano, V. (2012) Sempre alto l'interesse per i centri spirituali. *Il Sole 24 Ore* 26 October.

Shackley, M. (2001) *Managing Sacred Sites. Service Provision and Visitor Experience*. Thompson, London.

Shinde, K.A. (2007) Pilgrimage and environment: challenger in a pilgrimage centre. *Current Issues in Tourism* 10(4), 343–365.

Smith, V.L. (1992) Introduction: the quest in guest. *Annals of Tourism Research* 19(1), 1–17.

Trono, A. (2014) Cultural and religious routes: a new opportunity for regional development. In: Lois-González, R.C., Santos-Solla, X.M. and Taboada-de-Zúñiga, P. (eds) *New Tourism in the 21st Century: Culture, the City, Nature and Spirituality*. Cambridge Scholars Publishing, Cambridge, pp. 5–25.

Vantaggiato, L. (2010) *Pellegrinaggi Giudiziari. Dalla Fiandra a San Nicola di Bari, a Santiago di Compostella e ad altri santuari (secc. XIV–XV)*. Edizioni Compostellane, Perugia-Pomigliano d'Arco, Italy.

Vantaggiato, L. (2012) Un contributo alla geografia del pellegrinaggio medievale. In: Trono, A. (ed.) *Via Francigena. Cammini di Fede e Turismo Culturale*. Mario Congedo Editore, Galatina (Lecce), Italy, pp. 111–113.

10 Protestants and Pilgrimages: The Protestant Infrastructure in Jerusalem

YAAKOV ARIEL*

University of North Carolina at Chapel Hill, Chapel Hill, USA

Introduction

In 1889, William Blackstone, a Protestant premillennial activist, travelled from Chicago to Jerusalem. Certain that Jerusalem was the focal point for what he saw as the impending End-of-Time events, Blackstone investigated the topography of the city in relation to biblical prophecies. He also paid attention to demographic and economic developments, interpreting what he saw in line with his Messianic faith (Blackstone, 1892). Encouraged by his visit, Blackstone came up, on his return, with global initiatives that were intended to bring the Jews back to Palestine in preparation for the End-of-Times events (Ariel, 1991).

Blackstone was one of a long series of Protestant devotees, mostly Evangelicals and Pietists, who came to Jerusalem on short- or long-term pilgrimages, and found meaning and inspiration in the city where Jesus preached, suffered, died and rose from the dead, and to which, many of them believed, he was about to return. In their turn, such pilgrims have affected Jerusalem and Palestine at large in meaningful ways, developing infrastructures that helped transform the place and enlarged the opportunities the city has come to offer Christian visitors as well as local inhabitants (Ariel, 2010). Many of the Protestant endeavours were intended to accommodate pilgrims, provide a large variety of services and enable visitors to connect more effectively with local communities.

Exploring the institutions which such Protestants established to accommodate and encourage pilgrimage offers an opportunity to look at relatively neglected aspects of Protestant attitudes towards the Holy Land and its populations, as well as the priorities and agendas of Evangelicals and Pietists when visiting, exploring and investing in a city that they often viewed as an historical, spiritual and

*yariel@email.unc.edu

eschatological ground zero. Such investigation can also reveal specific Protestant manners of reading and understanding the Old and New Testaments, and point to Messianic hopes that motivated much of the pilgrims' interest and zeal.

A Protestant Holy Land?

Protestants arrived in Palestine relatively late. In theory, the Protestant segment of Christianity did not recognize the concept of holy spaces and sites. Protestants had rejected shrines, relics and pilgrimages. Between the 16th and 18th centuries very few Protestants took pilgrimages to the Holy Land, or *Terra Sancta*, as it was known to Catholics, who, like their Orthodox and Monophysite counterparts, kept their interest in Palestine alive. Catholicism had been represented in the country by faithful local communities of adherents, whose presence went back to Crusader rule in the 12th and 13th centuries. European powers helped in the church's struggle to maintain Catholic rights in spaces sacred to the faith, especially the Holy Sepulchre in Jerusalem and the Church of the Nativity in Bethlehem (Cohen, 2009). The Franciscan order was entrusted with being the 'custodian', overseeing Catholic activity, running churches and operating hostels for pilgrims. Until the early 19th century, Protestants had neither institutions nor local communities that could offer them an infrastructure ready to host and offer services to pilgrims. For lack of other alternatives, early Protestant visitors often chose to stay in Catholic institutions, such as the Franciscan San Salvador monastery and pilgrims' center in Jerusalem.

The Protestant relationship with Jerusalem and the Holy Land changed dramatically in the 19th century, coming to resemble that of Catholic, Orthodox and Monophysite Christians (Ben-Arieh, 1977). Protestants occasionally took interest in, and took pilgrimages to, other historical sites, such as Wittenberg where Luther started his Protest, but Palestine and Jerusalem were different – associated both with the Old and the New Testaments, with Jesus' life and ministry, and with the Messianic hope for his return and the establishment of the Kingdom of God on earth. Moreover, attachment to the Holy Land was not restricted to just one brand of Protestants: Lutherans, Anglicans, Presbyterians and Baptists, to mention just a few examples, have all been fascinated by the place, its history, sites and peoples. Protestants have been active in various sites in Palestine, however, unlike Catholics, Orthodox and Monophysite churches that have established extensive strongholds in places such as Bethlehem or Mount Tabor, Protestant interest in locales outside of Jerusalem has not been as strong. While most Protestants have not related to Jerusalem as the Holy City, they have devoted the largest share of their hopes, engagement and resources in Jerusalem.

Between the 1830s and the 1840s, when the first long-lasting Protestant institutions opened in Jerusalem and the turn of the 20th century, dozens of Protestant groups and hundreds of individuals turned Palestine in general and Jerusalem in particular into a focal point of pilgrimage, exploration and welfare, competing with other Christian groups for visibility and prominence (Schur, 1988). The change in Protestant attitudes and presence reflects internal developments in Protestant thought and agendas as well as new external realities that allowed for and encouraged Protestants to invest resources and efforts in the Holy Land.

Western interest in Palestine grew considerably in the early decades of the 19th century, with world powers paying greater attention to that land. In the wake of the Napoleonic wars, Protestant countries, such as Britain, became more involved in the Mediterranean world and the Middle East, and thus, initiated measures to protect and encourage travellers to a country that became more important and meaningful than before (Bar Yosef, 2005). Palestine became more accessible as Protestant power gained more standing in the Ottoman Empire and could ensure more respect for citizens who were visiting the area. Political and religious motivations intermingled at times. Influenced by Protestant Reformed, Pietist and Evangelical faiths and values, as well as missionary agendas, Protestant powers, including Prussia and Britain, were willing to invest in creating an infrastructure for pilgrims in the Holy Land.

Motivated by their attachment to biblical narratives, and, at times, Messianic faith, and encouraged by the growth in security and accommodation facilities, Protestants began arriving as tourists, missionaries, explorers of the land, biblical scholars, archaeologists, artists and diplomats. By the turn of the 20th century tens of thousands of Protestants had gone on pilgrimage to the Holy Land, a term they have come to embrace. Hundreds wrote travelogues and thousands settled, for longer or shorter durations, in the country, many of them in Jerusalem. Dozens of Protestant denominations and societies sent representatives to the city, establishing hospices for pilgrims, hospitals, schools, cemeteries and at times residential neighbourhoods and economic enterprises, often directed to serve the needs of pilgrims. As Western powers began looking upon the Holy Land as an important arena of geopolitical influence, they were willing to sponsor and often actively encourage religious activities and the building of infrastructure for pilgrims there.

Among the most active proponents were Messianically oriented Evangelical and Pietist Protestants, who related to Jerusalem as the place where the great events of the End Times were about to take place. They often came to the city wishing to affect the realities of the place and leave their mark on its infrastructure.

Early Protestants in Jerusalem

When Blackstone arrived in Jerusalem, he encountered a diverse and vibrant presence of Protestants in the city. By the 1880s, Jerusalem attracted a series of Evangelical and Pietist groups. The first among them began arriving in the 1830s–1840s when British Evangelicals and German Pietists established missionary stations and a united bishopric, as well as consulates to protect Protestant activity and promote economic and political interests. This was a particular moment in the history of Prussian Pietists and British Evangelicals whose influence on the ruling elites in their respective countries reached a zenith. They were thus able to bring their governments to support the establishment or the strengthening of their institutions in Palestine. This Prussian and British diplomatic and religious presence provided security and served as a catalyst and an example to other Protestants who continued arriving in the city.

The London Society for Promoting Christianity among the Jews established a compound near the Jaffa Gate in the old city of Jerusalem, as well as a hospital and school on the western slope of Mount Zion, outside the city walls. Constructed with the help of Maltese masons, the chapel, Christ Church, gave evidence to the attitudes of Evangelical missionaries towards the Jews. Devoid of iconographic representation of any kind, it was designed to resemble a synagogue. The audience sat facing east, towards the Temple Mount (Ariel, 2013). The eastern wall was decorated with a semblance of the Arc of the Covenant, complete with Hebrew inscriptions on wooden tablets listing the Ten Commandments. The compound included homes for members of the society and visitors. As the number of pilgrims grew as well as the number of local enterprises and communities, the Church of England established, in the early 20th century, a cathedral, named in honour of Saint George, on Nablus Road. This centre also included a hospice for pilgrims and a school.

German Lutherans also strengthened their presence. Establishing their first pilgrims' centre in the Old City of Jerusalem in the 1860s, at the turn of the 20th century they created, among other institutions, a particularly large pilgrims' centre on the Mount of Olives, the *Kaiserin Auguste Viktoria Stiftung*, as well as a large church, a school and a tower in the Muristan, near the Holy Sepulchre, inside the city walls. By that time, Britain and Germany were competing over their influence in the Holy Land and the respective governments were lavishly backing initiatives of their citizens in the country. Pilgrimage centres became assets, representing their countries' ambitions. Queen Victoria, perhaps symbolically, contributed a baptistery to Saint George's Cathedral. In his turn, her grandson, the German emperor, set out on a pilgrimage of the Holy Land, visiting German enterprises and meeting with German residents of the land, signalling a German imperial promotion of pilgrimage to Jerusalem and the Holy Land. As historians of Jerusalem have noted, the resources Western institutions have poured into the city affected its topography as more and more buildings were built or rehabilitated and more facilities greeted arriving pilgrims (Ben-Arieh, 1977). The growing Protestant infrastructure also affected the local populations, the material realities they came to live in, the educational and medical opportunities available to them and their encounters with European and American cultures and languages.

Numerous Protestant groups sent emissaries to Jerusalem to maintain the new posts, propagate the Gospel and serve as representatives of their faiths, cultures and agendas. One noted group was the London Society. By the 1840s, the society was fully Anglican, although the mission's theology and outreach messages mostly represented the Evangelical and premillennialist sections in the church. One of the more gifted members of the mission was actually the German-born Conrad Schick (1822–1901), who left his mark on the city and its environs as an archaeologist and an architect. Schick initially came to Jerusalem in 1846 as an emissary of the Swiss *Pilgermission St. Chrischona*, but transferred to the more experienced and affluent London Society. The English mission allowed Schick ample time to pursue his archaeological and architectural endeavours.

Schick designed a number of the newly established Protestant institutions in the city: schools, orphanages, hospitals and hospices. His style combined local architectural traditions, manifested by building with stone and the usage of arches and round roofs, together with the German neo-Gothic, a synthesis that made his buildings exceptional. William Blackstone took special interest in Schick's work. Like Blackstone, Schick researched the topography of ancient Jerusalem and, among other projects, had built a model of the Temple.

Schick was not alone. A series of long- and short-term Protestant pilgrims, among them writers, artists, explorers, missionaries, educators and physicians holding to a biblical-Messianic vision, created their own sociocultural and religious circle in Jerusalem. One example of long-term pilgrims, who took interest in the city and its people beyond the official call of duty, were the British consul and his wife, James and Elizabeth Finn. Motivated by a premillennialist Messianic faith, they too left their mark on the topography and economic life of the city.

Elizabeth was the daughter of Alexander McCaul, a premillennialist missionary and theologian of the London Society. Like McCaul, the Finns considered the Jews to be heirs and continuers of historical Israel and a people who were destined to revive their position as God's first nation. Arriving in Jerusalem in 1845, Finn used his position as consul to protect Jews and offer assistance when they got into trouble, either with the authorities or members of other communities. The Finns also sponsored projects that aimed at helping Jews acquire skills and livelihoods as well as settle the land. Among other endeavours, they facilitated the purchase of lands along the road from Jerusalem to Jaffa, where a number of Jews established an agricultural village, Mottza, which included an inn for pilgrims. The couple also took interest in the Arab community, with the counsel settling disputes within the local communities, and Elizabeth writing ethnographic studies of Arabs and other groups in Palestine (Finn and Finn, 1878). Almost needless to state, they offered hospitality and protection to a long stream of Protestant visitors who came to explore the city, among them the Prince of Wales, the future Edward VII, who visited the country in 1862.

Another early, long-term pilgrim was William Hunt, one of England's noted pre-Raphaelite painters. Arriving in Jerusalem in 1854, Hunt lived on the Prophet's Road outside the city's walls. The Messianically inclined painter resided in the city intermittently for a few years, not turning Jerusalem into his home, but rather a source of inspiration (Daly, 1989). His Palestinian-era art gave expression to his biblical Messianic outlook. One set of paintings focused on the scapegoat mentioned in the Old Testament and its role in bringing about human redemption. The goat in Hunt's paintings represents Jesus, ready to be sacrificed in order to atone for the sins of humanity. The scapegoat is white, symbolizing his total innocence, and dignified, even regal, with a red imperial crown on his head. Accepting his suffering without resentment, he is the true king of the Jews, and during the Messianic age he will turn into the ruler of the entire planet.

Protestant pilgrims, such as Schick, Finn and Hunt, were able to maintain their peace of mind and give expression to their gifts in a socially accepted manner. For them the liminal state of pilgrimage, which Victor Turner has strongly emphasized, was only marginally correct. For some Protestant pilgrims, however, the encounter with Jerusalem stirred unexpected emotions and expectations. The term *the Jerusalem syndrome* had not yet been coined, but the symptoms were already apparent during the 19th century. The scientist, traveller and author Ada Goodrich-Freer describes an almost surreal scene among Protestants in

Jerusalem. Well versed in the biblical narratives, and often expecting the Messiah to arrive, many mistook themselves for biblical figures or would daily await the return of Jesus. She offers a colourful description:

> On the north of the Holy City is the settlement of the American Colony, commonly known for their founder Spaffordites, on the south that of the Templars or Hofmannites, both societies admirable for their order and their industry, if somewhat creative in theological opinions. On the west we have the immense ruin of the unfinished building in which, half a century ago, some wealthy lady ... proposed to house the hundred and forty and four thousand ... To the east, we have the Mount of Olives, geographically the rallying-place of an extraordinary variety of enthusiasts, including a worthy Englishwoman who is ... in constant readiness to welcome our Lord's return thither with a cup of tea ... We have a colony profanely known as the Tishbites – English and American – presided over by 'the prophet Elijah.' Scarcely a year goes by without the arrival of someone who dares to assume a personality still more sacred.

(Goodrich-Freer, 1904, p. 80)

As the passage signifies, Protestants either brought with them or developed in Jerusalem a sense of Messianic anticipation that coloured their experience in the city.

American Protestant Pilgrims

American Protestants had already shown up in Jerusalem in the 1820s, but it was only in later decades that they began to create their own infrastructure in the city, including a consulate, missionary posts, churches, guest houses for pilgrims, schools, tourist shops and tourist agencies. These American individuals and groups often enlarged the infrastructure available to pilgrims in the city.

One such group of American Evangelicals, who arrived as pilgrims and served as hosts to other visitors, was the 'American Colony' or as Goodrich-Freer called them, the Spaffordites. Settling in Jerusalem in the early 1880s, the group started with a handful of families and individuals from Chicago, and grew within a few years into a major presence in Jerusalem, influencing the economic life and social welfare of the city. The first leader of the community, Horatio Spafford (1827–1888) was a businessman and lawyer who became dedicated to urban revivalism. During the 1860s, Horatio and his wife Anna were among a number of Evangelicals in the commercial classes in Chicago who adopted the dispensational premillennialist faith and became convinced of Jesus' imminent return. The Spaffords also became followers of the Holiness movement, viewing the current era, the period preceding the Messianic age, as a time of outpouring of the Holy Spirit. In 1874, the Spaffords encountered a tragedy. En route to vacation in Europe, Anna and the couple's four daughters sailed on the passenger ship *Ville du Havre*, which sank and the four children drowned. In 1880 the Spaffords' son, born after the *Ville du Havre* tragedy, died of scarlet fever. The bereaved couple came to believe in universal salvation, claiming that there was no hell and that children in particular would not suffer eternally. They gathered a small group of relatives and friends around them that became a religious community of its own.

The Spaffords considered their journey to Jerusalem in 1881 to be a pilgrimage, explained in spiritual, moral and Messianic terms.

Like other Evangelicals who came to Jerusalem, they hoped that the city where Jesus had taught and suffered, and to which they believed he would soon return, would have a profound effect on their spiritual well-being, and they were convinced that they had a role to play in the millennial scheme. Anna Spafford described the group's motivation: 'We wished to go there when God brought the Jews back; we wanted to see the prophecies fulfilled' (Spafford, 1895, quoted in Ariel and Kark, 1996). The Spaffords and their friends decided to live a communal life similar to that described in Acts, with property held in common. At first they settled in the Muslim Quarter of the Old City and took daily walks to the Mount of Olives, where they expected Jesus and his saints to arrive imminently. The community also practised sexual abstinence. Men and women lived in separate quarters, and for over two decades there were no marriages in the group. Ada Goodrich-Freer explained its 'condition of chastity as giving up on earthly love for the sake of the love of God' (Goodrich-Freer, 1904). For Protestants visiting Jerusalem, the community offered hospitality as well as serving as an attraction in its own right.

After Horatio Spafford's death in 1888, his wife Anna became the spiritual leader of the community, whose members considered her to hold charismatic powers. Anna abandoned Universalist convictions and adopted understandings of perfect life, sin and death more in line with standard Holiness teachings. She considered the Colony to be the biblical 'Bride' awaiting reunion with God and saw its mission as setting an example of love, purity and peace. The Colony carried out extensive welfare and medical work, which reached a peak during World War I.

A Swedish American Evangelical group from Chicago headed by Olof Larson (1842–1919) decided to join the American group in Jerusalem. In 1889, Larson held revival meetings in Dalarna, in central Sweden, and established a local community there as well. The Swedish Nobel Prize laureate Selma Lagerlöf provided a lively description of the rise of this Evangelical group of farmers and artisans and their eventual immigration to Jerusalem (Lagerlöf, 1915). The group believed that Jesus was returning soon and that true Christians would meet him upon his arrival in Jerusalem. In 1895, Anna Spafford visited Chicago, met Larson's group, and the groups in Chicago and Dalarna decided to move to Jerusalem and join the Americans.

The Colony, which now numbered more than 150 people, moved from the Muslim Quarter to a compound in Nablus Road, which in the 1890s was not yet a densely built-up urban area, and the American–Swedish Colony could develop both urban commercial enterprises and agricultural ones. These included a dairy farm, a bakery, a furniture shop, a guest house, a tourist shop and a photography studio, becoming a major economic and charitable organization in Jerusalem.

While the group encountered opposition within the local Protestant community, Holiness groups and individuals more easily accepted the ideas and religious practices of the Colony. Evangelists, such as William Blackstone and Dwight Moody, paid visits to the Colony. Likewise, friendships developed between the Colony and other Holiness groups in Jerusalem, such as the Christian and Missionary Alliance. This missionary organization, founded in 1888 by

A.B. Simpson, had accepted premillennialist and Holiness teachings and its leaders in Jerusalem became friendly with the Colony's leaders and sent their children to the Colony's school. The British general Charles 'Chinese' Gordon, an ardent Evangelical and premillennialist, befriended the Spaffords and lived in the Colony for a time during his visit to Jerusalem (1882–1883). Among Gordon's ventures in Jerusalem was the excavation of the Garden Tomb, which he and Evangelicals ever since have identified with Jesus's burial site. The place became a Protestant pilgrimage site. Catholic, Orthodox and Monophysite churches have their own traditional site of Jesus's tomb, the Holy Sepulchre, but thousands of Evangelicals have visited the Garden Tomb during their pilgrimages to Jerusalem. Excavations and the opening of historical sites were part of the infrastructure that Protestant explorers created for incoming pilgrims, thus enlarging and enriching the scope of attractions and points of interest.

While the American Colony as a religious commune disbanded half a century after its establishment, its influence on all spheres of life in the city, from pilgrimage to education, was remarkable. In this it was not alone: other Evangelical groups and individuals also left their mark on the city. In the 1880s–1890s, a number of Holiness churches, including the Church of the Nazarene and the Christian and Missionary Alliance, established congregations, educational enterprises and guest houses. The Christian and Missionary Alliance built a tin roofed 'Tabernacle' in the Prophet's Road in 1890 and in 1908 a large stone church and a guest house for pilgrims. These constructions, in two different compounds, offered more than statements of denominational and missionary presence. They signified to potential visitors that they could rely on solid and welcoming communities of compatriots and fellowships of people who shared the same faith.

By the turn of the 20th century, Protestant pilgrimages became more systematized. The region was now connected to Western Europe and North America by steamboats and railways. Commercial companies, such as Thomas Cook, which served Protestant clientele, began offering tour packages in the Holy Land, often in conjunction with visits to other countries associated with the Christian biblical world, such as Greece. Starting in 1869, these tours on horses or camels were intended for no more than a handful of pilgrims in each group. The company relied on Protestant agents operating in the country. Here again, recently arrived and often temporary, Protestant residents of the country proved to be pivotal for the building and running of pilgrimage infrastructure. Herbert Clark and Rolla Floyd, members of the defunct American messianic colony in Jaffa became two such early representatives and tourist guides, facilitating the pilgrimages of dignitaries, such as Ulysses Grant in 1871. A lively description of such pilgrimages is provided by Mark Twain in *The Innocents Abroad* (Twain, 1869). Twain, as could be expected, deviated from the standard genre of Protestant travelogues. Devoid of piety or spiritual yearning, the American author was not an enthusiastic pilgrim. He did not like the country and found fault with what he considered to be a misguided attempt to follow in the footsteps of Jesus. His was a minority opinion. Hundreds of Protestants wrote favourably about their travel experiences. Starting in 1876, the German Protestant Karl Baedeker published guides to the Holy Land that enjoyed great popularity (Baedeker, 1876).

Following World War I and Towards a Jewish State

World War I brought an era to an end. During the war years Protestant pilgrimages came to a halt and many Protestant representatives had to leave the country as the Ottomans considered them to be agents of hostile powers. The extended personnel of British and American missions that operated and supervised much of the infrastructure to serve pilgrims had to go home. Amazingly, women often stayed behind, watching over and keeping some of the infrastructure intact, while men, who feared arrest, left. When the British took over the country in 1917–1918, realities reversed. The conquering British rounded up German Protestants and interred them in Egypt.

These difficulties and others aside, the British rule of the country proved beneficial to the Protestant infrastructure in the country. A number of Protestant groups took advantage of British rule to establish or enlarge their presence in the country. In the interwar years, the Young Men's Christian Association (YMCA) established a major centre in Jerusalem, complete with an auditorium, sports facilities, a library, educational classes and a large guest house intended for pilgrims. The Church of Scotland had established missionary posts, medical facilities and pilgrimage hospices in Tzfat and Tiberias before World War I. Now it established a new compound in Jerusalem, which included a church, dedicated to St Andrew, as well as a lively guest house. Many Protestant pilgrims continued to take advantage of the extensive infrastructure awaiting them in the country. Especially in Jerusalem they could choose between numerous Protestant hospices and guest houses, many of which are still in operation. But gradually pilgrims could choose to stay in privately owned hotels, such as King David, which was built during the period. An alternative infrastructure of Arab and Jewish commercial enterprises came to intermingle with and complement the Protestant infrastructure, although many Protestant pilgrims still felt more at home in Protestant institutions.

During the British period, more Protestant denominations established posts in the country. This included the Southern Baptists, who after World War I built one of the largest Evangelical networks in Palestine, attracting Arabs and Jews to their congregations, as well as Americans and members of other nations who stayed temporarily in the country. In the 1920s and 1930s, a number of Pentecostal groups established congregations or missions in Palestine, including followers of Aimee Semple McPherson's Four Square Gospel (Newberg, 2012). Such Evangelicals often looked upon the Jews as a special people who were building a commonwealth that would serve as precursor to Christ's kingdom. Fascination with the country and its people would continue through the years, with new waves of Evangelical activists arriving after the birth of the State of Israel in 1948 (Ariel, 2000).

The war between Jews and Arabs, which lasted from November 1947 to January 1949, left many Protestant institutions in the Holy Land vulnerable, if not paralysed. The division of British Palestine and its capital, Jerusalem, into two separate political zones, one Jordanian, the other Israeli, challenged Protestant infrastructure. Under the British rule of Palestine, Christian churches in general, and Protestant activities in particular, enjoyed the government's full protection, if not outright encouragement. Protestants were now worried that the end of

British rule would give rise to anti-missionary or even anti-Christian sentiments and that Jews or Arabs might harass or attack converts to Christianity. Gershon Nerel, a historian of Messianic Judaism, has concluded that such worries were exaggerated, if not completely unwarranted (Nerel, 2009, 2014). Still, the London Jews' Society (originally the London Society for Promoting Christianity among the Jews) initiated, in the spring of 1948, in cooperation with the British government and the British army in Palestine, an evacuation plan for Christian Jewish residents, Operation Mercy.

After the birth of Israel, Pietists and Evangelicals who were invested spiritually in the country and held an extensive infrastructure there, observed the young Jewish state both in an attempt to interpret its significance for the advancement of God's plans and to determine if their operations could continue intact. They were not enthusiastic about the secular character of the Israeli government and culture, and they wanted more freedom within Israeli society to propagate their messages. However, many of the things they saw filled them with hope, as they meshed well with their Messianic expectations. The mass immigration of Jews to Israel in the late 1940s and 1950s from many parts of the world, including Asian, African and East European countries, was one cause for encouragement. In Evangelical opinion, this was a significant development, one that had been prophesied in the Bible. While the political changes upset pilgrimage plans, at least for a while, the establishment of the new state served as an additional incentive for Protestants to visit the land.

The new state allowed Protestants to maintain their infrastructure, pursue their work and guaranteed freedom of worship, although they had to re-group and re-orient their work and efforts. One Protestant activist who succeeded in building close relations with Israelis and worked to enlarge the Evangelical presence and the pilgrims' infrastructure in the country was Robert Lindsey, leader of the Southern Baptist community in Israel from the 1940s to the 1970s. A scholar of the New Testament, Lindsey founded a new school of New Testament Studies, which consisted of the very unlikely match of Evangelical Christians and Orthodox Jews. The Evangelical and Jewish scholars were interested in comparing the Gospels with Jewish teaching of the period, claiming that Jesus' message was not very different from that of Jewish sages of His time. Lindsey and other Baptist representatives also built working relationships with the Canaanites, a group of secular Jews that demanded the separation of synagogue and state, a topic on which they found a common language with Baptists.

The Baptists wished to propagate Christianity among members of the country's social, political and cultural elite and built their centres in fashionable areas of Israeli cities, such as Rehavia in Jerusalem and Dizingof Street in Tel Aviv. They opened a series of bookshops in Israeli cities, promoting Evangelical literature alongside books and albums intended for Christian pilgrims. Lindsey sat on an Israeli government board and helped design special medals for Christian pilgrims. His understanding of the Jewish people and their role in history was Messianic and very similar to that of dispensationalist premillennialists. For him, the Jews were the chosen people, and he believed God's promises for the rejuvenation of Israel in its land to be valid. The Jews, he was convinced, needed to convert to Christianity and accept Jesus before they could be fully rehabilitated. Under Lindsey's leadership, the Baptists built a large convention and retreat centre near Tel Aviv, which has since hosted delegates and pilgrims from around the world.

Contrary to a commonly held view, Evangelical groups, including the Southern Baptists, the Christian and Missionary Alliance, the Assemblies of God and the Plymouth Brethren, continued their work on the Jordanian side of the border and were active in maintaining a pilgrimage infrastructure there, in addition to extensive educational, medical and charitable activities. Although many of them criticized continued Arab opposition to the creation of Israel, Evangelicals, such as John Walvoord, president of Dallas Theological Seminary, emphasized that the Land of Israel could maintain both Arab and Jewish populations (Walvoord, 1962). They insisted that Israel had an obligation to respect human rights and treat the Arabs fairly. Many Protestant groups travelled to Jordan and Israel taking advantage of the pilgrimage facilities and attractions in both countries. In the West Bank of Jordan they would often visit historical Christian attractions, while in Israel they also took interest in the new state, its institutions and cultures. Visiting kibbutzim and Tel Aviv's city centre became part of the itinerary. Often, Evangelical leaders and journalists also wished to talk with or interview Israeli leaders. When Oral Roberts visited Israel in 1959, he met with Ben-Gurion, and in 1961, when the Pentecostals decided to gather for a global convention in Jerusalem, the Israeli prime minister wrote a speech welcoming the delegates.

1967 and Beyond

The 1967 Arab–Israeli War had a dramatic effect on Evangelical attitudes towards the Holy Land, much more so than the birth of the State of Israel in 1948. No other political military event during that era had provided so much hope for prophetic expectations as the short war between Israel and its neighbours on 5–11 June 1967. The unexpected Israeli victory, which included taking over the historical sites of Jerusalem, strengthened the conviction of premillennialist Evangelicals that their understanding of Scripture was correct and that Israel was to play an important role in the events that would precede the arrival of the Messiah. Conservative Evangelicals became ardent supporters of Israel, and their interest in the land increased. In 1972, for example, Billy Graham produced a movie, *His Land*, which equated the State of Israel with Jesus's territory.

It was no wonder that the years following the Six-Day War saw a huge increase in the presence and activity of Evangelical Christians in Israel. Pilgrimages of Evangelicals to that country took many forms and included field-study seminars and volunteer work in kibbutzim or archaeological digs, organized by groups such as Project Kibbutz. Evangelicals even established institutions of higher education in Israel. One of these was the Holy Land Institute (currently Jerusalem University College), set up by Douglas Young, a premillennialist with a pro-Zionist orientation. This Evangelical college centres on studies related to the history, archaeology and languages of the Holy Land, as well as Christian scriptures, and many of its students come to Jerusalem for a semester or a year. In addition, thousands of Evangelical Christians have settled in Israel since the 1970s, turning the country into their temporary home. Motivated by a Messianic faith, attracted to the land of the Bible or engaged in missionary activities, Evangelical Christians from around the globe have built new congregations in Israel. Many have joined or helped form communities of Jewish believers in Jesus. Others have established 'Gentile' congregations, such as the King of Kings in Jerusalem. Founded in the early 1980s by American and Canadian Pentecostals, the King of Kings is a vibrant community consisting of hundreds of charismatic Christian pilgrims from around the world, who come for short periods of time to live in a city which they regard as holding a special place in human history.

A number of pro-Israel Evangelical organizations have begun playing a growing role in bringing committed Christians to visit. Headquartered in Jerusalem, one of the larger and better-known Evangelical organizations is the International Christian Embassy Jerusalem (ICEJ). Its story tells a great deal about growing Evangelical activity in Israel and the organization of pilgrimage based on Protestant biblical notions.

In the 1970s, Evangelical activists in Jerusalem founded a number of organizations that were intended to stir interest in and support for Israel among Protestants. These included the non-Charismatic Bridges for Peace and the Charismatic Almond Tree Branch. This group of Jerusalemite Evangelicals met regularly for prayer, singing and discussions. One of the more dynamic participants was Jan Willem van der Hoeven, a Dutch minister who had served from 1968 until 1975 as the warden of the Garden Tomb. Van der Hoeven came up with the idea of organizing large annual pilgrimages of Christian supporters of Israel as part of Sukkot, the Jewish harvest festival commemorating the tent sanctuaries, or tabernacles, used during the Exodus. His theological rationale was twofold. First, according to the Bible (Zechariah 14: 15), Gentiles were also commanded to gather in Jerusalem during the festival. Secondly, he pointed out that whereas Christians celebrated two of the 'pilgrimage festivals' commanded in the Bible – Easter and Pentecost – there was no general Christian celebration of Sukkot. In 1979 the Almond Tree Branch launched its first yearly Tabernacles festival, a week-long assembly of Evangelical supporters of Israel, highlighted by a march through the streets of Jerusalem. Soon the celebrations would entail inviting thousands of pilgrims from all around the world (Ariel, 1994).

In 1980 the Israeli Knesset passed the 'Jerusalem Law', which declared the whole of the city to be the capital of the State of Israel. In protest, almost all countries with embassies and consulates in Jerusalem moved their diplomatic staff to Tel Aviv. This evacuation provided a dramatic point at which the Almond Tree activists announced the creation of the International Christian Embassy in Jerusalem, presenting it as an act of sympathy and support for Israel on the part of true Christians at a time when even friendly or neutral countries had betrayed her (Ariel, 1994). The ICEJ chose as its logo two olive branches hovering over a globe with Jerusalem at its centre. The ICEJ's leaders announced: 'This symbolizes the great day when Zechariah's prophecy will be fulfilled, and all nations will come up to Jerusalem to keep the Feast of Tabernacles during Messiah's reign on earth' (van der Hoeven et al., 1984, p. 4). Van der Hoeven as well as other workers and participants in the activities of the ICEJ, pointed to the geographical scope of Evangelical interest in Israel. While Evangelicals have exercised a high degree of visibility and political influence in America, large constituencies of Evangelicals in other regions where this movement is on the rise, such as Latin America, have taken interest in Israel and the Holy Land and have begun visiting on pilgrimage in growing numbers. The organization has wished to represent Christianity worldwide and has made great efforts to open branches and gain supporters in as many countries as possible, but pilgrims who participate in the group's tours and gatherings in Israel come mostly from Protestant populations, including thousands of Latin Americans.

Since the late 1970s, the Feast of Tabernacles serves as a colourful focal point of the year for the ICEJ, creating a visible presence in the capital of Israel and noting elsewhere that Evangelical Christians support Israel. The activities include tours of the country for the pilgrims, a march through Jerusalem's main streets, a 'biblical meal' and a series of assemblies and exhibitions in Jerusalem. Since the 1960s, Israeli officials have: (i) encouraged pilgrimages of supportive Christians; (ii) met with Evangelists who come on visits; (iii) greeted groups of pilgrims; and (iv) spoken at gatherings such as those organized by the ICEJ.

The ICEJ is not the only group to develop the scope and variety of the Protestant pilgrimage infrastructure in the Holy Land. Hundreds of churches, colleges, pro-Israel groups and even journals organize yearly visits to the country. These Protestant visits have become a major component of tourism to Israel, with the Israeli hotel industry as well as the Palestinian one relying on such ventures. These Protestant visits are more than journeys of piety. They are also journeys of discovery as the pilgrims study the history, politics and topographies of the place. Such pilgrimages have taken varied forms. For example, while more conservative Protestants prefer to interact with those who are more approving of Israel and its goals, many liberal or mainstream Protestant groups have chosen to encounter and interview Palestinians and peace activists (Hewitt, 1995). Peace and Justice Pilgrimages have become prevalent among Progressive Christians or those wishing to take a more neutral stand.

While Protestant guest houses can currently accommodate only a fraction of the growing Protestant waves of pilgrims, such centres have found other means of being involved and putting their imprint on the visitors and the experience. Certain local Christian and Messianic Jewish tourist agencies have come to specialize in Protestant tourism, with bespoke tours, experiences, meetings and services. Most of the guides accompanying the tourists are committed Protestants, some with theological and biblical education. Many local guides, likewise, share the tourists' faith. These include Protestants who settled in the country and Messianic Jews who combine their love for the country and their zeal to promote its cause with practical commercial motivations. A number of Messianic Jews have entered the tourist–pilgrimage industry, initiating and investing in guest houses, hotels and at times in additional museums or archaeological sites. The venues, volume, technologies and means of transportation have changed, but Protestant interest in the land and the infrastructure which local and global groups have established, has, if anything, been on the rise.

Conclusion

The Protestant relationship with Jerusalem and the Holy Land changed dramatically in the 19th century, with the first long-lasting Protestant institutions opening between the 1830s and the turn of the 20th century. Dozens of groups turned Palestine in general and Jerusalem in particular into a focal point of pilgrimage, with tourists, missionaries, explorers of the land, biblical scholars, archaeologists, artists and diplomats arriving. Numerous groups sent emissaries to Jerusalem to maintain posts, propagate the Gospel and serve as representatives of their faiths, cultures and agendas. These long- and short-term European and American pilgrims created congregations, educational enterprises and guest houses and formed their own sociocultural and religious circles, thereby leaving their mark on the topography and economy of the city. At the beginning of the 20th century, the arrival of pilgrims became more systematized, facilitated by steamboats, railways and commercial travel companies. The introduction of British rule in the post-World War I period proved beneficial to the Protestant infrastructure, and many pilgrims took advantage of the resultant facilities. Hospices and guest houses were still popular during this period, but gradually pilgrims began staying in newly emerging privately owned hotels.

Pentecostal and other groups of Evangelicals continued to arrive after the birth of the State of Israel, but many were not overly enthusiastic about the secular nature of the government and culture. However, they were filled with hope with the mass immigration of Jews in the late 1940s and 1950s. This new state allowed Protestants to maintain their infrastructure and undertake their work and worship, and following the 1967 war some Evangelicals became ardent supporters of Israel. Since the 1970s many Evangelical Christians built new congregations, established institutions of higher education and settled in Israel. In more recent times these and other Protestant groups have focused their energy on bringing Christians to visit Israel, organizing visits, and thus supporting the Israeli and Palestinian hotel industries. While Protestant guest houses still exist, they only accommodate a fraction of the visiting pilgrims, and groups have instead focused on putting their imprint on the visitors and the experience. While the pilgrim visit itself has changed in nature and character, Protestant interest in the land and the infrastructure they have created is on the rise.

References

Ariel, Y. (1991) *On Behalf of Israel: American Fundamentalist Attitudes toward Jews, Judaism, and Zionism, 1865–1945*. Carlson, New York.

Ariel, Y. (1994) *Fundamentalist Christian Zionism: a Portrait of a Pro-Israeli Christian Organization*. The Leonard Davis Institute, the Hebrew University of Jerusalem, Jerusalem.

Ariel, Y. (2000) *Evangelizing the Chosen People: Missions to the Jews in America, 1880–2000*. University of North Carolina Press, Chapel Hill, North Carolina.

Ariel, Y. (2010) Messianic expectations among Christians and Jews in the late Ottoman Empire. In: Bartal, I. and Goren, H. (eds) *Jerusalem in the Late Ottoman Period*. Yad Ben-Zvi, Jerusalem, pp. 83–94.

Ariel, Y. (2013) *An Unusual Relationship: Evangelical Christians and Jews*. New York University Press, New York.

Ariel, Y. and Kark, R. (1996) Messianism, holiness, charisma, and community: the American–Swedish Colony in Jerusalem, 1881–1993. *Church History* 65(4), 641–657.

Baedeker, K. (1876) *Jerusalem and its Surroundings: Handbook for Travellers*. Karl Baedeker, Leipzig, Germany.

Bar Yosef, E. (2005) *The Holy Land in English Culture, 1799–1917*. Oxford University Press, New York.

Ben-Arieh, Y. (1977) *A City Reflected in its Time: Jerusalem in the Nineteenth Century*. Yad Izhak Ben-Zvi Publications, Jerusalem.

Blackstone, W. (1892) Jerusalem. *The Jewish Era* 1, pp. 67–71.

Cohen, R. (2009) *Saving the Holy Sepulcher: How Rival Christians Came Together to Rescue Their Holiest Shrine*. Oxford University Press, New York.

Daly, G. (1989) *Pre-Raphaelites in Love*. Ticknor and Fields, London.

Finn, J. and Finn, E.A. (1878) *Stirring Times, or Records from Jerusalem Consular Chronicles of 1853–1856*. Kegan Paul, London.

Goodrich-Freer, A. (1904) *Inner Jerusalem*. Dutton, New York.

Hewitt, G. (1995) *Pilgrims and Peacemakers: a Journey through Lent towards Jerusalem*. Bible Reading Fellowship, Oxford.

Lagerlöf, S. (1915) *Jerusalem*. Doubleday, Garden City, New York.

Nerel, N. (2009) Operation Mercy before establishment of the State of Israel. *MISHKAN* 61, 21–32.

Nerel, N. (2014) From American mission to Israeli Messianic Assembly: theology and deed in Jerusalem's Street of the Prophets. *Cathedra* 154, 107–136. (in Hebrew)

Newberg, E.N. (2012) *The Pentecostal Mission in Palestine*. Pickwick Publications, Eugene, Oregon.

Schur, N. (1988) *The Book of Travelers to the Holy Land in the 19th Century*. Keter Books, Jerusalem.

Twain, M. (1869) *The Innocents Abroad*. American Publishing Company, Hartford, Connecticut.

van der Hoeven, J.W. *et al.* (1984) *Succot*. International Christian Embassy Jerusalem (ICEJ), Jerusalem.

Walvoord, J. (1962) *Israel in Prophecy*. Zondervan, Grand Rapids, Michigan.

11 The Impact of the Islamic State of Iraq and Syria's Campaign on Yezidi Religious Structures and Pilgrimage Practices

Ibrahim Al-Marashi*

California State University, San Marcos, USA

Introduction

The rise of the Islamic State of Iraq and Syria (ISIS) in the summer of 2014 disrupted the faith and pilgrimage practices of Iraq's historically vulnerable minority communities. ISIS has created a homogenous neo-Salafi space through 'religious cleansing' of persons and physical structures, antiquity sites related to the pre-Islamic past, and religious structures used by minority and 'heterodox communities'. The expulsion of Iraqi Christian Chaldeans from Mosul, the extermination and enslavement of Yezidi communities and the destruction of both communities' religious structures, sites of local religious pilgrimage, is justified by the doctrinal beliefs of ISIS, but also serves a secular goal of consolidating recently conquered land. Expelling heterodox communities in the name of the faith eliminates potential 'fifth columns'. ISIS' allegations of Yezidis as 'devil worshippers' and the images of the destruction of their sites also gains approval of ISIS' inner core of supporters. The choreographed and mediated destruction of these sites concurrently generates coverage by international media, communicating ISIS' deliberate rejection of the Western liberal state and normative notions of protecting minority rights. The dismantling of the Iraqi–Syrian border and the expulsion of the minority communities that straddled both sides of the border serves in ISIS' view to rectify the borders of the Arab world drawn by such Western states after World War I. The ramifications of such a campaign stretch beyond local communities in Iraq and Syria, in that ISIS' elimination of these religious sites removes opportunities for veneration and pilgrimage. Thus these actions destroy a religious geospatial link between these local communities and their respective

*ialmarashi@csusm.edu

diaspora, particularly in the USA and Western Europe, which continue to grow in exile as a result of a decade of religious persecution that ensued in the instability unleashed by the 2003 Iraq War.

An Overview of Iconoclasm and Destruction of Pilgrimage Sites in the Muslim World

ISIS' strategy towards shrines can be contextualized within, but is not necessarily a deterministic outcome of an iconoclastic history that took root among the 18th-century religious puritanical movement in the Najd region of Saudi Arabia. Referred to as Wahhabism today, one of the tenets of the movement was the rejection of any form of Muslim veneration of burial sites of ancestors or sacred figures, an act deemed as a form of idol worship or *shirk*, dividing the worshipper's attention and devotion from the unity of God. That this movement vehemently objected to this practice attests to a legacy for the veneration of grave sites for some time, and that believing Muslims did not necessarily see paying their respects at graveyards as a violation of Islam's prohibitions on idolatry. Stephennie Mulder, an art historian from the University of Texas, reiterates that veneration at tombs and grave sites served as an historic practice among Muslims: 'I should say that Muslims have worshipped at saints' shrines from the beginning of the faith' (Quinton, 2015). Mulder coined ISIS' destruction as 'heritage terror', the goal of which is 'to destroy sense of identity, by removing these objects that are key to locals' sense of cultural pride and understanding' (Quinton, 2015).

Thus, the destruction of religious sites might be couched by ISIS in iconoclastic terms of destroying idols and graven images, but ISIS' strategy has a profane value, in that it is a tactic of an insurgent movement, whose legitimacy may derive from a religious genealogy, but whose priority is to consolidate political power over recently conquered territory. The establishment of political power over a newly conquered space is demonstrated by this insurgent group's ability to reconfigure the pre-existing religious order, whether it be multi-confessional in the case of Mosul, Yezidi in the case of Jabal Sinjar, or Shi'i in the case of Tal Afar, all of which witnessed the destruction of religious sites, shrines and tombs in 2014.

The destruction and sacking of enemy religious sites and architecture is not a new historical phenomenon in the Middle East. However, the destruction of tombs and shrines situated within the 20th century coincides with insurgent movements that are not only puritanical in their belief, but seeking to consolidate power in the form of a modern nation state, combining religiously inspired motivations for conformity and hegemony, while establishing relatively new political entities in the region following the post-World War I era and collapse of the Ottoman Empire.

One of the most high-profile acts of tomb destruction occurred in 1926, when forces aligned with the al-Sa'ud tribe, the Wahhabi-inspired tribal levies known as the Ikhwan, entered the city of Madina and destroyed the mausoleum in the al-Baqi cemetery, a site encompassing graves of the prophet Mohammed's grandchildren and descendants, dating back as early as the seventh century. James Noyes, author of *The Politics of Iconoclasm*, stated in an interview that the destruction of the site 'shocked the international Muslim community' at the time (Beauchamp, 2015). His comment indicates that the destruction of shrines was by no means embraced by the greater Muslim world then, and was seen as an abhorrent act, a reaction that Muslims in the 21st century have expressed regarding ISIS' destruction of sites, including mosques such as the one in Mosul that housed the tomb of the Prophet Yunus, or Jonah.

The Saudi-Ikhwan forces were essentially an insurgent group establishing a nascent Saudi state, whose strategy to consolidate territory included incorporating Madina, and the recently captured Mecca, into the eventual Kingdom of Saudi Arabia. While controlling these religious sites enhanced the legitimacy of what had essentially been a quasi-tribal state, they also demonstrated their power by dictating to the entire Muslim world how the pilgrimage to these sites would be conducted. Since iconoclasm and anti-Shi'ism were integral to their movement, any visitation by the Shi'a or Sufi pilgrims during the Hajj to sites deemed idolatrous in Mecca and Madina would no longer be tolerated. However, unlike ISIS today, which is engaging in a similar state-building project, Saudi Arabia did tolerate the presence of pre-Islamic heritage on its soil, including Nabatean sites to the north of the country. In fact Saudi Arabia has gradually embraced the promotion of these sites for tourism, unlike ISIS, which has destroyed pre-Islamic antiquity sites.

The Saudi-Ikhwan alliance established in the early 20th century provides an example of a non-state actor, motivated by an austere and iconoclastic ideology, destroying non-Islamic sites as orthopraxy. The Taliban's history also resonates with the Saudi precedent. This was a non-state army seeking to create a state in Afghanistan, whose Deobandi interpretation of the faith shares similarities with the Wahabism of the Arabian Peninsula. However, when the Taliban destroyed the twin statues of Buddha in the Bamiyan valley on 26 March 2001, Jamal Elias (2013) argues that it did deliberate over this decision and was wary of the potential international response. This deliberative process indicates that the leader of the Taliban, Mulla Omar, did factor in the rational calculation of how this act would deprive the organization of international legitimacy at a time when only three countries recognized their government – Saudi Arabia, the United Arab Emirates and Pakistan.

Similar non-state actors inspired by similar religious interpretation have conducted heritage terrorism in sub-Saharan Africa. In 2008, the Al-Qaida-affiliated al-Shabab group in Somalia destroyed Sufi shrines in the city of Kismayo. In 2012, the al-Qaeda-affiliated Ansar Dine destroyed the Sidi Yahya mosque in Timbuktu, along with numerous other shrines in the city (Fisher, 2012).

While these precedents demonstrate an ideological genealogy among groups that could be grouped as Wahabi, Salafi and Deobandi, all of which have an iconoclasm embedded in their doctrine, one must not assume that adherents to any of these three Muslim movements are necessarily consumed with destroying shrines in their orthopraxy. In the cases of Madina, Bamiyan, Kismayo, Timbuktu and Mosul, insurgent groups that shared this religious interpretation were also engaged in long-term goals of controlling territory, where destruction of shrines couched in terms of orthopraxy had the secular objective of intimidating heterodox communities, compelling them to leave their territory, or instilling fear among those communities who chose to stay to accept the new political order.

Destruction of shrines in all of these cases ultimately served to enforce a group's hegemony couched in an austere form of Islam.

These precedents demonstrate how armed conflict has disrupted networks of pilgrimage, destroying sites of veneration, and in the process, eliminating foci of identity for groups within a faith, or for an entire faith, as in the case of the Yezidis.

The case of a conflict disrupting Yezidi pilgrimage in 2014, while a tragic and localized case, can be situated in the geographical context of the relationship between conflict and pilgrimage in the greater Mediterranean Basin, using Braudel's historical definition (1996) of this area, encompassing the Red and Black Seas as well. In the final years of the establishment of Islam as a faith during Muhammad's lifetime, one of the last series of battles between his forces and the pagan-Meccan elite was over the right for his new community of believers to practise pilgrimage at the Ka'aba, the house of worship whose construction was attributed to the patriarch Abraham. The final culminating act in the victory of the Muslims over the Meccans took place when Muslims could enter Mecca and conduct the pilgrimage, eliminating the idols that were once venerated in the structure by pagan pilgrims and replacing it as a site of pilgrimage to the monotheistic deity of the Abrahamic faiths. Centuries later the emergence of the Camino Santiago can also be related to the process of conflict and pilgrimage, as the trail could only emerge once the front line had established between the Muslim forces in Spain and various northern Christian kingdoms during the series of battles that have been collectively referred to as the 'Reconquista'. The eight Crusades that ensued since 1095 serve as further examples of the interrelationship of conflict establishing or disrupting pilgrimage routes. Groups that have taken on mythic status in Western popular historical memory, such as the Knights Templar and the Knights Hospitaller, owe their fame to their piety and fighting prowess, but in terms of institutions they emerged to maintain the Christian pilgrimage routes, or the health of the pilgrims on that journey. Jumping to the 21st century, ISIS and its former affiliate, the Al-Qaida-linked Jabhat al-Nusra are movements that re-emerged in a Mediterranean struggle, the Syrian civil war, with affiliated elements damaging the Syriac and Aramaic fabric of the country in towns like Ma'alula, and the potential to destroy further sites in Palmyra.

The Yezidi plight situated within the greater history of the Mediterranean is that of a community suffering depredation in the later phases of the Crusades, at one time meeting the wrath of an Ottoman governor in the 19th century, and now facing a non-state actor which emerged as a result of the Syrian civil war. Martin Lewis (2010), a geographer at Stanford University, delineates a sub-unit within the greater Mediterranean basin as 'The Heterodox Zone', a mountainous terrain stretching from the Levantine coast to the mountains of the Anatolian Peninsula and the Fertile Crescent. On the eastern Mediterranean, this zone includes communities such as the Syrian Alawites, Druze and Syriac Christians, to Lebanon's mosaic of confessional communities. The zone expands and continues along the mountains between the Tigris and Euphrates Rivers, encompassing Turkey, Syria and Iraq. The Yezidis would straddle the entirety of this mountainous area, with communities in Syria, the south of Turkey and predominantly in the north of Iraq. Mountainous terrain often provided protection for minority groups from large imperial armies in the region. Isolated topography also often led to isolated communities, providing spaces for groups' beliefs to evolve on their own. This would explain the history of the Yezidis, who ostensibly revered a Sufi Muslim figure, but in their isolation evolved into a syncretic faith that lost most of its Muslim element, while maintaining a mélange of Zoroastrian and possibly Mithraic and gnostic elements.

The History of Yezidis

The Yezidi faith can be described as an esoteric syncretism that incorporates ancient Iranian religions, and then Muslim Sufism after the 12th century, inspired by the 'Adawiyya Sufi order that was established by 'Adi ibn Musafir in a mountainous area inhabited by Kurdish tribes. The Sufi layer in Yezidism emerged due to the legacy of Shaykh 'Adi, as he is known by his adherents, who was born in 1075 CE in the Biqa Valley of Lebanon. After studying in Baghdad under the illustrious scholar 'Abd al-Qadir al-Jaylani, he settled in the Lalish Valley, north-east of Mosul. The community inhabiting this area included pockets of Kurdish tribes evidently still influenced by aspects of ancient Iranian beliefs, among the majority of Kurds who were mostly Muslim. While Shaykh 'Adi himself was a devout Muslim, he was embraced by these local non-Muslim communities, and when he died in 1162, his tomb in Lalish emerged as a focal point of Yezidi spiritual devotion (Acikyildiz, 2014, p. 39). Yezidism evolved and grew in the area under Zangid Atabeg rule, often at odds with this dynasty. The Atabeg commander Lu'lu killed Shaykh Hasan, the leader of the Yezidis in 1254 and desecrated the Shaykh's remains (Acikyildiz, 2014, pp. 41–42, 144). This tension was not over their beliefs per se, but the community's challenge of the Atabeg's territorial ambitions. Yezidis, in the area of Mount Sinjar, had been attacked by Mongols in 1261–1262, Shaykh 'Adi's tomb was sacked by a local dynasty in 1414, and their communities were attacked by an Ottoman governor in 1890, whereupon the shrine was converted into an Islamic school for a brief period (Acikyildiz, 2014, pp. 43, 45, 56). According to the Yezidis, they have faced 72 concerted massacres in the history of their community (Shelton, 2014).

Yezidi communities settled in the foothills outside of Mosul, in Lalish and the Shaykan area, including the towns of Bashiqa and Bahzane, and another community emerged around Mount Sinjar, some 80 km west of Mosul. The community eventually spread to what is today Syria and Turkey, and during the period of the Ottoman Empire eventually migrated to what is today Armenia.

The Ba'athist government of Iraq attempted to re-categorize the Yezidis' Kurdish identity as Arab, by forging a lineage between their name and Yazid ibn Mu'awiyya, the leader of the Umayyad dynasty based in Damascus, who ruled from 661 to 680 CE. However, Yezidis often stress their name is derived from the ancient Iranian Pahlavi language and the word for 'angel' (*Ezidi* or *Izidi* based on differing transliterations) (Acikyildiz, 2014, p. 35). As the Ba'ath government that took power in 1968 was in a continuous war against Kurdish parties in the north of Iraq, this divide-and-rule tactic of bestowing upon the Yezidis an Arab identity was resisted by most members of the community. However, during the Iran–Iraq

War, the Yezidis did suffer the fate of other Kurds, who were resettled from their villages into *mujammas*, a series of collective towns in the plains as a means to better maintain state surveillance over the Kurdish communities in the rebellious mountains and destroy the population base that was supporting the rebellion, a process that included destroying villages in the process (Acikyildiz, 2014, p. 60). After the fall of the Ba'ath government in 2003, Yezidis, as a good number of their villages were destroyed, continued living in *mujammas* like Qahtaniyya or Jazira in the plains of Sinjar district (Maisel, 2008).

This legacy of Saddam Hussein had a tragic consequence for the Yezidis, as it collected them in concentrated urban spaces where they could easily be targeted by the Islamic State of Iraq, the Al-Qaida-affiliated precursor to ISIS. On 14 August 2007 four simultaneous truck bombings killed more than 500 Yezidis in these collective towns (Acikyildiz, 2014, p. 61). After the attack the Islamic State of Iraq continued to urge its members to kill Yezidis wherever they came across them (Human Rights Watch, 2009, pp. 41–42). This campaign against the Yezidis only intensified once ISIS pushed back into Mosul in 2014, pursuing a strategy of not just attacking the Yezidis with terrorist attacks, but eliminating them entirely, destroying any physical vestige of their culture, destroying structures they venerated, killing Yezidi men and enslaving their women. The ISIS offensive in the summer of 2014 led to the displacement of 130,000 Yezidis, including 40,000 stranded on Mount Sinjar (Chulov, 2014). Many sought refuge in the town of Lalish itself, or Irbil, the capital of the Kurdistan Regional Government (Jalabi, 2014), or sought asylum in the USA and Europe.

The current population of the Yezidis is estimated to be between 600,000 and 620,000, with the vast majority concentrated in northern Iraq (Acikyildiz, 2014, p. 34). Yezidi diaspora communities are primarily located in Germany, the UK, the USA and Canada. The recent violence conducted by ISIS and its predecessor in Iraq has led to more Iraq Yezidis seeking asylum in Europe, with 70,000 people, or about 15% of the Yezidi in Iraq, leaving the country (Salih, 2014).

Yezidi Pilgrimages and Ceremonies

Over the last century, information on the Yezidi faith had been gleaned from European travellers, often fascinated by the Orientalist allure of a community of 'devil worshippers' living among Muslims. Up until the 1960s, travellers to the Yezidi community would observe Yezidi practices and relate them to religions of antiquity they were familiar with. For example, John Godolphin Bennett (1962) writes of the Yezidi faith: 'It became clear to me that the Yezidi religion is a survival of true Mithraism, which has thus remained alive for fifteen thousand years after the downfall of the Sassanian Empire' (Bennett, 1962, pp. 303–304).

Travel to the shrine of Shaykh 'Adi has been undertaken by the Yezidi faithful and non-Yezidis, particularly Europeans, curious about this syncretic faith. What emerged as of the summer of 2014 was a history of religious heritage tourism coming to an end due to religious 'heritage terrorism'.

Yezidism is a faith based on an oral tradition and orthopraxy, with rituals governing all aspects of life. The ritualistic aspects, from pilgrimage to processions of the faith, maintain the community more than liturgical texts and formal religious education. According to Yezidi cosmogony, the eternal God (*Xwede*) created the world in the form of 'a pearl', a belief shared by another Iraqi 'heterodox' community, the Ahl-e Haqq. The pearl remained in this state for either 40 or 40,000 years, sacred numbers in Yezidi numerology. God then created a Heptad of angelic entities, referred to as the 'Seven Mysteries' (*haft serr*), and delegated them dominion over the Earth. *Xwede*'s pre-eminent regent is Malak Taus, or the Peacock Angel, and the sayings of the Peacock Angel are documented in the 'Book of Illumination' (*Keteba Jelwa*), which describes his responsibilities as bestowing blessing or misfortune on humans, the race of Adam. Thus, Yezidism is a monotheistic not dualistic faith, with a distant, single God conceived almost along Deist lines. The faith shares similarities to Zoroastrianism, but is not a form of Zoroastrianism per se, as while Yezidis share similar cosmogonies, they venerate a benign demiurge responsible for the state of the world, whereas the Zoroastrian demiurge, Ahriman, is the entity responsible for evil among humans, a precursor to the Devil, Satan or *Shaytan*, 'the adversary' in the Abrahamic faiths. Since the Peacock Angel is associated with the Fallen Angel or Satan in these three faiths, it has led to appellation of Yezidis as 'devil worshippers' (Acikyildiz, 2014, pp. 1–2, 71, 74). So offensive is this association among Yezidis, they have a taboo against uttering the name '*Shaytan*' so as to not link this name to the Peacock Angel.

Rather as portraying the Peacock Angel as the Fallen Angel for his refusal to bow down to Adam, which according to Abrahamic tradition led to his expulsion from Heaven, the Peacock Angel's refusal to submit to Adam was an indication of his loyalty to God, as bowing down to Adam would have been a challenge to the monotheism of the supreme divine entity. According to Yezidis, the creator God redeemed the Peacock Angel's refusal by granting him the prime regency within the Heptad (Acikyildiz, 2014, p. 75). As a result of this belief, Yezidis have no conception of eternal sin or hell, but believe in transmigration of souls and reincarnation. It is not a cosmic dualism between God and the Devil which leads to evil in human beings, but rather Yezidi belief is that evil lies collectively in the hearts of humans, a belief similar to early Judaism.

The holiest site for Yezidis is the tomb of Shaykh 'Adi in Lalish, a valley that includes numerous other shrines. Metempsychosis is central to Yezidi belief, so the Heptad can be manifest in human form called *kassa*. Thus, Shaykh 'Adi was considered a human form of the Peacock Angel. The other Yezidi shrines are often the burial sites of humans considered as reincarnations of the Heptad entities.

The most significant event for the Yezidis is the 'Feast of the Assembly' (*Jazna Jama'iyya*), sometimes referred to as the 'Autumn Assembly', a 7-day festivity held from 23 to 27 September at Lalish when the Heptad in their angelic form 'assemble' in Lalish. This event and location becomes the focus of the Yezidi pilgrimage, known as '*ziyaret*' (Acikyildiz, 2014, pp. 72, 104). Pilgrims approach Lalish, crossing the Serat Bridge (*pirra selat*) (Acikyildiz, 2014, p. 106). The tomb is characterized by several *qobs*, structures topped by ribbed triangular domes, with 12 ridges symbolizing the rays of the sun. The entrance features a black snake, which according to Yezidi belief saved Noah's ark by plugging a hole in the vessel. Each of the angels in the Heptad is represented by a tomb in Lalish, with a different coloured piece of silk corresponding to each tomb. Pilgrims tie knots on the cloth covering the tombs, with each knot representing a wish. Untying the knot in a future pilgrimage would bring about the fulfilment of that wish. During the Assembly each cloth is baptized in the 'White Spring' (*kaniya spi*), a spring in a cave under the tomb of Shaykh 'Adi where Yezidi children are also baptized, akin to Christianity (Acikyildiz, 2014, p. 95) or Mandaean practice (an Iraqi faith devoted to John the Baptist). Water from this spring is also mixed with earth from the Valley to make *barat*, small clay-like moulded balls, taken away by the pilgrim and used as sacred objects in marriages and funerary rites. Tying ribbons and collecting dust from sacred ground is not unique to Yezidism, as these are practices similar to Shi'i and Sufi visits to sacred sites.

The Yezidi faithful living away from Lalish in more distant locations in Iraq, the region or the diaspora, make at least one pilgrimage to Shaykh 'Adi's tomb in their lifetime, akin to the Hajj, the Muslim pilgrimage to Mecca. Those living in the north of Iraq often make the pilgrimage on an annual basis. The 7-day event promotes contact among various members of the faith and serves to reaffirm their identity. When Iraq in the 1990s was separated by an armistice line between the Kurdish-run north and Saddam Hussein's Iraq, it was difficult for most Yezidis to attend the festival. After 2003, due to the continuous threat of terrorism, the event has witnessed low attendance or has been cancelled entirely (Jalabi, 2014).

Yezidis also observe their New Year ceremony in Lalish, although for them it falls on the first Wednesday of April, a bit later than the 21 March of the Persian Nowruz (Acikyildiz, 2014, p. 108). Elements of Yezidism demonstrate similarities to Zoroastrianism and the Zoroastrian influences that are evident in Nowruz, still commemorated by Iranians today. The egg in Nowruz is also featured in Yezidi New Year, representing the 'white pearl' in its cosmogony, which burst apart spreading colourful flowers and lush vegetation on the previously barren terrain of the Lalish Valley. Fire, a sacred element in Zoroastrianism is also prevalent in Yezidism, where fires are lit every evening in the Lalish Valley.

Other Yezidi ceremonies are also under threat, such as Parading of the Peacock, when a class of religious reciters (*qewwals*) recite sacred texts in a procession, along with a bronze representation of a peacock, known as a *sanjak*. Serving as a pilgrimage in reverse, the sacred comes to the faithful, as this procession tours the Yezidi villages. Given that Yezidism is an oral faith, these mobile recitations in areas around the former Yezidi heartland of Mount Sinjar would have served as an opportunity for the Yezidis to receive religious education and learn concepts and traditions of their faith.

The Disruption and Destruction of the Yezidi Cultural Fabric

In the summer of 2014, ISIS successfully captured the town of Sinjar, home to a large Yezidi community, sending them fleeing to the mountains as they faced the ultimatum to convert to Islam or face death. While the central Yezidi tomb of Shaykh 'Adi has not been destroyed, ISIS has declared that it has sought to conquer the area (Shelton, 2014).

Primary sources for the destruction of Yezidi pilgrimage sites are often difficult to corroborate, but Sam Hardy, the manager of the Conflict Antiquities blog, demands several sources of verification of destruction before declaring a site has been destroyed. An example of this verification process is indicated by one blog entry: 'Double, triple, quadruple-checking: is this evidence that the Shrine of Sayeda Zeinab has been destroyed?' (Hardy, 2014c).

On 7 August 2014, the website indicated that a Yezidi shrine of Quba Shaykh Sherefedin in the Sinjar area had not been destroyed, despite previous reports that indicated so. Apparently the shrine survived since units of the Kurdish Peshmerga and 3000 Yezidi volunteers defended the structure (Hardy, 2014a). Rumours also emerged that the site of Shaykh 'Adi in Lalish had been destroyed, but proved unfounded (Hardy, 2014b). ISIS uploaded videos of their destruction of other Yezidi shrines; however, the videos have been removed from YouTube. By 29 October, a Twitter image documented the actual destruction of a Yezidi shrine (Hardy, 2014d).

The images of the structure, which had the conical dome usually used by the Yezidis, were circulated in a 'press release' from the Islamic State, but did not indicate the name of the shrine. In November, another two Yezidi structures, the Temple of Shaykh Sin and the Temple of Shaykh Mikhfiya, were destroyed in the town of Babila (Hardy, 2014e).

The destruction of these aforementioned shrines is tragic, but represents an effect greater than the erasure of physical Yezidi structures. Their destruction represents the disruption of a network of sites that define this community. According to Matthew Barber (2014), a scholar who studies Yezidism and was present in the north of Iraq during the ISIS offensive, this religious community's faith is integrally linked to the physical space that is now the Islamic State:

> Yezidi religious practice is connected to a network of sacred places within the essential areas of the homeland; if contact with Sinjar's holy places is severed and its population dispersed, the religious tradition will be further endangered as Yezidism moves a step closer to extinction.
>
> (Barber, 2014)

Michael Danti, an archaeologist at Boston University, states (2015) that ISIS' destruction of pre-Islamic sites, such as the sack of the Mosul Museum and vandalism inflicted on Nimrud, Nineveh and Hatra, generate media attention, but represent less than 4% of their 'heritage terrorism'. In Iraq's Nineveh province alone he estimates that 200 incidents have occurred, the vast majority of attacks are on sites that have sacred value for Iraq's communities, destroying hundreds of pilgrimage sites of Yezidis, Shi'a and Sunni Muslims, Christians and other communities. He presents this destruction as a campaign to obliterate the area's cultural fabric and patrimony, 'the cornerstone of cultural identity and conceptions of community'.

The destruction of shrines and thus, their related pilgrimage rituals, are elements of an ISIS determination to stay in the region they have conquered. In a sense ISIS differs from Al-Qaida, an organization designed to use spectacular acts of terrorism to galvanize the Muslim world. Al-Qaida was specifically seen as a 'base' to conduct a strategy of targeting the USA and its allied regimes in the region. ISIS, on the other hand, is engaging in a nation-building project. Given that a lot of its commanders are former Ba'athist Iraqis, ISIS serves as a vehicle for them to reconquer the land they were dispossessed from as a result of the 2003 invasion, as long as they abandon their former secular affiliation with the Party and publicly profess their new-found faith. Since ISIS' *raison d'être* is to hold territory, 'heritage terrorism' is a way to purge this territory according to Islamic, Salafi doctrine. While both Al-Qaida and ISIS engage in a war unbounded by space and time, ISIS does have a spatial element in that it seeks to govern its territory, whereas Al-Qaida operated as cells in failed states. As a 'state', ISIS seeks to maintain hegemony, albeit a hegemony that also proselytizes and eliminates those who fail to submit to its definition of Islam and statehood. The Islamic State thus emerges as a paradox, invoking a secular notion of a state and sovereignty, yet does not seek international legitimacy and recognition by joining the United Nations (UN), or comply with any of the rules of an international system of nations that emerged after Westphalia. It is not a nation bound by an ethnic or a traditional social contract, but a nation of 'believers', who have to follow the only one permissible 'Salafi-jihadi' interpretation of the faith as dictated by ISIS. Thus, anyone who fails to convert or practise their form of Islam is either expelled or exterminated.

Not only does ISIS refuse to accept heterodox communities within its borders, when ISIS dropped the 'Iraq and Syria' aspect of its name, rebranding itself as the 'Islamic State', its caliph could claim global loyalty of Muslims, without them actually travelling to the Muslim state. To this end, ISIS chose to destroy all 'non-Muslims' under their jurisdiction, an actual abuse of history, as caliphs in the past have tended to rule over heterogeneous societies, such as the caliphs of Umayyad Spain who ruled over Muslims, Christians and Jews under the oft-invoked historical lens of *convivencia*. Ironically, ISIS is following the 1492 precedent of the Catholic monarchs of Spain, Isabel and Ferdinand, who set a policy of expelling the Jews and eventually expelling Muslims for the sake of creating a single political space for a single population defined by a uniform Catholic belief.

The destruction of heterodox sites of pilgrimage serves as part of a campaign where these Iraqi minorities' homes and property are also confiscated, constituting a religious and demographic project to create a puritan state. Thus, it has uprooted the locals, and their traditions, rooted and embedded in Iraq since antiquity, and imported Muslims from around the world who share the vision of ISIS. The destruction of sites of non-Muslim sacred architecture is embedded in a process of deporting Iraq's minorities, and crushing any religious focal point that could unite their respective diaspora to the area controlled by Islamic State, resembling the destruction of the Temple by the Roman Empire. Despite its anti-colonial rhetoric vis-à-vis the Sykes–Picot Treaty, ISIS has engaged in its own colonial-settler project. The advantage of importing foreign Muslims to its domains gives ISIS a loyal population base to rally in case local Iraqi and Syrian Sunni Muslims start to chafe and agitate against the Islamic State's rule, which happened between 2006 and 2008 when Iraqis in the Anbar province rose up against the Islamic State of Iraq, ISIS' predecessor.

Conclusion

The destruction of Yezidi shrines, the continuous threat to their communities and their ability to perform religious pilgrimage to the site of Shaykh'Adi in Lalish have served an integral part of an ISIS project of creating a homogenous, Salafi space. In addition to the threatened Yezidi community, Christian Chaldeans and Assyrians were targeted and then expelled from Mosul. Other syncretic minority faiths in Mosul and the north of Iraq, such as the Shabak, Kakais and Ahl-e Haqq have been targeted or are threatened by ISIS. The Shi'a Turkmen of Tel Afar fled or were massacred by ISIS forces when they took the town in the summer of 2014. The destruction of the Church of Jonah, sacred to the Chaldeans, or the Mandeans who have fled Iraq, and thus lost access to baptismal rites in the Euphrates and Tigris Rivers, a practice unique to them, has severed the only spiritual link these exiled, refugee communities possess to their ancestral lands.

While other Iraqi religious communities are transnational, such as the Iraqi Shi'a who could conduct religious pilgrimages to Shi'a shrines in Syria and Iran when visits to Shi'a shrines were curtailed in Iraq under Saddam Hussein, many other threatened Iraqi minorities are not transnational communities, and their identity is solely tied to the locale, within the boundaries of the Iraqi state. These identities and the related religious practices have now been severed.

References

Acikyildiz, B. (2014) *The Yezidis: the History of a Community, Culture and Religion*. I.B. Tauris, London.

Barber, M. (2014) IS Routs Peshmerga, takes control of Sinjar Mountains, jeopardizes Yezidi homeland. *Syria Comment*, 3 August. Available at: http://www.joshualandis.com/blog/routs-peshmerga-takes-control-sinjar-mountains-jeapordizes-Yezidi-homeland/ (accessed 6 May 2015).

Beauchamp, Z. (2015) Why ISIS is Destroying Syrian and Iraqi Heritage Sites. Vox.com, 19 August. Available at: http://www.vox.com/2015/3/11/8184207/islamist-monuments (accessed 15 October 2015).

Bennett, J.G. (1962) *Witness: the Story of a Search*. Hodder and Stoughton, London.

Braudel, F. (1996) *The Mediterranean and the Mediterranean World in the Age of Philip II*. University of California Press, Berkeley, California.

Chulov, M. (2014) 40,000 Iraqis stranded on mountain as ISIS jihadists threaten death. *The Guardian*, 7 August. Available at: http://www.theguardian.com/world/2014/aug/07/40000-iraqis-stranded-mountain-isis-death-threat (accessed 8 May 2015).

Danti, M. (2015) Why the Islamic State's annihilation of ancient cultures matters. *Washington Post*, 29 May. Available at: http://www.washingtonpost.com/blogs/monkey-cage/wp/2015/05/29/the-islamic-states-threat-to-cultural-heritage/ (accessed 5 May 2015).

Elias, J. (2013) The Taliban, Bamiyan, and revisionist iconoclasm. In: Boldrick, S., Brubaker, L. and Clay, R.S. (eds) *Striking Images, Iconoclasms Past and Present*. Ashgate, Burlington, Vermont, pp. 145–164.

Fisher, M. (2012) These 600-year-old World Heritage Sites might be rubble by August. *The Atlantic*, 3 July. Available at: http://www.theatlantic.com/international/archive/2012/07/these-600-year-old-world-heritage-sites-might-be-rubble-by-august/259360/ (accessed 8 May 2015).

Hardy, S. (2014a) The Islamic State has not been able to destroy the Yezidi Shrine of Sherfedin (Quba Şêx Şerfedîn). 7 August. Available at: https://conflictantiquities.wordpress.com/2014/08/07/iraq-sinjar-shrine-sherfedin-quba-sex-serfedin-not-destroyed/ (accessed 5 May 2015).

Hardy, S. (2014b) There is no evidence (yet) that the Islamic State has destroyed the Yezidi Shrine of Sheikh Adi ibn Musafir (Şêx Adî) in Lalish. 7 August. Available at: https://conflictantiquities.wordpress.com/2014/08/07/iraq-lalish-shrine-sheikh-adi-ibn-musafir-sex-adi-destruction-evidence/#more-6231 (accessed 5 May 2015).

Hardy, S. (2014c) Double, triple, quadruple-checking: is this evidence that the Shrine of Sayeda Zeinab has been destroyed? 9 August. Available at: https://conflictantiquities.wordpress.com/2014/08/09/iraq-sinjar-shrine-sayeda-zeinab-destruction-evidence-question/ (accessed 5 May 2015).

Hardy, S. (2014d) Islamic State destroyed the Shia Shrine of Imam al-Daur (Samarra, Iraq). 23 October. Available at: https://conflictantiquities.wordpress.com/2014/10/30/iraq-samarra-islamic-state-destruction-shia-shrine-imam-al-daur/ (accessed 5 May 2015).

Hardy, S. (2014e) Fresh evidence points to destruction of Yezidi temples by Islamic State. 25 November. Available at: https://conflictantiquities.wordpress.com/2014/11/25/hyperallergic-iraq-destruction-yezidi-temples-sheikh-sin-sheikh-mikhfiya-video-confirmation/ (accessed 5 May 2015).

Human Rights Watch (2009) On vulnerable ground: Violence against minority communities in Nineveh province's disputed territories. *Human Rights Watch*, 2009. Available at: https://www.hrw.org/report/2009/11/10/vulnerable-ground/violence-against-minority-communities-nineveh-provinces-disputed (accessed 15 May 2015).

Jalabi, R. (2014) Who are the Yazidis and why is ISIS hunting them? *The Guardian*, 11 August. Available at: http://www.theguardian.com/world/2014/aug/07/who-Yezidi-isis-iraq-religion-ethnicity-mountains (accessed 5 May 2015).

Lewis, M.W. (2010) The Heterodox Zone. GeoCurrents.com, 26 January. Available at: http://www.geocurrents.info/geopolitics/the-heterodox-zone (accessed 5 May 2015).

Maisel, S. (2008) Social change amidst terror and discrimination: Yezidis in the new Iraq. The Middle East Institute, 1 August. Available at: http://www.mei.edu/content/social-change-amidst-terror-and-discrimination-yezidis-new-iraq (accessed 5 May 2015).

Quinton, L. (2015) ISIS isn't randomly destroying art – it's another form of terrorism. 28 April. Available at: http://www.texasstandard.org/shows/current/isis-isnt-randomly-destroying-art-its-another-form-of-terrorism/ (accessed 5 May 2015).

Salih, C. (2014) Islamic extremists pose new risks for religious minorities in Iraq. *New York Times*, 24 June. Available at: http://kristof.blogs.nytimes.com/2014/06/24/islamic-extremists-pose-new-risks-for-religious-minorities-in-iraq/ (accessed 25 April 2015).

Shelton, T. (2014) There are reports of the Islamic State executing dozens of Yazidis. *Global Post*, 3 August. Available at: http://www.globalpost.com/dispatch/news/regions/middle-east/iraq/140803/islamic-state-captures-sinjar-yazidis (accessed 5 May 2015).

12 Ambassadors for the Kingdom: Evangelical Volunteers in Israel as Long-term Pilgrims

ARON ENGBERG*

Lund University, Lund, Sweden

Introduction

The Bridges for Peace food bank is located in a modest warehouse in Talpiyot, a suburb south of Jerusalem city centre. The shelves along the walls are filled with packs of rice, couscous, spaghetti, tomato sauce, beans, sugar, flour, tea and corn-flakes; food stuffs that are to be packed on pallets which will be distributed to Jewish communities in Israel and on the West Bank. Together with an elderly American man and a middle-aged Japanese woman I am walking between the shelves and the pallets, carefully selecting the groceries that are marked on the food order and packing them in a neat pile. From the sticker I understand that this pallet is destined for Ariel, a Jewish community located across the green line that separates Israel proper from the Palestinian territories.[1] An armed Jewish settler comes in and talks jokingly with some of the volunteers, he is here to pick up the pallet.[2] After the pallet is sent away a friendly Canadian woman explains to me about the different aid-related services that are coordinated from the relief centre: 'Home Repair', 'Operation Rescue' and 'Feed a Child' – three different programmes that are designed primarily to help the poorer segments of Israeli society, in particular, new Jewish immigrants. The best part about her work, she says, is registering the newly arrived on her desktop. It is then that she feels most closely connected to what she came here to do.

At first glance, the activities in the warehouse in Talpiyot are difficult to connect to scholarly discourses about 'tourism' and 'pilgrimage'. International volunteer workers engaged in humanitarian work in Israel seem to have little, if anything, to do with pilgrimage as it has traditionally been understood (i.e. as a religiously motivated journey to sacred destinations; Barber, 1993). Yet, when one explores the discursive processes by which the evangelical volunteers make

---

*aron.engberg@ctr.lu.se

these activities meaningful, a quite different picture emerges: (i) the distribution of food to Jewish communities is connected to ideas about 'blessing the chosen people'; (ii) Jewish immigration to Israel is understood as part of an eschatological restoration that precedes the second coming of Christ; and (iii) the volunteers locate themselves in this narrative as ambassadors for this coming Kingdom. Coming to Israel, they claim, is a spiritual journey of discovery, learning and self-transformation.

Drawing from several years of field work and about 30 life story interviews, this chapter will present a case of contemporary evangelical mobility that cannot be squarely placed within any of the related academic debates about '(religious) tourism', 'pilgrimage', 'short-term missions', 'international volunteering' or 'migration' simply because the phenomenon is intrinsically related to all these phenomena at the same time.[3] Pro-Zionist evangelical Christians come to Jerusalem from all parts of the world; some of them as part of biblical tours, some for Christian conferences or for Hebrew courses and yet others come as volunteers.[4] This latter group is engaged in what often looks like secular humanitarian work, or sometimes even political activism, but explains these activities almost exclusively in religious terms. Initially, they come for a short period of time but often end up staying in Jerusalem for 10 years or more. What looks like a temporary adventure often turns out to be something more akin to a 'way of life'. Thus, I will explore this phenomenon as a case of 'long-term pilgrimage' in order to discuss the religious meanings that the volunteers attach to their time in Israel, the practices that they are involved in and to the place itself. Apart from providing more data on contemporary religiously motivated travel patterns I hope that this case will prove useful in reconsidering the traditional boundaries between 'tourism', 'volunteer work' and 'pilgrimage', and perhaps also illuminate something of the underlying theoretical quagmires about the relationship between 'the secular' and 'the religious'.

Pilgrimage and Religion

Much pilgrimage research in the past 50 years has been concerned with boundary making; that is, specifying the differences and similarities between different modes of travel such as 'pilgrimage' and 'tourism' (Collins-Kreiner, 2010). Many of these distinctions have relied on some kind of opposition between the 'religious' and the 'secular' as observed for instance in the motivations of travellers, the kinds of sites they visit, or the things they do when they visit them. Recent years, however, have seen a growing awareness among scholars about the fuzziness of the borders between tourism and pilgrimage. This more recent trend has given rise to a range of new 'transboundary' terms such as 'religious tourism', 'heritage journeys' and 'secular pilgrimage' (Collins-Kreiner, 2010). In addition, related terms such as 'civil religion' implicitly questions the theoretical divide between religion and society, if yet not necessarily within pilgrimage studies. Some pilgrimage scholars, however, such as Badone and Roseman (2004), have ventured further and tried to undermine the dichotomy altogether by opting for more constructivist approaches; sites aren't inherently sacred but are constructed thus by visitors. The same might of course be said about practices that travellers (or volunteer workers) are involved in. Similarly, Eade and Sallnow (1991) have explored pilgrimages as sites of competing secular and religious discourses. From such a perspective, it becomes important to explore what kind of narratives tour organizers, tour guides and travellers draw upon in making the trips feel meaningful and successful. Consequently, the ideological context of the journeys and the narratives put to work in the trips deserves a closer examination. In the case under survey here, 'Christian Zionism' is the most immediate such ideological context.

'Christian Zionism'

'Christian Zionism' is a controversial concept that is meant to capture a phenomenon within contemporary protestant Christianity that has spurred quite an interest among scholars in the last 10 years (Weber, 2004; Goldman, 2009; Spector, 2009; Shapiro, 2011; Carenen, 2012; Engberg, 2012; Ariel, 2013; Durbin, 2013a, b; Smith, 2013; Gunner and Smith, 2014). Generally speaking, 'Christian Zionist' refers to Christians for whom the Zionist movement and the State of Israel represent a fulfilment of certain biblical prophecies about the end times and the expected millennial kingdom. In other words, for Christian Zionists, the State of Israel is linked to religious narratives that leave the country shimmering with a unique other-worldly light. Historically, premillenial dispensationalism served a formative role in the development and spread of these ideas,[5] particularly in the USA. Among contemporary Christian Zionists, political, moral and economic support of Israel is viewed as encompassing moral obligation, religious duty, responsible political position and as a way to locate oneself in the eschatological drama that is currently unfolding. Apart from these fundamental aspects of the phenomenon, contemporary expressions vary widely: (i) one may or may not self-identify as a dispensationalist; (ii) one may or may not have a clear view of the political realities involved in the conflict; *and* (iii) one may or may not support a two-state solution (although the latter is the norm). Differences aside, what remains at the heart of the phenomenon is the symbolic value attributed to Israel and the idea that Christians – if they are indeed real Christians – should be committed to supporting Israel morally, economically and politically; support which is understood and explained primarily in religious terms.[6]

Christian Zionism has often been assumed to be, and often been approached as, a paradigmatically North American phenomenon. This assumption is wrong. As a Pew Research Center's Forum report quite recently showed, these ideas are widely represented within global evangelicalism, particularly in sub-Saharan Africa, and these ideas are steadily growing (Pew Forum on Religion and Public Life, 2011). The global character of the phenomenon is visible also among the volunteers in Jerusalem who come from a wide range of countries and from all continents. The International Christian Embassy Jerusalem (ICEJ) – the most influential Christian Zionist ministry in Jerusalem – has representatives in as many as 80 countries, annually organizes a conference that draws thousands of evangelicals to Jerusalem from all over the world, and regularly sends their staff on preaching trips to Africa, Asia, Latin America and the Pacific region.[7] Among the volunteers, North Americans are perhaps still in a slight majority, but the centre of gravity is shifting, here as in Christianity more generally.

Evangelical Pilgrimage

In conjunction with growing interest in Christian Zionism, evangelical pilgrimage to Israel has lately started to attract the attention of scholars (Bowman, 1991; Belhassen and Santos, 2006; Bajc, 2007; Feldman, 2007, 2011; Shapiro, 2008; Hutt, 2014; Kaell, 2014). This is partly due to the rising numbers of evangelicals travelling to Israel, but also because of some of the particular characteristics of evangelicals' relationship to Israel. Many scholarly accounts have emphasized the specific blend of spirituality and politics that evangelical pilgrimage manifests. While evangelicals certainly travel to Israel to 'walk where Jesus walked', as Hillary Kaell has suggested, and to experience the land of the Bible, they also go there to visit the land of the 'restoration'. That is, pilgrimage in its contemporary evangelical expression is not only a return to the source of the faith, but also to witness the 'miraculous rebirth' of the Jewish nation, God's chosen people. Israel, for them, is a sacred place both because of its past, but also, notably, because of its present and its expected future (Figs 12.1 and 12.2). It is often in this latter dimension of evangelical pilgrimages that politics becomes most visible.

Many evangelical tour groups follow traditional pilgrimage itineraries by visiting the sites associated with the life and death of Jesus, and places of importance in the history of Christianity. These include the Garden Tomb (the Protestant alternative to the Holy Sepulchre), the garden of Gethsemane, Mount Tabor, the Sea of Galilee, Nazareth, Yardenit (a Jordan river baptismal site) and Megiddo (the valley where the battle of Armageddon is expected to take place). However, these itineraries often also include visits to places that are more associated with the history of modern Israel such as the Knesset (the Israeli parliament), the Holocaust museum Yad Vashem, the hall where Israeli independence was declared, the military cemetery on Har Herzl and social institutions such as immigration centres. In a sense, evangelical itineraries can be seen as a fusion between Christian biblical imaginaries and Israeli civil religion; they juxtapose the ancient and modern history (and usually pay little attention to the time between the 1st and the 20th century CE) in the construction of Israel as 'the land of the Bible' (Feldman, 2007; for Israeli civil religion see: Liebman and Don-Yehiya, 1983).

Additionally, while modern sites do not fit the classic imagery of Christian sites it is clear that evangelical pilgrims often experience them as such. Sometimes they even seem to have a deeper effect on the pilgrims than the traditionally Christian sites have (Shapiro, 2008; Hutt, 2014). Faydra L. Shapiro has argued that her interviewees approached the traditionally religious sites (such as the Holy Sepulchre) not with the expected piety but rather with a manifest distance, almost distaste, that has its root in Protestant scepticism towards Orthodox and Catholic material piety. 'Protestant sites of Jesus's life and ministry', in turn were 'eagerly anticipated', yet often as easily forgotten. Instead, what made the strongest impression on the evangelical pilgrims were 'places and experiences associated with

Fig. 12.1. Bolivian evangelicals taking part in the Jerusalem March to display solidarity with Israel. The Jerusalem March takes place annually as part of the Feast of Tabernacles celebration organized by the International Christian Embassy Jerusalem (ICEJ) and draws several thousand evangelicals from at least 70 different countries. (Photograph by Aron Engberg, 2011.)

Fig. 12.2. Chinese evangelicals, here dressed up as brides, taking part in the Jerusalem March. (Photograph by Aron Engberg, 2011.)

the modern, political state' (Shapiro, 2008, p. 301). In other words, evangelical tours seem to turn the dichotomy between pilgrimage and tourism on its head; traditional pilgrimage sites are approached as religious tourists, and modern sites are encountered as pilgrims. The former are visited primarily for their cultural and historical significance, while the latter – in spite of appearance – are visited for their religious significance.

The same kind of transition of religious meaning was expressed to me in an interview with an elderly couple who have been volunteering in Israel on and off for the past 20 years. In the interview, the man explains to me what made the greatest impression on them the first time they came to Israel were precisely the encounters with the modern history:

> Because what we saw was what God is doing in this country with His people now – not necessarily what happened a long time ago in the Bible. Now we did see the Bible places, but what impacted us I think more than anything was that God is doing something even now in this land with this people – the fact that they are returning, the fact that the land is blooming again and all of that.
>
> (Tom and Susan, 2013)

For this American couple, the most significant part of their first trip to Israel was not to see the biblical places, to 'walk where Jesus walked', but rather to have first-hand experience of 'the restoration'. It was not the biblical past that caught their attention, but the 'biblical' present; *what God is doing in the Land now*. If pilgrimage is about connecting yourself to other-worldly forces by visiting holy places, about locating oneself in sacred history, these modern sites were more 'pilgrimage-like' than the traditionally 'religious' sites associated with the life and death of Jesus. It was through them that this couple experienced God as real and present.

In the above-mentioned article, Shapiro criticizes distinctions between 'tourism' and 'pilgrimage' that are based on the kind of sites the travellers visit. In her view, these distinctions easily lead to a circular argument: 'because a site is a sacred centre, travel there is pilgrimage and because people make pilgrimage there, the site is sacred' (Shapiro, 2008, p. 313). One might add to this that whether a site – or a practice for that matter – is 'religious' or 'secular' cannot be determined a priori but depends on how that particular site or practice is experienced by visitors or practitioners. A site doesn't possess meaning; it is *made meaningful* by those that consider it worth a visit.

While the dichotomy between tourism and pilgrimage is shaky when it comes to evangelical trips to Israel, so is the distinction between tourism and volunteer work. In addition to visits to these seemingly secular sites it is not uncommon that evangelical tours also include possibilities of short-term volunteering and charitable activities such as the distribution of food and handing over of gifts that they have brought with them on the tour (Shapiro, 2008; Belhassen, 2009). Since 'blessing Israel' – a trope which is derived from Genesis 12 – is a unifying idea among these evangelicals, it is perhaps unsurprising that their pilgrimages include some social activism on behalf of Jewish Israelis. However, the point here is not that visits to 'secular' sites and charitable work are practices that are somehow added to the 'pilgrimage proper' but rather that they form a constitutive part of the *pilgrimage as pilgrimage*. It is through visits to modern sites that the journey is experienced as *religiously* meaningful; it is through 'blessing Israel' that the evangelicals are connecting to the religious narratives that makes the journey spiritually important in the first place.

Some evangelicals, however, feel compelled to do more than just be part of tours, and handing out gifts to Israelis. They look for a more long-term commitment. Many of these evangelicals sign up for volunteer work in one of several Christian Zionist ministries in Jerusalem. Here they can make the pilgrimage last for years, perhaps even prolong it indefinitely.

Volunteering as Long-term Pilgrimage

The activities of volunteers, some of which were mentioned in the beginning of this chapter, look very much like Christian humanitarian work, and in many respects are.[8] Organizationally, financially and practically the Christian Zionist ministries in Jerusalem function more or less like Christian non-governmental organizations (NGOs) and are registered as Israeli charities (*amutah*). However, it is important to note that the work in Israel, in addition to general Christian humanitarian ideals, also emerges from a quite specific ideational context. In the discourses of the volunteers the activities are made meaningful not primarily with references to general Christian ideas about 'loving your neighbour' or 'serving the poor', or in relation to modern ideas about 'development' or 'poverty relief', but rather with reference to the particularity and uniqueness of Israel and the Jewish people. For them the connection between Israel and Christian eschatological narratives sets Israel – the state and the people – apart as ontologically unique in the community of nations. Precisely because it has come to be integrated in evangelical theology and practice throughout the 20th century, Israel is perceived and approached as a *religious symbol*. Modern Israeli history, due to its connection to eschatology, is perceived as sacred history. Similar to religious symbols in other contexts, Israel is able to mediate divine presence and make religious belief uniquely felt and experienced. Following this line of thought, volunteering in Israel – in addition (not in opposition) to political action – can be seen as *ritual acts*; practices that are discursively produced as 'consecrated behaviour' (Geertz, 1973).

To be sure, the volunteers never use these terms; they do not call their work 'ritual', they generally do not refer to themselves as 'pilgrims', they do not call Israel a 'symbol', but they do emphasize the spiritual nature of their work over and against my suggestions of other interpretative frameworks. In their stories, the volunteers often make distinctions between themselves and 'less committed' travellers to Israel, such as Christian pilgrims, tourists, activists and journalists. In contrast to these categories of people the volunteers see their work as long term and committed, and they generally contextualize their experience theologically, as a 'walk with God'. In other words, volunteering in Israel is part of their calling as Christians, a particular way of being Christian in the world. These life stories implicitly draw from a long history of Christian thinking about pilgrimage, not in the sense of a one-time journey, but rather as a metaphor for Christian experience of being a foreigner in the world.[9] While the anthropology of pilgrimage, at least in the Turners' tradition (Turner and Turner, 1978), has tended to see pilgrimage as characterized by liminality, a place between old social structures and new ones, much Christian theology has presented the whole Christian life in terms of a pilgrimage. In this tradition, Christians are never at home in the world (they are 'in' the world, but not 'of' it) and they are always on the way to a 'new Jerusalem', to the real home in heaven. John Bunyan popularized this metaphorical tradition in his widely influential *The Pilgrim's Progress* (originally published in 1678) but the roots of the pilgrim as a metaphor for Christian life goes back to biblical times (for a more recent work see: Horton, 2011).

The most visible aspect of this perspective emerges when the volunteers present their life stories in terms of personal transformation, and the spiritual effect that their work in Israel has upon them as Christians. This sense of personal transformation is illustrated well by Mary, a middle-aged woman from South Africa who came to Israel for the first time 2 years ago. When asked to describe her first trip to Israel she says that her 'whole life changed' and that 'the Lord turned everything inside-out'. When I asked her to elaborate, she continues:

> Yes. It changed everything in my heart. This is truly God's land ... It's, it's a spiritual place, there's a spiritual intensity in the land. Ideas that you formerly had, um, things change internally, it's as though everything is brought into the proper perspective – your understanding of the Bible, of the land, of yourself. Your priorities change. For me so many of my priorities changed personally, on a broader level, everything changed. Everything changed.
>
> (Mary, 2013)

These narratives of transformation are illustrative also when it comes to interpreting the volunteers' discourses about their work in Israel. One volunteer explains her work as a special 'assignment from God':

> I feel this season more than any, it's an absolute privilege because I feel that God is absolutely doing something through the ICEJ in the nations, concerning this nation. And so to be a part of that. It's really about making the nations and the body of Christ aware of their responsibility to this nation because this is God's chosen people and God has a plan and He's working out His plan. And according to the Bible, we have a responsibility, you know. So I feel that it is, it's an absolute privilege to be a part of this organization now and I see it as a specific assignment from God.
>
> (Cindy, 2013)

Through these narratives the volunteers locate themselves as agents in the unfolding sacred history. Not in the sense of 'forcing God's hand' (Halsell, 2003) – none of them would believe that possible in any case – but at least as workers for the coming kingdom. From this perspective, every task – no matter how seemingly mundane – has a deep spiritual purpose. Packing pallets of food to be sent to Ariel, registering new immigrants, writing articles for magazines or preparing conferences are all part of an individual calling that places the volunteer in relation to God, and to God's purposes with history.

Ambassadors for the Kingdom

The obvious question facing a researcher among evangelical volunteers in Israel – a question that undoubtedly faces them as well – is what about politics? The distribution of food to Ariel has certain quite obvious political ramifications, so has the volunteer's advocacy work, their media productions and their work with newly arrived Jewish immigrants. Yet, the volunteers obviously prefer to construct their identities and to motivate their activities along religious rather than along political lines. The American historian George Marsden has pointed out that evangelicalism historically has harboured a deep ambivalence towards the world of politics (Marsden, 1991). Among the volunteers, 'political' is often attributed to ideological opponents but very rarely adopted in relation to one's own practices or beliefs. Part of the reason for this is that politics is understood in opposition to sincere faith; faith which is meant to be universal and hence something that transcends political preferences. Politics, in the volunteers' discourses, emerges as *desacralizing*, because 'politics' locates a phenomenon within the world, within the sphere of 'the secular'. When asked, for instance, about sending pallets of food to Ariel, the Canadian woman mentioned in the beginning of this chapter replied:

> It's the centre of Samaria and I don't like to call it the West Bank, I like to call it Samaria, so delivering food to Ariel there's, there's needy people there for sure. I actually saw some of the homes where the people that had been removed from Gaza had been relocated and it was, it was pretty horrifying, um, for them and so it's a privilege to be able to help the people in Ariel. Um, the 'green line' – green line, schmeen line ... I mean [chuckles] ... Time will tell and my take on this is that the green line will disappear certainly and go into a different place altogether ... Much further out.
>
> (Karen, 2013)

This quote is illustrative of several aspects of the evangelical discourse about their work in Israel. Instead of reflecting on the politics of the situation, the discourse is framed in terms of humanitarian aid, sympathy for suffering people and spiced with eschatological and biblical references. This could be understood as a purely rhetorical move – or as simple ignorance of the context – but it also indicates the world view from which the situation is approached, interpreted and understood. Even though Karen does not use much explicit religious language, her whole discourse arises from a distinctly religious worldview. She claims that she 'does not like' the term West Bank – instead she prefers the biblical term 'Samaria' – and that 'the green line, schmeen line' is a non-issue. Ultimately – that is, in the eschatological future – it will go away altogether. The green line is the armistice line from 1949, which in most international negotiations is taken as the starting point from which a viable solution to the conflict will be built. Karen, however, views it differently. For her, the green line is irrelevant primarily because it is not biblical; the green line has no place in God's plan for the future. Prophetically speaking, Israel will – in its future glory – stretch from 'the Nile to the Euphrates'. The green line is a political border, and as such it is a human construct bound to disappear in the future.

Puzzling with these questions, towards the end of an interview with another volunteer who is involved in media production and advocacy work, I decided to ask this question explicitly. When questioned about the 'political nature of his work' he immediately refused my interpretation: 'No, no, no, no ...', he says, 'personally I don't, I don't wanna mix politics and my belief in God.' But when I repeated the question he reconsidered and said that, well, 'It's political in the sense that, in the sense that I want to advance the Kingdom of God, if you see the Kingdom of God as a nation, which it is. So political in that sense.' His work, Adam seems to say, is political *but only* in a religious framework.

The 'both-and' nature of the volunteers' self-understanding connects well to theological ideas about Christian life as a journey, indeed as a pilgrimage. They are 'in' the world, but not 'of' it, they are involved in seemingly mundane – sometimes even political – tasks but fill these practices with spiritual meaning. One volunteer (aptly enough she is employed by the International Christian Embassy) explains this self-understanding in terms of ambassadorship:

> We are called to establish the Kingdom of God on earth ... we are called to be ambassadors of God. And what does it mean to be ambassadors of God? It means even in the worldly sense I think we see that ambassadors are those who are in one country while representing another country. And so that, that's what defines us as ambassadors of Christ – that we represent the Kingdom of God.
>
> (Anna, 2012)

Conclusion

Ideology – the ideology of the researcher as well as the ideology of those that the researcher studies – matters. It matters for how pilgrimages are approached, described and analysed. It even matters for what is conceptualized as a pilgrimage in the first place. In this brief chapter about evangelical travellers to Israel I have tried to show that what we conceptualize as pilgrimages are highly dependent on context, not only in the sense of concrete places that travellers visit, but also in terms of the narratives that they carry with them, and the inherited practices that they have for making sense of what they experience there. I have chosen to characterize the volunteers in Jerusalem as 'long-term pilgrims' because this approach is faithful to their discourses about themselves, and their practices in Jerusalem. I have not, however, intended to say that rather than viewing the volunteers' activities as 'political action' we should see them as 'religious ritual'. Such an argument would only serve to re-inscribe the dichotomy that I have here tried to de-stabilize. Being an ambassador for the Kingdom of God certainly entails a bit of both, it means being 'in' the world but not 'of' it, and it means being a pilgrim, theologically speaking.

Notes

[1] Ariel, established in 1978, is one of the largest settlements on the West Bank with a population of around 20,000. As Ariel is located east of the green line it is considered an illegal settlement by the United Nations (UN) and the international community. The Israeli government generally disputes this and declared Ariel as a city in 1998.

[2] Gun ownership, as well as carrying firearms in public in Israel requires a licence. Settlers are eligible for licences for hand guns (and sometimes automatic rifles) under Israeli law due to security reasons. Generally speaking, when civilians in Israel are seen to carry guns in public they are often residents of the West Bank settlements (for more information see: Alpers and Wilson, 2015).

[3] Field diary 20130214. This chapter is based on the author's field work among evangelical volunteer workers at three Christian ministries in Jerusalem (see Note 6) that was conducted between 2011 and 2013. All interviews quoted in this chapter were audio recorded and transcribed verbatim. All names of volunteers that appear here are pseudonyms.

[4] The term 'evangelical' is understood differently in different geographical and ecclesial contexts but generally refers to a particular type of protestant Christian that emphasizes the experience of being 'born again' as a defining moment in Christian life and faith.

[5] Dispensationalism is an intricate theological system developed primarily by the British theologian John Nelson Darby in the 1800s. Dispensationalism is well known for its meta-historical perspective that divides the history of the world into several distinct eras and locates the different biblical passages in relation to these 'dispensations'. The 'return' of the Jews to Palestine was seen by Darby as an eschatological event that would eventually usher mankind into the seventh and final dispensation which would ultimately lead to Jesus's return and the establishing of his millennial kingdom. Through several missionary trips in the USA dispensationalism became embedded in the growing fundamentalist movement in the early 1900s (for more information on the history of dispensationalism in the USA see: Weber, 2004).

[6] Apocalyptic or eschatological ideas, particularly dispensationalism, have been given explanatory priority in much previous research on evangelicals travelling to or working in Israel (for instance: Belhassen, 2009). However, this focus on apocalyptic heritage needs to be nuanced. Time spent among the volunteers makes it obvious that dispensationalism's cultural capital is rather limited; very few volunteers are familiar with the finer details of the theological system, many of its central ideas are forgotten or even explicitly rejected by modern-day evangelicals.

[7] When the Israeli parliament passed the 'Basic Law: Jerusalem' which specified the united Jerusalem as the capital of Israel, most of the official embassies that still remained in Jerusalem were relocated to Tel Aviv in critique of the law. As a political response to this, a group of concerned evangelical Christians established the International Christian Embassy Jerusalem (ICEJ) to show support for Jerusalem as the undivided capital of Israel. The Bridges for Peace was established in 1975 as a Christian educational institution and the Christian Friends of Israel in 1985, partly as a result of a split within the ICEJ. Taken together the three organizations represent millions of evangelical Christians worldwide.

[8] At least this goes for the volunteers involved in aid-related work, caring for the poorer segments of (Jewish) Israeli society, and those involved in home repair and construction. Other areas the volunteers work with that are less related to humanitarianism are advocacy, administration, media and the planning and preparation of conferences such as the ICEJ-hosted Feast of Tabernacles.

[9] The English word 'pilgrim' is etymologically derived from the Latin *peregrinus* which means 'foreigner'.

References

Alpers, P. and Wilson, M. (2015) Israel – Gun facts, figures and the law. Sydney School of Public Health, The University of Sydney, 11 May. GunPolicy.org. Available at: http://www.gunpolicy.org/firearms/region/israel (accessed 25 May 2016).

Ariel, Y.S. (2013) *An Unusual Relationship: Evangelical Christians and Jews*. New York University Press, New York.

Badone, E. and Roseman, S. (2004) *Intersecting Journeys: the Anthropology of Pilgrimage and Tourism*. University of Illinois Press, Champaign, Illinois.

Bajc, V. (2007) Creating ritual through narrative, place and performance in evangelical protestant pilgrimage in the Holy Land. *Mobilities* 2, 395–412.

Barber, R. (1993) *Pilgrimages*. The Boydell Press, London.

Belhassen, Y. (2009) Fundamentalist Christian pilgrimages as a political and cultural force. *Journal of Heritage Tourism* 4, 131–144.

Belhassen, Y. and Santos, C. (2006) An American evangelical pilgrimage to Israel: a case study on politics and triangulation. *Journal of Travel Research* 44, 431–441.

Bowman, G. (1991) Christian ideology and the image of a Holy Land: the place of pilgrimage in the various Christianities. In: Eade, J. and Sallnow, M.J. (eds) *Contesting the Sacred: the Anthropology of Christian Pilgrimage*. Routledge, London, pp. 98–121.

Carenen, C. (2012) *The Fervent Embrace: Liberal Protestants, Evangelicals, and Israel*. New York University Press, New York.

Collins-Kreiner, N. (2010) Researching pilgrimage: continuity and transformations. *Annals of Tourism Research* 2, 440–456.

Durbin, S. (2013a) 'I am an Israeli': Christian Zionism as American redemption. *Culture and Religion: an Interdisciplinary Journal* 10, 1–24.

Durbin, S. (2013b) 'I will bless those who bless you': Christian Zionism, fetishism, and unleashing the blessings of God. *Journal of Contemporary Religion* 28, 507–521.

Eade, J. and Sallnow, M.J. (1991) *Contesting the Sacred: the Anthropology of Christian Pilgrimage*. Routledge, London.

Engberg, A. (2012) Evangelicalism in the interspaces: the construction of Judeo-Christian identity in a Messianic community in Jerusalem. *Swedish Missiological Themes* 100, 263–281.

Feldman, J. (2007) Constructing a shared Bible land: Jewish Israeli guiding performances for Protestant pilgrims. *American Ethnologist* 34, 351–374.

Feldman, J. (2011) Abraham the settler, Jesus the refugee: contemporary conflict and Christianity on the road to Bethlehem. *History & Memory* 23, 62–95.

Geertz, C. (1973) *The Interpretation of Cultures: Selected Essays*. Basic Books, New York.

Goldman, S. (2009) *Zeal for Zion: Christians, Jews, and the Idea of the Promised Land*. University of North Carolina Press, Chapel Hill, North Carolina.

Gunner, G. and Smith, R.O. (2014) *Comprehending Christian Zionism: Perspectives in Comparison*. Fortress Press, Minneapolis, Minnesota.

Halsell, G. (2003) *Forcing God's Hand: Why Millions Pray for a Quick Rapture and Destruction of Planet Earth*. Amana Publications, Beltsville, Maryland.

Horton, M. (2011) *The Christian Faith: a Systematic Theology for Pilgrims on the Way*. Zondervan, Grand Rapids, Michigan.

Hutt, C. (2014) Christian Zionist pilgrimage in the twenty-first century. In: Gunner, G. and Smith, R.O. (eds) *Comprehending Christian Zionism: Perspectives in Comparison*. Fortress Press, Minneapolis, Minnesota, pp. 137–160.

Kaell, H. (2014) *Walking Where Jesus Walked: American Christians and Holy Land Pilgrimage*. New York University Press, New York.

Liebman, C.S. and Don-Yehiya, E. (1983) *Civil Religion in Israel: Traditional Judaism and Political Culture in the Jewish State*. University of California Press, Berkeley, California.

Marsden, G. (1991) *Understanding Fundamentalism and Evangelicalism*. Eerdmans, Grand Rapids, Michigan.

Pew Forum on Religion and Public Life (2011) *Global Survey of Evangelical Protestant Leaders*. Pew Research Center, Washington, DC.

Shapiro, F. (2008) To the apple of God's eye: Christian Zionist travel to Israel. *Journal of Contemporary Religion* 23, 307–320.

Shapiro, F. (2011) The Messiah and Rabbi Jesus: policing the Jewish–Christian border in Christian Zionism. *Culture and Religion* 12, 463–477.

Smith, R.O. (2013) *More Desired than our Owne Salvation: The Roots of Christian Zionism*. Oxford University Press, New York.

Spector, S. (2009) *Evangelicals and Israel: the Story of American Christian Zionism*. Oxford University Press, New York.

Turner, V. and Turner, E. (1978) *Image and Pilgrimage in Christian Culture: Anthropological Perspectives*. Blackwell, Oxford.

Weber, T. (2004) *On the Road to Armageddon: How Evangelicals Became Israel's Best Friend*. Baker Academic, Grand Rapids, Michigan.

Closing Words

13 Redeeming Western Holy Places and Contested Holy Cities

MARIA LEPPÄKARI*

Swedish Theological Institute in Jerusalem and Åbo Akademi University, Finland

Introduction

This chapter addresses 'holy places' in relation to 'holy cities' and problematizes the challenges which pilgrimage and tourism research faces when addressing such religious concepts. Within the sphere of religion we find that certain geographical sites are of intrinsic importance as sacred places and attract people in a very special way. Settlements described as 'holy cities' are cities like any others, yet they are not; perhaps they are more complex in their characteristics than ordinary urban settlements. Such sites have come to signify something 'holy' – they are not only to be considered as physical, they also comprise humans as moral subjects, inhabiting symbolic sets and references to specific places.

The author reflects on the collective impact of the chapters in this book, and argues that they provide new perspectives on old, familiar and well-documented themes and thus constitute a fresh approach in relation to themes such as ideological motives, ethics and justice, history, management, mental health and religious perceptions. Sustainable development in dialogue and conflict settings is addressed as part of a delicate societal development. Here, identity-making abilities and living symbolisms become identified, highlighted and further described in order to expand the reader's perspectives and thereby this volume takes management beyond the topic. In the end, visitors might think they are redeeming a place but it is perhaps the opposite, a place redeeming the visitor.

*maria.leppakari@abo.fi

Holy City versus Holy Place

What makes a place holy? In extension to this question one can ask what makes a city holy. The two questions are not easily answered since what we can describe and define as something 'holy' is not so much a specific quality to be observed. In order to understand this perspective one needs to address complex historical processes, the construction and reference of theological texts and their interpretations through history, and finally, and perhaps most importantly, how individuals and groups describe themselves – as something 'holy' – and how one refers to it, in specific contexts through time and in specific places.

If a place is described as 'holy' it usually refers to something that people ascribe to the place when thinking and talking about it. In academic settings 'holiness' is not something that we can grab or easily point out. Therefore, what distinguishes places described as 'holy' from ordinary places are the traditions, the symbols and meanings attached to the place. If a place then is regarded and described as holy, it is generally due to the apparition or the sustained presence of something beyond the ordinary, something rather superhuman. As a term, 'holy place' refers to the accounts and stories of spaces where supernatural encounters have taken place in a natural environment. Not only is the place referred to as a meeting point of superhuman encounters in the past, more so, it is also believed to host the presence of continuous encounters with the supernatural. For some, the place is significant due to continuous superhuman encounters and functions, as a gateway where the natural meets the unnatural. The presence of the supernatural is then continuously present in the space. Its presence is sustained and therefore can generate new superhuman apparitions and a sense of belonging for those engaged in expressions of beliefs connected to the specific space. Whether the place is believed to be holy in relation to some specific events or persons, is not relevant. What is relevant are the qualities ascribed to it. The connection might be purely historical, linked to events that have taken place or it might be described as a sense visitors have at the spot.

'Holy cities' then, are cities like any other, but yet, they are not. Such sites come to signify something 'holy'. In Hinduism, Varanasi is a place of worship and pilgrimage; in Catholic Christianity, Rome has been referred to as a City of God, to mention but two examples. As the late Professor R.Z. Werblowsky put it, there are holy places distinct from holy lands, and there are holy cities as distinct from holy places (Werblowsky, 1998). The city commonly referred to as holy in the three monotheistic faiths of Judaism, Christianity and Islam is Jerusalem. Jerusalem is special since no other historical city evokes such claims to this day. For each of the three religions, Jerusalem has a different meaning, but we find at least two factors in the religiously motivated longing for Jerusalem that unites the three faiths: (i) the actual geographical spot of Jerusalem including the role ascribed by the faith traditions as the Mountain of the Lord; and, equally importantly, (ii) the role the city plays in futuristic visions of life on earth (Leppäkari, 2006). Similar to holy places, holy cities are not only characterized by the presence of an amalgam of 'holy elements', but rather the intensity and the magnitude of the holy place(s) are such that they distort the normal urban functions of the city and produce anomalous institutions, investments and demographics (Peters, 2004).

Representations of a 'Holy Place' and a 'Holy City'

When cities are described as holy, they can be studied and treated as symbols. As such they have through the ages drawn to them special attention. As a far-reaching symbol, the city is embodied with multiple representations created and constructed in people's minds, in people's physical environment and cultural heritage. The suggestion here, of a place being evocative of inner affective structures implies that perception of a place is not fixed in a cemented structure in a social context, but rather, is related to both human and non-human surroundings in transformative ways. It is thus important to take note of a psychological framework here, a transformative dialogue between place, individuals and various fragments of societies.

As a 'holy city', Jerusalem is not only a geographical spot close to the Mediterranean coastline, but it is also present in people's dreams and future-oriented visions of a kingdom of heaven. These visions of Jerusalem are not restricted to history but are very much alive today. Bearing the epithet the 'Holy City', Jerusalem is at the moment in focus for both world politics and religious attention. Few cities in the world harbour so many holy sites as Jerusalem. This is why the city can serve as a 'prototype' of an extended holy place and as an example of a contested 'holy city'. Being a holy city for Jews, Christians and Muslims, the respective sites and shrines are divided among these three religious traditions. A study of the city's relevance to the different monotheistic faith-traditions is expressed in what is perceived as a sustained presence of the supernatural in the likes of: (i) God's presence (in the Temple) on Temple Mount; (ii) the tomb of Jesus (the Church of the Holy Sepulchre); and (iii) the presence of a saint in Muhammad's Night Journey from Al Quds (*Haram esh-Sharif*, the Noble Sanctuary with its mosques). Jerusalem's sanctity has, to a great extent, shaped and stretched the 'normal' functions of a city, since the theological traditions linked to the place continue to nourish representations of the sacred in relation to this specific place and city itself.

Jerusalem is a holy city to Jews in the sense that it is regarded both as a national capital and as a religious centre in reference to the biblical tradition of the 'Promised Land', and later, its concentration of sanctification as the 'City of God'. Jerusalem is a holy city for Christians in the sense that it is the setting of important events in relation to Jesus and as such, is linked into a sacred narrative of the history and future of mankind. Jerusalem is holy to Muslims for its association with the Bible (both Old and New Testaments) and Muhammad's life.

The most well-known among all the holy sites is what the Jewish tradition knows as the *Har ha-Bayit* or the Temple Mount, and in the Muslim tradition the *Haram esh-Sharif* (Fig. 13.1). The different names indicate the different functions the site has in tradition. Within the Jewish tradition, this marks the site of the ancient temples and in the Muslim tradition it is referred to as the third most important place of prayer after Mecca and Medina. The location itself comprises 155,000 m^2 and is built on bedrock between the Kidron and Tyropoeon valleys (Bengtsson, 2015).

Fig. 13.1. A panoramic view of the Holy City, picturing the *Har ha-Bayit* (the Temple Mount) or *Haram esh-Sharif*. Photograph taken from the Mount of Olives in Jerusalem.

Sadly, in Jerusalem disputes in relation to sacred sites have a history of conflict, which is why there are formal agreements in place to facilitate practical workings in the city. In 2000 a survey was undertaken to quantify religious shrines in the Old City of Jerusalem, and according to the findings, a total of 326 shrines exist, with an estimated 25 synagogues, 15 mosques and around 70 churches. The number is exceptional, not only in relation to shrines per square kilometre but also in relation to the religious diversity displayed in the city (Bengtsson, 2015).

Internationally, the vast majority of sacred shrines and holy sites host pilgrims united by strong degrees of cultural homogeneity. But, since the city is considered holy by the three monotheistic religious traditions, Jerusalem differs on this point, drawing pilgrims from a vast multitude of nations and cultural traditions. The representatives of these traditions partly go to different places at different times, where they engage in different forms of worship. From time to time, these visits are marked by clashes at the holy places.

During the Ottoman administration in the mid-19th century, at the time before the British Mandate, the number of holy shrines was much lower, still an order called *Status Quo* was confirmed in order to settle religious disputes in relation to sacred sites. In 1852, when the ruling sultan established the latest Status Quo firman (a 'firman' is a decree/contract) to tackle the main problem at that time – that Christian communities were fighting with each other about replacing a lost artefact in the Church of the Nativity in Bethlehem. The Status Quo agreement referred also to other Christian sites, and to Jewish and Muslim shrines alike. The basic idea behind the agreement was to let each religious community administrate and care for their own places of worship. What the Status Quo did not regulate nor anticipate were changes in religious demographics and changes in the political scene (Bengtsson, 2015).

What then, can be described as a holy place in Jerusalem? Synagogues, mosques and churches are venues for worship and do in fact not qualify as 'holy places' as such. Although the place of worship can be referred to as 'holy' in itself, as pointed out above, a holy place requires more. According to a classical definition proposed by Mircea Eliade, for a place to be referred to as 'holy' it needs somehow to be connected to some kind of superhuman occurrences. Practitioners of a religious tradition, that is believers and pilgrims who enter such a place, still view a visit as entering another realm. In other words, the sacred place is perceived as separated from this worldly existence – and therefore referred to as an opposite to the profane or mundane. When groups and individuals come to visit Jerusalem as a distinguished 'holy city', this view is still relevant in many respects, especially in relation to visiting the Temple Mount or *Haram esh-Sharif* where there are specific foundational myths connected to the site. The myths are not simply confined to history and ancient times but also include ritual elements, such as religiously motivated restrictions for entering the site itself. Yet, the place is still venerated by Muslims and Jews however prescribed and interpreted through different theological explanations and motives. None the less, people dwell in and travel to such a venerated city.

Significant changes to the city have taken place here, and the historical events are too vast to address in an article of this length. The current problems in this contested city are, however, related to provocations, riots and violent clashes linked to additional perspectives, those of archology, hegemony, identity, power and politics. In this respect both local residents as worshippers in the city, and visiting pilgrims/tourists alike, experience how sanctity and conflict are simultaneously overlapping in this complex place. Concurrently, people of different faith traditions live their lives side by side in this city. From both perspectives in the Israeli–Palestine conflict, disparate political realities including archaeological endeavours and different political provocations, along with constant hostile fundamentalist rhetoric, add fuel to the tensions in the city. From time to time these tensions spark into physical confrontation and violence. These actions and the reports they generate internationally, continuously contribute to the process of generating and deepening certain specific representations of the city.

These multiple layers of experienced reality and sacredness make Jerusalem not appear so much as a 'holy city' but rather as a multiplicity of holy cities, due to the fact that multiple religious communities worship at many of the sites. These faith groups are more or less contending over the same spot, operating at the same moment, each party striving for hegemony (Bowman, 1991). By looking at contemporary Western Protestant Christian expressions of the city alone, we find that what makes Jerusalem holy for Christians today is not so much about something found in the city, but rather something brought to it from outside (Leppäkari, 2015). Representations of the city are then matched up on the spot by individuals and groups in the presence of monuments and spaces as physical markers of sacredness. These various imaginations and expressions of Jerusalem are representations of the city, and function as signs in the diverse discourses on religion, power and identity of the visiting groups.

Though religious traditions around the world share the same biblical sources, their interpretations of them, especially in relation to Jerusalem, differ. Here the different cultural environments and their development play an important intrinsic role. To a great extent, the distinctions between the major strains of Christianity lie in the interpretation of their substantial differences between epistemologies and soteriologies. Thus, it is impossible to grasp the complexity of the phenomena, settings and sociopolitical expressions of Jerusalem today without referring to the place's demography, geography, history and theology. Furthermore, individual emotions and perceptions connected to the place play a significant role in a contemporary understanding of the 'Holy City' today.

'Religion' is a complex term, and scholars in the field tend to argue extensively about defining the phenomenon. In general, the term stands for a meaning-creating function, and is regarded as an expression of how individuals and groups construct meaningful perspectives and orientations in their lives. As an umbrella term, it comprises questions and matters that are existentially important to humans and includes behavioural concepts in relation to codes of conduct, morality and admiration. As an attitude and a form of praxis, religion is expressed in various ways. Included in these expressions we find rituals and particularly rich symbolic use of language. In this way, religion can be viewed as a combination of physical elements, symbolic meanings and functions attached to its physical realities.

People are drawn to 'holy places' in 'holy cities'. They visit shrines and sanctuaries, attend festivals, games and spectacles. Among such visits, pilgrimage is perhaps the most well-known form of established religious tourism. Religious sensitivities keep many from referring to pilgrims as mere 'tourists', while the pilgrim is generally seen as being driven by deeply spiritual motives. Development within the field of tourism and religion, including pilgrimage, is well accounted in recent research which is increasingly addressing the complicated relationship and dynamics between pilgrimage and tourism. Research challenges are currently being met with interdisciplinary approaches in order to emphasize the complexity of the phenomenon itself (Raj and Griffin, 2015).

The Impact of Travel and Tourism on a 'Holy City'

The motivating factors for participation in pilgrimage and religious tourism are currently identified and discussed in intriguing ways. According to Ruth Blackwell (2007), religious tourism encompasses all kinds of travel motivated by religion, where the destination is a religious site. The main question remains: how should we then distinguish between pilgrims and religious tourists, or should we? Blackwell argues that we can do this by observing the way people behave: pilgrims make the journey a ritual by, for example, chanting or reciting religious songs at critical moments, while the religious tourists do not. Simply travelling to a religious site does not make one a pilgrim (Blackwell, 2007).

The study of transformative trends in relation to sacred spaces within contemporary and contested 'holy cities' allows scholars to identify the impact of religion in relation to the above-outlined, specific theoretical quest. It is obvious that the role of religion in contemporary society is still a relevant one. The strategic choice in this book, to focus on 'holy cities', seeks to uncover present and past religious characteristics in contextual ritual patterns, which tourism management studies seek to explore in different ways of interaction, in specific contexts. This enables both academics and managers who share specific common interests in 'holy cities', to deal with late modern locations of 'religion' in people's personal lives and in surrounding environments.

Tourism is also a voluntary practice, whereby many people expose themselves to 'other' religions and cultures. People who rarely visit a church at home may enjoy visits to sacred sites. Even if devotional objects no longer find a place in secular homes, one might happily bring religious items belonging to 'other religions' as souvenirs and integrate them as part of home decor, visual design or curios for admiration. Through such activities, religion then is re-emerging as part of leisure-based activity.

Secular Western travellers heading to 'holy cities' in Israel and Palestine encounter other Christian denominations (Armenian, Catholic, Orthodox, Ethiopian, Coptic, etc.) and meet various expressions of Jewish and Muslim traditions. Eventually, travellers end up visiting 'holy cities', including religiously important sites and places that the visitor may not necessarily be familiar with, and yet encounter devoted travellers. Such encounters have the potentiality of transformation and open up a perspective that would allow scholars to also address questions in relation to human encounters, dialogue, research and social striving for peace and well-being. Tourism to holy cities can be a vehicle for the international community to become advocates of peace. Definitions of 'peace' still come in various embedded preferences with reference to different religious communities and their internal contest for hegemony.

In recent times, there is an emergence of tours that embark on themes such as 'sustainable tourism' and 'justice tourism', addressing relevant topics that post-secular, meaning-searching Westerners dwell upon (Solomon, 2005). Tour organizers in 'Holy Lands' and 'Holy Cities' compete for customers, particularly in relation to the more traditional, religiously designed tours, and indeed, through their activities, they often contest and challenge political hegemonies. While currently requiring more study to validate and explore the idea further, these tours bring forth a new paradigm in tourism, as they aim to contest media reports and popular simplification in relation to visits and presentations of holy places and holy cities.

When assessing the impact of tourism in local contexts and on local religion, with respect to both the travellers and the residents at the destination, the consequences of tourism are enormous. Paramount in this are processes of commoditization of place and services, which affect religion/culture in various ways, including: (i) re-traditionalization; (ii) stylization of various performances and rituals; (iii) creation or reproduction of artefacts serving as souvenirs and gifts; (iv) promotion of certain heritage sites that may have been of much less importance previously; (v) changes in the access to 'holy sites'; (vi) changes in the structure of sites, adding further components in order to accommodate the needs of the visitors; and not to forget (vii) changing conceptions of gender and age. Some of these seemingly superficial changes are often interlinked with processes of substantial transformation and renegotiation that affect the power structure of local or host communities and their constructions of identities. On the one hand, tourism may provide a certain shield of protection in an otherwise hostile environment (e.g. some locations in Israel and Palestine). On the other hand, it may provoke engagement and conflict.

Encounters in 'Holy Cities'

Eventually, for some scholars the aim of academic curiosity and study is to create a deeper understanding of the negotiated processes through which contemporary religious identities are constantly being formed and re-formed. Such formation can be addressed as dialogic processes, which take place inside the human mind and are then intrapersonal, but also interpersonal as they become expressed between individuals and groups. In Israel/Palestine the contesting parties who conceive of each other as 'other', open up an interreligious and intercultural perspective. Such encounters can in character be both positive and negative. Encounters can promote peace and reconciliation, and are then dialogic in their character. When negative, encounters may promote hatred and conflict. Jewish, Christian and Islamic faith traditions become empirically central if we want to understand various approaches to holy cities, especially with justice and societal peace in mind. The formation of more theoretical implications and perspectives is related to themes like spatiality, dialogue, human relatedness and transformation. Research efforts would surely contribute to a common, over-arching and multi-facetted understanding of the research topic, but it can never be understood as comprehensive. It will always have its limitations, since both individual and social variations in interpretation and perception of a space are continuous. This fact will keep on challenging pilgrimage and tourism studies, and continuously call for diversified approaches.

A 'place' or 'city' in this book has not only been considered as physical, it is also a constituent factor of humans as moral subjects, inhabiting symbolic sets and references. A comprehensive model for the existential dimension of a 'place' brings the varying foci of different theoretical perspectives together on a more general level. In this book 'place' and 'city' are viewed as central to meaning, shaped by memories, expectations, stories of real and imagined events and visceral feelings. As a symbol, the 'city' or 'place' sensitizes and clarifies the boundaries between the world and us. On a more conceptual level, a central assumption is that a theoretical model of place, with existential references, also acknowledges psychological, interpretative and phenomenological dimensions.

Reflective, qualitative methods allow scholars to observe, analyse and explore the potential relevance of different traits as underlying structures in a theoretical model of the existential dimension when travelling to a place. Such themes can be explored with the help of case studies. Due to the methodological difficulties related to working with underlying affective structures, experiences of contrasting, conflicting and complementary spaces should be a matter to be considered as we highlight the evocative dimension of a place. Analyses of meanings embedded in contrasting sacred places and urban environments address effects and attitudes as they are expressed in ritualistic fashions.

Ruth Illman, in undertaking her study of interreligious dialogue, employs modern research approaches of moral philosophy and dialogue philosophy, an approach that takes an interest in interpersonal encounters in order to create a deeper understanding of how the boundaries of 'us' and 'them' are created and crossed in such encounters. The 'other' can either be met as an 'idealized other', a 'radical other' or an 'autonomous other' (Illman, 2004). An interesting question arises: can religious convictions make way for mutuality and respect between persons of different faiths, if we were to address what inspires the persons involved in such dialogues to cross the spatial and symbolic boundaries of otherness? In a pilgrimage and religious tourism perspective this would suggest an 'opening of personal spaces'. Rephrased, what happens when we enable meetings between Jews, Christians and Muslims with each other, allowing the presence of cultural, political and religious differences in a specific context? Here, the referred context equates to the contemporary 'Holy City' Jerusalem, but it could also be Bethlehem or Hebron.

Ethical issues can be addressed in pilgrimage studies. The ability to discern humanity in the persons we meet is understood as a cornerstone of interreligious dialogue (Illman, 2004). A challenge for future research is to gain deeper understanding of religious symbolic self-understanding of the persons involved in such interreligious dialogue encounters. Individual travellers, persons who regard their religious conviction as a call for respect, humility and communion are crossing the spatial boundaries of specific faith traditions.

The above-described research would comprise a comprehensive understanding of contemporary religiosity as it is expressed in relation to religiously motivated travel with specific locations in mind and challenges for ethical perspectives in relation to political, economic and religious aspects.

Since humans have the ability to adapt and continuously create meaning while engaging in encounters, we also contribute to the transformation of the notion of 'sacred space' and become engaged in the re-construction of what is perceived as a 'holy city'. This we do in relation to both spatiality and movement. It is vitally important to take this into consideration when, in contemporary and changing social situations, religions are increasingly being used and referred to as interpretive tools when explaining conflicts and hatred between peoples. Pilgrims and religious tourists might think that they, by their visit, are redeeming a city but it is perhaps quite the opposite; the place is redeeming the individual.

References

Bengtsson, H. (2015) The role of the holy sites in the old city of Jerusalem in the Israeli–Palestinian conflict. Paper presented at the conference *Mending the World? Possibilities and Obstacles for Religion, Church, and Theology*, 14 October 2015, The Church of Sweden, Uppsala. Available at: https://www.svenskakyrkan.se/default.aspx?id=1288140 (accessed 14 February 2016).

Blackwell, R. (2007) Motivations for religious tourism, pilgrimage, festivals and events. In: Raj, R. and Morpeth, N.D. (eds) *Religious Tourism and Pilgrimage Management: an International Perspective*. CAB International, Wallingford, UK, pp. 35–47.

Bowman, G. (1991) Christian ideology and the image of a Holy Land: the place of pilgrimage in the various Christianities. In: Eade, J. and Sallnow, M.J. (eds) *Contesting the Sacred.The Anthropology of Christian Pilgrimage*. Routledge, London, pp. 98–121.

Illman, R. (2004) *Gränser och gränsöverskridanden. Skildrade erfarenheter av kulturella möten i internationellt projektarbete*. Åbo Akademis förlag, Åbo, Finland.

Leppäkari, M. (2006) *Apocalyptic Representations of Jerusalem*. Brill Academic Publisher, Leiden, The Netherlands.

Leppäkari, M. (2015) Nordic pilgrimage to Israel: a case of Christian Zionism. In: Raj, R. and Griffin, K. (eds) *Religious Tourism and Pilgrimage Management: an International Perspective*. CAB International, Wallingford, UK, pp. 205–217.

Peters, F.E. (2004) *Jerusalem. City of God, City of Fire*. Barns & Noble Audio, New York.

Raj, R. and Griffin, K. (eds) (2015) *Religious Tourism and Pilgrimage Management: an International Perspective*, 2nd edn. CAB International, Wallingford, UK.

Solomon, R. (2005) Pilgrimages for Transformation. Papers and findings from a study workshop on *Interfaith Co-operation for Justice in the Occupied Territories – Human encounters for peace and reconciliation through tourism*, 21–24 October 2005. Ecumenical Coalition on Tourism, Alexandria, Egypt.

Werblowsky, R.J.Z. (1998) Introduction: mindscape and landscape. In: Kedar, B.Z. and Werblosky, R.J.Z. (eds) *Sacred Space, Shrine, City, Land*. Macmillan, London, pp. 9–17.

Appendix – Discussion Points

Chapter 2

- Comparing the Jewish pilgrimage ritual to the Temple in Jerusalem during antiquity with present-day pilgrimages, what similarities and differences can you identify?
- How do national and international pilgrimages assist in telling the Zionist story?
- In the context of this chapter, discuss the rabbinical concepts of exile and redemption.

Chapter 3

- While some authors suggest that the importance of religion is declining in an increasingly globalized, secularized world, Christian pilgrimage is still very popular, and indeed many sites are experiencing increased numbers and pressures. Why do you think this is the case?
- The nature of Christian pilgrimage appears to currently be in a period of change, how is this being manifest, and how will sites cope with such changes?
- What are the main differences and similarities when one compares the pilgrimage experience at the start of the 20th and 21st centuries?

Chapter 4

- How and why did the view of Jerusalem evolve for Swedish Christians throughout the 19th century?
- In the early 20th century, how did travel writers idealize day-to-day life in the Holy Land, for their readers 'back home' in Sweden?

- In relation to visitors to the Holy Land, what are your thoughts on the way in which travel writers can challenge or perpetuate a political ideal due to their representation of the place they are visiting?

Chapter 5

- How does the relationship between tourists and their beliefs play a part in influencing individuals when visiting religious sites?
- Why is the mosque such an important element of Islamic society, and thus, how might a regular tourism destination facilitate an experience suited to the needs and requirements of a practising Muslim?
- What place does pilgrimage hold for a modern Muslim?

Chapter 6

- How does a deeper understanding of the Qur'an impact a person's visit to an Islamic site or Mosque?
- In what ways do the teachings in the Qur'an inform the pilgrim in their actions, and how can this be influenced by use of the Qur'anic Cognitive Model?
- It is suggested in this chapter that most studies of Muslim travel or pilgrimage demonstrate a lack of interpretation and authentication by Muslim scholars, why is this an issue for the author?

Chapter 7

- How can the defensive model of sustainability outlined in this chapter be reconciled with an alternative model, which encourages flexibility of movement and action among visitors?
- Why does travel to holy places seem to be on the increase in many parts of Europe?
- Who should have ultimate control over the use of a shrine: religious authorities, municipal authorities, commercial businesses, national governments or visitors themselves?

Chapter 8

- In what ways does the 'search for centre' influence a pilgrim, and why does this sometimes manifest in extreme episodes?
- Why does visiting Jerusalem have such an extreme impact on some visitors?
- Why is it suggested by the authors that managers of religious sites should understand and recognize behaviour such as exhilaration, disturbance of sleep, odd behaviour or odd verbal content, and what measures should be in place to avoid extreme episodes?

Chapter 9

- How do the pilgrims' reasons for travel align to the motives of those who organize and manage the journeys?
- Discuss how, in recent years, the market positioning of religious locations has adopted the same approach as regular tourist destinations.
- Does the management of logistics at holy places impact on the pilgrimage experience of visitors, and if so, how can managers ensure that focusing on sources of income does not damage a site?

Chapter 10

- How has the work of 'Protestant devotees' over many generations altered the landscape of modern Jerusalem and its offering of accommodation and hospitality to visiting pilgrims?
- The Spaffords are an interesting group who established a 'colony' in Jerusalem. What motivated these and other American organizations to establish a presence in the Holy City?
- What type of relationship have evangelical groups and other organizations had with the Israeli state, and how does this relationship influence how they interact and operate?

Chapter 11

- Why is the destruction and sacking of enemy religious sites and architecture seen to be such a serious 'crime'?
- Do minority religions really need to have their own pilgrimage sites?
- How do you think the identity of minority groups is affected when they are severed from their religious sites and territories?

Chapter 12

- What reasons (historical, traditional, theoretical, ideological) do we have to classify certain sites or practices as 'religious'?
- To what extent are the secular and the religious separate spheres and to what extent are they intertwined in pilgrimage?
- Is it reasonable to see religiously motivated volunteer work abroad as a case of long-term pilgrimage or would other labels (religious activism/volunteering, missionary work, faith-based development) be more apt?
- Do you know of any other examples and contexts where seemingly secular sites have become the object of religiously motivated travel?

Index

Note: Page numbers in **bold** type refer to **figures**; page numbers in *italic* type refer to *tables*; page numbers followed by 'n' refer to notes.